SOCIETY SHAPED BY THEOLOGY

Robin Gill is the best kind of academic theologian. He has taken the conventional 'soft' science of 'sociology of religion' and turned it upside down, showing how, over and over again, the same evidence of apparent decline can lead into what is, in effect, a new branch of theology. This is a stimulating, intriguing, and exciting book for anyone interested in modern theology, social theory, or, more simply, where we find ourselves today. It is also a very good read – accessible, free of jargon, and always intelligently expressed. I recommend it strongly.

Stephen Prickett, University of Kent, UK

Society Shaped by Theology explores the possibility that theological concepts may sometimes still be influential in the modern world. It follows in the tradition of Max Weber, arguing that theological virtues and debates can at times be transposed, wittingly or unwittingly, into society at large. Robin Gill examines the unusual instance of the public debate about *Honest to God* in the 1960s, but then turns to the current debate about faith and social capital, adding fresh and unexpected evidence. Finally Gill argues that bioethics in the public domain, especially on global issues such as AIDS, can be enriched and deepened by a judicious use of theological virtues.

Over the last 30 years a number of theologians have been using aspects of sociology alongside the more traditional resources of philosophy. In turn, sociologists with an interest in theology have also contributed to an interaction between theology and sociology. The time is right to revisit the dialogue between theologians and sociologists. In his new trilogy on Sociological Theology, Robin Gill makes a renewed contribution to the mapping of three abiding ways of relating theology and sociology, with the three volumes covering: *Theology in a Social Context*; *Theology Shaped by Society*; *Society Shaped by Theology*.

Ashgate Contemporary Ecclesiology

The field of ecclesiology has grown remarkably in the last decade, and most especially in relation to the study of the contemporary church. Recently, theological attention has turned once more to the nature of the church, its practices and proclivities, and to interpretative readings and understandings on its role, function and ethos in contemporary society.

This new series draws from a range of disciplines and established scholars to further the study of contemporary ecclesiology and publish an important cluster of landmark titles in this field. The Series Editors represent a range of Christian traditions and disciplines, and this reflects the breadth and depth of books developing in the Series. This Ashgate series presents a clear focus on the contemporary situation of churches worldwide, offering an invaluable resource for students, researchers, ministers and other interested readers around the world working or interested in the diverse areas of contemporary ecclesiology and the important changing shape of the church worldwide.

Society Shaped by Theology
Sociological Theology Volume 3

ROBIN GILL
University of Kent, Canterbury, UK

ASHGATE

© Robin Gill 2013

Published by
Ashgate Publishing Limited
Wey Court East
Union Road
Farnham
Surrey, GU9 7PT
England

Ashgate Publishing Company
110 Cherry Street
Suite 3-1
Burlington, VT 05401-3818
USA

www.ashgate.com

British Library Cataloguing in Publication Data
Gill, Robin.
  Society shaped by theology : sociological theology.
  Volume 3. -- (Ashgate contemporary ecclesiology)
  1. Religion and civilization. 2. Religion and sociology.
  I. Title II. Series
  306.6-dc23

The Library of Congress has cataloged the printed edition as follows:
Gill, Robin.
  Sociological theology / Robin Gill.
     v. cm. -- (Ashgate contemporary ecclesiology)
  Includes index.
  Contents: v. 1. Theology in a social context
  ISBN 978-1-4094-2595-3 (v. 1 : hardcover) -- ISBN 978-1-4094-2594-6 (v. 1 : pbk.)
  -- ISBN 978-1-4094-2596-0 (ebook) 1. Christian sociology. 2.
  Theology--Methodology. I. Title.
  BT738.G465 2012
  261.5--dc23

                                                                              2011041806

ISBN 9781409426011 (hbk)
ISBN 9781409426004 (pbk)
ISBN 9781409426028 (ebk – PDF)
ISBN 9781472402943 (ebk – ePUB)

Printed and bound in Great Britain by the
MPG Books Group, UK.

To David Martin

Contents

Introduction

In many respects *Society Shaped by Theology* is the most challenging and risky of the three volumes in this trilogy. It is not difficult to see that theology is always written in a particular social context and that, as a result, it is shaped by that context. Nor is it particularly difficult to imagine that in an age of faith Catholic theology, Protestant theology, Islamic theology, Hindu theology, or whatever, left its mark on wider society. But it is much less obvious that theology in any form might still shape pluralistic, let alone 'secular', societies in the West today. Many intellectuals would simply dismiss such a possibility. A few, however, do not. With growing scepticism about the validity of the secularization paradigm, the latter might even be on the increase. Be that as it may, those engaged in sociological theology will surely be interested to explore this theme further. For me it is quite irresistible.

Once again this book is written in three parts, with the first addressing methodological points and the second and third more substantive issues. There is a narrative running throughout. My task is first to establish just what is involved in examining theology for its possible social significance. I offer an analysis of a rare instance of a modern theological debate spilling out into wider society, namely the debate generated by Bishop John Robinson's *Honest to God*. I admit to a personal affection for this debate, since *Honest to God* was published in 1963, my first year as a theology undergraduate. We debated its contents endlessly with fellow students, whether they were studying theology or not. The Archbishop of Canterbury, the saintly Michael Ramsey, even came to address our naïve questions. For a 19-year-old, nurtured on the splendours of Choral Matins accompanied by purely conventional sermons, these were thrilling times. For the first time in my life I was meeting Christians who brought critical intelligence to their faith. John Robinson, as my local bishop, even sent a hand-written letter later in the same year saying that I had been selected to train for ordination. Of course, it was glued at once to the inside cover of *Honest to God* where it still remains.

Inevitably this particular debate looks antique today, but, as I shall argue, it can still be instructive. Less antique, paradoxically, was the wartime debate among church leaders and theologians, such as Archbishop William Temple, Professor Charles Raven at Oxford and Professor John Baillie at Edinburgh, a Moderator of the Church of Scotland, about values or virtues in wider society. All made a crucial link between Christian virtues and the virtues that still informed wider society. I shall argue that they offered an important clue about the social significance of theology, namely that it may be theological virtues transposed into wider society that are most likely to be socially significant.

Part II tests this possibility against Robert Putnam's startling claims about religion and social capital. The growing literature on social capital does not seem to have been noticed by many theologians or even by all sociologists of religion. Or perhaps they have noticed it but concluded that it is too elusive and untestable. As will be seen, Putnam himself is sceptical about the relevance of theology as such to social capital, regarding the social networks of churchgoers as far more socially significant than their theological convictions. I intend to test Putnam's claims as rigorously as possible using new quantitative data. The results, I believe, are surprising.

Part III tests the social significance of theology in a very different area. Drawing on recent work that I have done on bioethics in Britain and on AIDS in Sub-Saharan Africa, I suggest at length how theological virtues might make a significant contribution to wider public discourse. I will argue that there are signs that this is already happening even in 'secular' Britain.

It has been a huge pleasure and privilege writing these three volumes of *Sociological Theology*. I am particularly grateful to the editors of the series and to Sarah Lloyd at Ashgate for suggesting this project and, as ever, to David Martin for endorsing it so fulsomely. David examined my original Master's thesis in sociology four decades ago, wrote the Foreword to my very first book, acted as a referee and mentor at every stage of my academic career, and still remains a hugely valued friend. This final volume is dedicated in gratitude to him.

In a recent, but as yet unpublished, account of his intellectual development he finds strong resonances with Peter Berger:

The resemblances are striking, above all the indirect way we have stumbled on the necessity of sociology as a natural extension of our immersion in theology and as a way of sorting out what were to us urgent issues about religion, social understanding, and human betterment. Coming to sociology by this route seems to have caused us similar problems, one being our ambivalent attitude to what was taken for granted in sociology, and the other being our unease about what was taken for granted in theology. Unease only increased when the theologians supposed they had taken sociology on board. We had problems with the appropriation of sociology by the churches, especially the confident embrace of secularisation as a Christian imperative by 'secular theologians' ... We felt the force of the neo-orthodox critique of theological liberalism but were not in the end convinced, however much we suspected liberalism in general of not grappling realistically with politics, especially problems of power and violence. I expect we might count as liberal in our *attitudes*, but at the same time we were dubious about the liberal grasp of the world ... We were, and remain, mistrustful across the board rather than liberals across the board. For us the proper work of a sociologist is to sniff cautiously at *everything*, sociology included.[1]

This matches almost exactly my own stumbling and sniffing. All three of us are nourished by theistic, Christocentric (and, as it happens, Anglican) worship and tradition. From my perspective grounded in virtue ethics it would make little sense to claim that I was not shaped by a particular tradition, even while remaining distrustful of both confident critics and, especially, defenders of that tradition. Sociological theology, properly understood, might encourage intellectual and spiritual humility, if only from the realization that even our most heart-felt convictions can give rise to unintended social consequences.

A small, poignant and fascinating book by Dan Frank (with Graham Howes), *The Word and the World: Religion after the Sociology of Knowledge*, has reminded me of this quite clearly. It is poignant because Dan Frank died of heart failure at the age of just 24. Graham Howes, a wise veteran of the Blackfriars Symposia on theology and sociology and Dan's supervisor at Cambridge, made it possible to publish his sparkling 10,000-word student essay as a book by adding a thoughtful response of equal length. Dan summarizes the debate about using the sociology

---

[1]   Used with permission from David Martin.

of knowledge within theology, concluding with a careful and mostly sympathetic account of my own work. However, as Graham Howes notes: 'He does ... in a final paragraph on Gill, unerringly locate what many of the latter's academic peers have long seen as his sociological Achilles heel: his belief in the incontestable ontological primacy of the Gospel in constructing social reality.'[2] In Dan's own words:

> Gill makes it clear that it is not for theology to critique the Gospel or debate the existence of God. Rather its role is to interpret the message of the Gospel in the light of an evolving social reality. Yet this is the paradox at the heart of his work: he recognizes the contextual nature of religious knowledge, yet makes exclusive exception for that contained in canonical scripture. He refuses to accept the consequence of his own critique of theology, which is that *all* knowledge—religious and secular, 'revealed' and rational, *including* the scriptural basis of theology—must be considered open to critical evaluation. In seeking correlations between scripture and contemporary social needs, he is trying to build a dynamic, contextual and self-aware theology on a static and absolutist foundation. Scripture is the problem, not the solution.[3]

This, of course, was entirely my own fault for making claims about 'the Gospel as a whole' in my early books. Trained as an undergraduate by exponents of liberal, critical biblical scholarship, it never occurred to me that my language would convey that I believed in an 'absolutist' or 'incontestable' scriptural foundation. For me, even before I started a theology degree, the pluralism of scripture was self-evident and deeply challenging. Yet (and this is where I possibly differ from Dan) scripture was also a crucial part of the tradition within which I worshipped. A contextual approach to scripture – especially to the virtues in tension within its various and diverging strands – is a key feature of the present volume.

Once again, as with the other two volumes, I have needed to re-fashion, change and supplement some early material, while writing other chapters anew. Parts of Chapters 1 and 2 come from *Theology and Social Structure* and 3 to 5

---

[2]   Graham Howes, 'A Response to Dan Frank', in Dan Frank, *The Word and the World: Religion after the Sociology of Knowledge*, London: Continuum, 2007, p. 89.
[3]   Frank, *The Word and the World*, p. 45.

from *Prophecy and Praxis* (both long out of print), but all of these chapters also have much that is new and have left out much that is now just too embarrassing (including my claims about 'the Gospel as a whole'!). My debate with Robert Putnam in Chapters 6 and 7 is entirely new, although I have included data from *Churchgoing and Christian Ethics* (used with permission from CUP), alongside data calculated from three new major sources, in Chapter 7. I have included critical exegetical and hermeneutical scriptural discussion from *Health Care and Christian Ethics* (used with permission from CUP) in Chapter 8 and parts of Chapter 9, but the rest is new.

PART I
Social Significance

Chapter 1

The Social Significance of Theology

Theology is seldom treated by sociologists as anything other than epiphenomenal and the symbols and concepts generated by theology are typically ignored in sociological accounts of religion in Western society. In Chapter 6 it will be seen that even Robert Putnam, who has done more than almost any other social scientist to establish the social significance of religious belonging in the United States, tends to be dismissive of the relevance of theological differences to social capital. Sociological theology, in contrast, takes seriously the possibility that theology may at times be socially significant even in the modern world. More specifically, it is concerned to explore the claim that socially constructed theological ideas, once generated, may have an influence upon society at large. It will be the function of this chapter and the next to explore this claim.

There appear to be at least two reasons why sociologists have tended to ignore the possibility that theology may act at times as an independent variable within society. The first, already familiar from Volume 1, depends upon viewing theology as set firmly in a context of radical secularization. Among sociologists a generation ago who supported a thoroughgoing secularization paradigm,[1] there was a tendency to view contemporary theology as both the product and the result of secularization. Together with a number of theologians at the time,[2] they argued that theological movements like that of secular theology, or even ecumenical theology,[3] were themselves a part of the process of secularization, contributing

---

[1]   E.g. Bryan Wilson, *Religion in Secular Society*, London: C.A. Watts, 1966 and Harmondsworth, Middlesex: Penguin, 1969 and *Contemporary Transformations of Religion*, Oxford: Oxford University Press, 1976 and Peter L. Berger, *The Social Reality of Religion*, London: Faber and Faber, 1969 [US title, *The Sacred Canopy of Religion*, Garden City, NY: Doubleday, 1967].

[2]   Especially E.L. Mascall, *The Secularisation of Christianity*, London: Libra, 1967.

[3]   See Bryan S. Turner, 'The Sociological Explanation of Ecumenicalism', in C.L. Mitton (ed.), *The Social Sciences and the Churches*, Edinburgh: T&T Clark, 1972, pp. 231–245.

directly to the demise of the discipline as a whole. In addition (and somewhat paradoxically), they argued that, within a situation of radical secularization, theology had effectively ceased to be an influence upon society.

The second reason why sociologists tended to ignore this possibility perhaps involved a more general scepticism about the social efficacy of intellectual ideas. Those sociologists of knowledge, such as Berger and Luckmann,[4] who focused upon the social significance of everyday knowledge, tended at the same time to denigrate the significance of intellectual knowledge. So, specifically intellectualistic disciplines like theology were regarded as socially epiphenomenal – even when, as in the instance of Berger,[5] they were considered to be intrinsically interesting.

Once it is conceded that the secularization paradigm in its most radical form does less than justice to the ambiguity of religion in the modern world and that intellectual ideas may yet be socially significant, an adequate understanding of sociological theology needs to explore more seriously the possibility that theology may act, at times, as both a dependent and an independent variable within society. In the process a genuinely interactionist approach to theology becomes possible. In an important, recent summary of current British research in the sociology of religion, *Religion and Change in Modern Britain*, Linda Woodhead captures in the Introduction a change that is happening once the secularization paradigm is no longer assumed to be the only starting point:

> This book analyses and explains ... changes and apparent contradictions in the post-Second World War period. In order to do so it adopts an approach which considers religion not in isolation, but in relation to the wider social, political, economic and global changes in which it has been immersed. This means that it is implicitly critical of a characteristic assumption of the post-war period: that religion has become a purely private matter with no public or political significance. So long as this idea prevailed, both in scholarship and in society, it was possible to treat religions as discrete entities which could be analysed

---

[4]   Peter L. Berger and Thomas Luckmann, *The Social Construction of Reality*, New York: Anchor, 1966 and London: Penguin, 1971.

[5]   See Berger, *The Social Reality of Religion*, Appendix II 'Sociological and Theological Perspectives', pp. 181–190.

solely in terms of their inner logics and characteristic texts, beliefs, rituals and symbols. The alternative, integrated, approach developed in this volume views religion not only as affected by wider changes in the global economy, politics, media, the law and other arenas, but as integral to them. In other words, it takes the idea of strong social differentiation—which assumes that modern societies like Britain are made up of separate 'spheres' or 'domains' of which religion is one—as a loaded claim which should be the subject of empirical enquiry rather than the starting point.[6]

In the chapters that follow several of the contributors, despite differences on the usefulness of a secularization paradigm, agree that religion in the modern world is not 'a purely private matter with no public or political significance'. To give a single example, Kim Knott and Jolyon Mitchell argue that new forms of online media do not simply privatize religious belonging but may expand and globalize it as well. Online religion is expanded by religion-online 'where groups adapt their communicative practices in the wake of the new communication technologies which have ensured the flourishing of the internet ... [finding] new ways of expressing and experiencing ancient and contemporary religious traditions which regularly transcend national boundaries'. They conclude that 'even though one of the most recent phenomena, the internet, is little more than 20 years old, the way that it is being used by both religious institutions and individuals is transforming the daily practices and expressions of religion not only in Britain but also around the world today'.[7]

Nevertheless, a theologically sympathetic sociologist can assume too easily that various theological movements and concepts are indeed socially significant. It is one thing to allow for the possibility that theology may act at times as an independent variable, but quite another to demonstrate that particular features of the discipline actually influence specific social situations. Among those few sociologists of religion a generation ago who considered the social function of theology, a too facile jump was sometimes made from this general possibility to

---

[6] Linda Woodhead, 'Introduction', in Linda Woodhead and Rebecca Catto (eds), *Religion and Change in Modern Britain*, London: Routledge, 2012, p. 2.

[7] Kim Knott and Jolyon Mitchell, 'The Changing Faces of Media and Religion', in Linda Woodhead and Rebecca Catto (eds), *Religion and Change in Modern Britain*, London: Routledge, 2012, pp. 259–260.

an actual demonstration. The works of Roger Mehl in France and M.J. Jackson in Britain well illustrate this danger.

Even though he recognized the importance of an examination of the social determinants of theology, Mehl maintained that 'the common error of the sociologist is that of thinking that he does not have to take doctrinal elements into consideration, because these elements would be the intellectual superstructures which only record a religion's effort to adapt to the cultural level in which it lives'.[8] In contrast to other sociologists, Mehl insisted that, if Protestantism is to be understood adequately, particular attention must be paid to the role of theology:

> If a sociology of Christianity must take account of this fact, a sociology of Protestantism has even more reason to bear it in mind. For Protestantism was born of a doctrinal reform which was effected by doctors of theology. This reform was raised against the omnipotence of practices, of forms of piety, of the elements of sociological morphology. It aspired to reform the visible communities of the church according to a doctrinally determined archetype. It had desired that the line going from Christology through ecclesiology to the organisation of the parishes be as direct as possible. The question is not primarily one of knowing if the Reformation was perfectly successful in this enterprise and if 'non-theological factors' intervened in the constitution of the church and of the parishes. The primary obligation of the sociologist who studies the Protestant church is that of taking account of this intention, of this essence of Protestantism, following which he can investigate the manner in which they have operated or not operated.[9]

This quotation is attractive, since it apparently confirms that theology is indeed socially significant. None the less, it is open to criticism at a number of points. Sociologists of religion may feel that there is nothing in Protestantism, rather than Catholicism, which especially obliges them to take theology more or less seriously. Further, they might maintain that it is precisely the exploration of 'non-theological factors' within both Protestantism and Catholicism which constitutes the most interesting and original part of their study. In such exploration, sociologists have

---

8   Roger Mehl, *The Sociology of Protestantism*, London: SCM Press, 1970, p. 6.
9   Mehl, *Sociology of Protestantism*, p. 7.

been able to make their most important contribution to the study of religion as a whole. And finally, sociologists may feel less than happy with Mehl's apparently extra-sociological depiction of the 'essence' of Protestantism. After all, Mehl himself rejected the idea elsewhere that sociology should imagine that 'it reaches religion in its essence'.[10]

A similar unsubstantiated jump, from the general possibility to the actuality of the social significance of theology, was apparent in the work of M.J. Jackson. His analysis of the relation between sociology and theology began with and centred upon theology as an independent variable within society. He reviewed at some length Karl Barth's apparent rejection of 'religion' and natural theology in favour of 'revelation' through Jesus Christ and Hans Küng's 'Christian universalism', following Vatican II's *Constitution on the Church*. Of the latter, especially, Jackson argued that, in relation to world religions, 'the dangers of relativism are … apparent, as also danger of an end to dialogue, for why bother to talk if we are all going the same way to the same destination?'[11] In contrast, Barth's attitude towards 'religion' led to the whole-hearted missionary activity of men like Hendrik Kraemer, whereas Küng's 'universalism' tended to relax 'the urge to mission'.[12]

In the light of this analysis, Jackson argued strongly for the social significance of theology, seen as 'the understanding and explanation of the religious dimension of life':[13]

> The views of the theologian about religion are of the first importance to the sociology of religion. What the theologians say about religion has considerable impact on the belief and practice of religious bodies, on how their members see their functions, on how religious bodies relate themselves to the outside world, on their programmes of mission, on their attitudes to other religions. The views … of Barth and Küng, of quasi-rejection and acceptance of religion, are widely held and full of practical implications.[14]

---

[10]   Ibid., p. 2.
[11]   M.J. Jackson, *The Sociology of Religion*, London: Batsford, 1974, pp. 46–47.
[12]   Ibid., p. 47.
[13]   Ibid., p. 40.
[14]   Ibid.

Unfortunately, Jackson's thesis was stated rather than argued. The differing theological responses of these two theologians to 'religion' may well have been socially significant beyond the bounds of the theological world itself, but no evidence was given to demonstrate this. An end to dialogue was not the only possible response to Küng's 'universalism' and in practice Barthianism may or may not have been dominant among active missionaries. A more sophisticated analysis was essential if the possibility of theology acting as an independent variable within society was to be firmly established.

I argued at the time that if this was established, then it would be of interest to both theologians and sociologists of religion. Yet I cautioned that this might result in two quite different scenarios. Theologians may be heartened to know that their work has an influence beyond a small religious elite and sociologists of religion may be forced to take the work of theologians more seriously, whatever they might otherwise think of its validity. Alternatively, theologians may be somewhat dismayed at the unintended consequences of their writings, while sociologists become even more convinced than ever of the epiphenomenal nature of the specifically religious content of these writings.

Despite the obvious attractions of such a study for the theologian, the sociologist, as a sociologist, may at times explore possibilities which are apparently harmful to the theological enterprise. Jackson argued that a sociologist of religion should ideally be a believer, since 'neutrality' vis-à-vis religion is impossible and the believer 'enters religion sympathetically'.[15] Writing at the time Bryan Wilson, in particular, was unimpressed by such claims, regarding Jackson's own attempt to defend theology as an independent variable as itself theologically, rather than sociologically, motivated.[16] Even the theologically sympathetic sociologist Robert Towler argued that if sociologists are to examine theology adequately, they cannot be under continuous pressure from theologians.[17] Rather, like the critical biblical scholar or philosopher of religion, even within a theological faculty, sociologists of religion should pursue the consequences of their discipline wherever they might lead and 'as if' it were the only relevant discipline (as I argued at length in Volume 1).

---

[15]   Ibid., p. 50.

[16]   Bryan Wilson, 'The Debate Over "Secularization"', *Encounter*, Oct 1975.

[17]   Robert Towler, *Homo Religiosus: Sociological Problems in the Study of Religion*, London: Constable, 1974.

If this were not the case, then the possible correlations between certain types of theology and anti-Semitism[18] or racism[19] might never have been investigated. It is worth recalling one of Max Weber's footnotes to his *The Protestant Ethic and the 'Spirit' of Capitalism*:

> From theologians I have received numerous valuable suggestions in connection with this study. Its reception on their part has been in general friendly and impersonal, in spite of wide differences of opinion on particular points. This is the more welcome to me since I should not have wondered at a certain antipathy to the manner in which these matters must necessarily be treated here. What to a theologian is valuable in his religion cannot play a very large part in this study. We are concerned with what, from a religious point of view, are often quite superficial and unrefined aspects of religious life, but which, and precisely because they are superficial and unrefined, have often influenced outward behaviour most profoundly.[20]

Theology as an Independent Variable

In contrast to the neglect of theology by later sociologists of religion, two of the pioneers of the discipline took it more seriously. The theologian and church historian Ernst Troeltsch and the sociologist Max Weber were prepared to treat, not only religion, but also theology, as an independent variable within society: for both, specifically theological symbols and concepts could be socially significant. Further, major elements in their contributions towards a sociological understanding of religion would be negated if the possibility were removed of theology acting as an independent variable within society. For this reason alone the comparative neglect of this area by sociologists in the 1970s appeared strange.

---

[18]   Charles Y. Glock and Rodney Stark, *Christian Beliefs and Anti-Semitism*, New York: Harper, 1966.

[19]   Richard L. Gorsuch and Daniel Aleshire, 'Christian Faith and Prejudice: Review of Research', *Journal for the Scientific Study of Religion*, 13:3, 281–307, 1974.

[20]   Max Weber, *The Protestant Ethic and the 'Spirit' of Capitalism*, New York: Scribner, 1958 (1905), p. 187, n. 1.

The small amount of research that did exist in this area tended to be clustered around the Weberian thesis in *The Protestant Ethic and the 'Spirit' of Capitalism* and the post-Troeltsch Church/Sect typology. The first tended to examine continuing differences between Catholics and Protestants, based on their supposed theological differences, while the second tended to differentiate churches, denominations and sects, at least partially, on their varying theological responses to each other and to the world at large. Weber's thesis began with the empirical observations that business leaders and owners of capital within the West tended to be Protestant rather than Catholic and that Benjamin Franklin's self-acknowledged ethic involved 'the earning of more and more money, combined with the strict avoidance of all spontaneous enjoyment of life'.[21] Weber suggested that one of the cultural factors enabling capitalism to arise in the West may have been Calvinist theology. Naturally, the specific correlation that Weber sought to demonstrate between the Protestant doctrines of the calling, predestination, asceticism and sanctification and the 'spirit' of Western European and American capitalism is a complex one. Had it not been, it would scarcely have received so much attention from the academic community. But, inevitably, it was soon subjected to considerable criticism.[22] Several methodological points, however, are of immediate interest, but have often been overlooked in the research that the thesis has generated:

First, Weber consistently maintained that theology was just one variable involved in the rise of capitalism within the West. Other factors, such as rational book-keeping and transport, were equally, if not more, important. The modest role he adopted for his thesis was 'to ascertain whether and to what extent religious forces have taken part in the qualitative formation and the quantitative expansion' of the spirit of Capitalism over the world:[23] he made no claim that capitalism could never have arisen without the Reformation or that the latter was the sole cause of the former. While he treated certain theological ideas as being socially significant, he never suggested that they were exclusively significant.

---

[21]   Weber, p. 53.

[22]   See Gary D. Bouma, 'Recent "Protestant Ethic" Research', *Journal for the Scientific Study of Religion*, 21:2, pp. 141–155, 1973, and Charles Y. Glock and Phillip E. Hammond (eds), *Beyond the Classics? Essays in the Scientific Study of Religion*, New York: Harper & Row, 1973, pp. 113–130.

[23]   Weber, p. 91.

This point must be fundamental to any attempt to study the social significance of theology. Exaggerated claims about the extent of this significance, unsupported by rigorous empirical evidence, can play no part in it. So, for example, Kevin Clements' important claim that, following the Depression in New Zealand, theological considerations were socially significant, must be set in the context which he analyses. In the period 1925–31, he suggested, the churches tacitly and explicitly accepted the status quo: in the period 1931–34 they 'started developing social teaching that stood in radical contrast to earlier statements sympathetic to the maintenance of the status quo':[24] and only in the period 1934–35 did 'religious opinion leaders' adopt overtly radical political stances, giving considerable support to the Labour Party and helping it to win the election in 1935 by providing it with a religious legitimation. So, he argued that, at first religious and theological factors operated only as dependent variables, but that by 1934 'the religious variable exerted considerable independent influence on social change, by legitimating the agents of change – the Labour Party – and by suggesting specific innovations that the Labour Party might adopt in order to bring about a specifically Christian solution to the problem … it was by producing religious symbols to interpret the situation that the religious institutions exerted an independent influence on the changes that occurred'.[25] Clements claimed a relatively modest role for theology in this situation – that of producing legitimating symbols – and that only on the basis of rigorous research.[26] To have claimed more would have been to go beyond the evidence.

Secondly, Weber was concerned with interpreted or 'popular' theology, not with theology as produced by academics. A frequent criticism of the 'Protestant Ethic' thesis has been that it provides a thoroughly distorted account of Calvinism, imputing to it a misconceived conception of its doctrines of the calling, election and sanctification. So, it is maintained that neither Calvin nor Luther accepted these doctrines in the manner in which Weber depicted them. However, this criticism misses the point that Weber was more concerned with these doctrines

---

[24]   Kevin Clements, 'The Religious Variable: Dependent, Independent or Interdependent?', in Michael Hill (ed.), *A Sociological Yearbook of Religion in Britain*, London: SCM Press, 4, 1971, p. 40.

[25]   Clements, p. 45.

[26]   Kevin Clements, *The Churches and Social Policy: A Study in the Relationship of Ideology to Action*, Wellington, New Zealand: Victoria University of Wellington, 1970.

as they might have been perceived by followers of Calvin and Luther than by the theologians themselves. If theology is to be considered socially significant, the way that it is perceived by non-theologians becomes a matter of considerable importance, but the way that it is perceived by the theologians themselves may be of peripheral concern. If specific notions within Calvinism did indeed contribute to the rise of capitalism within the West, it must have been these notions, as generally perceived, rather than as originally intended, which had this effect.

A focus upon perceived, rather than academic, theology presents sociologists with a somewhat daunting task. They might distinguish four levels of analysis: theology among academic theologians (that is, the traditional focus); theology among preachers who are seeking to communicate it, whether in writing or orally, to a non-theological audience; theology among church attenders and readers of literature written by these preachers; and, finally, theology among those who neither attend church nor read religious literature with any degree of regularity. Typically for academic theologians theology is located at the first level and at the written part of the second level. Accordingly, the oral part of the second and the whole of the third and fourth levels are concerned for them more with the effects of theology rather than with theology itself. Precisely because they are oral rather than written, though, they can be less accessible for analysis. Just as Weber was forced to speculate about the 'probable' ways in which theology would be popularly perceived, so sociological theologians today are presented with the same intractable difficulty. I will return to this point in the next chapter, when I consider the four levels of reaction to *Honest to God*.

Finally, it is important to emphasize that Weber was concerned with the rise of capitalism, not with its continued maintenance (even though, confusingly, he began, as just noted, with an unreferenced observation about contemporary differences between Catholics and Protestants). Following Gerhard Lenski's[27] adaption of the thesis into a general hypothesis through which to examine ongoing differences between Catholics and Protestants, suggesting as it did that religious affiliation may indeed act as an independent variable within society (itself a significant finding, given the widespread indifference to the sociology of religion at the time he was writing), some research at the time focused upon these differences. But this research was an adaption of Weber's own thesis which

---

[27]   Gerhard E. Lenski, *The Religious Factor*, New York: Doubleday, 1961.

was concerned primarily with the rise of capitalism.[28] Weber argued that this rise owed something to moral values, such as thrift and hard work, detached from their original religious setting. Modern capitalism need owe nothing to contemporary religious affiliation: once effected the former can survive quite well without the latter. Similarly, in Clements' suggested correlation between religious symbols and political actualities, the modern-day Labour Party in New Zealand need have no special relationship with the contemporary churches there. The Labour Party, having received the religious legitimation offered by the churches and thus the respectability that it previously lacked (before 1934 members were often suspected of Communism), could continue to hold office with or without the blessing of the churches.[29]

The fact that Weber's thesis is essentially historical does raise difficulties for historians and sociologists alike. As subsequent critics of the thesis have found, it is difficult to test in any sufficiently empirical or rigorous manner. This difficulty is compounded by the two qualifications already given – namely, that the thesis is only concerned with one of many possible variables and that it is based upon perceived rather than academic theology. Ironically, Weber's sophistication as a sociologist, producing models that usually are carefully qualified, allied to his nuanced methodology, served to produce a thesis that may be neither verifiable nor falsifiable. Nevertheless, it has proved to be of enduring interest to theological sociologists. Gregory Baum, in particular, argued that the thesis offers a striking example of 'creative religion':

> An original, creative, religious breakthrough took place in Calvinistic Christianity. God's call was experienced as a secular calling. Christians experienced the meaning and power of the gospel in their dedication to hard work and personal enterprise, and they regarded the success of their undertakings as God's approval and blessing. This new spirituality removed the religious obstacles to capitalistic expansion, for in the Middle Ages the Church had not only regarded as gravely sinful the taking of interest on money loaned, but had also held up contemplation, other worldliness, patience in one's providential

---

[28] See Bouma, 'Recent "Protestant Ethic" Research'.

[29] Linda Woodhead makes a similar point about the British welfare state in her Introduction to *Religious Change in Modern Britain*, pp. 10–17.

position, and even elected poverty as the ideals to be followed by the most
dedicated Christians.[30]

Another example might be Ernst Troeltsch's Church/Sect typology – the study of
differing types and dynamics within religious institutions. It is clear that he believed
that his three types of religious organization – Churches, Sects and Mysticism
– each found its origins within different parts of the New Testament. Troeltsch
consistently maintained (a feature often ignored by sociologists of religion in the
past)[31] that the roots of his typology lay within Christian theology. For him, then,
theology was socially significant in so far as it served to create and maintain the
triadic structure of organizational responses to it. I argued in the previous volumes
that it is precisely this theological basis to his typology which creates difficulties
for the sociologist, since the latter usually wishes to maintain that Church/Sect
typology ought to be applicable to religions other than Christianity alone and that
a mixture of theological and social criteria is undesirable in rigorous research.
However, for the sociological theologian it presents no such difficulty. On the
contrary, as I argued in Volume 2, Troeltsch offers crucial *theological* insights
about a relational understanding of religious institutions.

Theology and Pacifism

In *A Textbook of Christian Ethics*[32] I suggested that theological response to war can
be analysed in terms of four 'ideal' types (itself a concept developed by Weber).
Since they are 'ideal' rather than 'actual' types, it is not, of course, necessary to
claim that they are all to be found in a pure form within existing groups in society,
or even that considerable overlap is not to be found in such groups. They are
intended, instead, to denote the theoretical range of possibilities in such a way that
actual responses to war can be better classified and compared. Ideal types are at
best heuristic devices: they are means for interpreting society, rather than direct

---

[30]   Gregory Baum, *Religion and Alienation: A Theological Reading of Sociology*, New
York: Paulist Press, 1975 [reprinted Ottawa: Novalis, 2006], p. 164.

[31]   But not by Betty Scharf, *The Sociological Study of Religion*, London: Hutchinson,
1970.

[32]   Robin Gill, *A Textbook of Christian Ethics*, 3rd edition, London: T&T Clark, 2006.

observations from society. Understood in this way, then, the four ideal types of response to war are as follows:

a. Thoroughgoing Militarism – understood as a willingness to fight anywhere, at any time and for any cause.
b. Selective Militarism – understood as a willingness to fight when one's country, or another, declares that the cause is just.
c. Selective Pacifism – understood as a willingness to fight only when one is convinced that the cause is just.
d. Thoroughgoing Pacifism – understood as an unwillingness to fight anywhere, at any time and for any cause.

It is clear that these four ideal types concentrate upon the willingness and intention of the individual confronted with war and make no attempt to account for other variables within this situation. It is also clear that B and C differ from A and D in their inclusion of the concept of perceived justice. As a result the sort of just-war theories discussed in Volume 2 apply only to them. The point of distinction between B and C lies in the fact that in B it is individuals' country or even another country/organization (this ambiguity is intentionally unresolved), which decides on the justice of a particular cause, whereas in C it is the individuals who so decide.

Within most, if not all, Christian organizations only types B, C and D would be considered to be possible Christian responses to war. Only non-idealistic mercenaries, perhaps, would conform to type A and they seldom find defenders within Christianity. Bainton's three historical attitudes to warfare in Christian and pre-Christian thinking, namely, the crusade, the just war and pacifism,[33] can be seen to be included in types B, C and D, although these types are naturally somewhat broader and not entirely coincidental with them. In particular, the distinction between C and D, both defended at times as varieties of Christian pacifism, becomes more evident. It is only the last type that will be considered here, although it must be admitted that, in practice, it may sometimes be hard to distinguish between C and D. So, for example, Bertrand Russell, in effect a clear instance of type D, in theory admitted to the futuristic possibility of legitimate

---

[33] Roland H. Bainton, *Christian Attitudes toward War and Peace*, Nashville, TN: Abingdon, 1960, p. 53f.

violent sanctions in a situation of world-government and as a result would be classified as type C. A similar problem will be noted presently in the context of the Jehovah's Witnesses' response to war. While admitting this difficulty in the exact classification of individual empirical instances of pacifism, it is none the less thoroughgoing pacifism which will form the focus of this analysis.

It is, perhaps, in thoroughgoing pacifism that the social significance of theology is likely to be most apparent. In other Christian responses to war the views of the individual, or of the particular religious organization, tend, by definition, to be coincidental with those of the state. Accordingly, it becomes extremely difficult to determine how far the formers' views are determined simply by the latter's, or how far they might also be determined by the legitimations offered by theological expressions of a just-war theory. In contrast, the thoroughgoing pacifist, whether as an individual or as a sect, represents a deviant type within either society in general or Christianity in particular. Numerically, at least, types B and C represent the majority Christian response to war: type D accounts only for a very small minority. Of course it is quite possible to propose social determinants even for this last type[34] – methodologically no response to war should be excluded from such analysis – but there is a strong possibility here that theological positions, even when viewed as socially constructed realities, may have acted as independent variables. This possibility may be investigated at the level both of the individual thoroughgoing pacifist theologian and of the thoroughgoing pacifist sect.

At the level of the individual thoroughgoing pacifist theologian, Charles Raven, used as an example in Volume 2, again provides an instructive example. Whatever social determinants may be isolated in causing him to change from types B or C to D during the 1920s, there is strong evidence to be found in his writings to suggest that specifically theological factors significantly affected the position he maintained from that time until his death in 1965. Among a series of books on Christian responses to war he even entitled one *The Theological Basis of Christian Pacifism*.[35] It is the attempt to provide such a basis which forms the focus of his other writings on the subject.

---

[34]   Cf. J. Milton Yinger, *The Scientific Study of Religion*, New York: Collier-Macmillan, 1970, p. 466f.

[35]   Charles E. Raven, *The Theological Basis of Christian Pacifism*, London: The Fellowship Publications, 1951.

Raven constantly rejected a variety of other social variables as the cause of his pacifism. Given the polemical nature of his books on the subject and the considerable criticism to which he was subjected, it is not surprising to find that, whereas he frequently admitted social determinants to the attitudes of some of his fellow pacifists, he was reluctant to admit their relevance to his own. So, he conceded that the movement towards pacifism in the 1920s in Britain 'was largely due to motives of which the Christian can only disapprove'.[36] Among these, he suggested, were 'disgust and fear, the accumulated effects of nervous exhaustion and disappointment'.[37] He constantly sought to disassociate himself from such emotional reactions to war, even to the extent of admitting that war could produce desirable moral characteristics in those participating in it.

The accuracy of Raven's analysis of the social determinants of pacifism is less important in the present context than the fact of his resolution to differentiate his own position from such determinants. In his self-estimation it was theological considerations which provided the motivation for his Christian pacifism and as a professional theologian he sought to communicate these as widely as possible in lectures, books, speeches and sermons. On several occasions he sought to show that Christian pacifism is derivable from the doctrine of the Trinity. Having argued that war is not to be condemned simply because it involves killing, suffering and the destruction of material resources, he maintained that it is to be condemned for theological reasons:

> War destroys the essential fellowship which exists and should be fostered between human beings as children of God and members one of another ... The Christian doctrine of God centres upon ... the personal qualities symbolised by love and life and light. The doctrine of the Incarnation bears witness to the sanctity of personality as the unique medium capable of revealing the Son of God. The Holy Spirit is primarily manifested in the *koinonia*, the communion and community of believers, the blessed society which is the body of Christ. This primary tenet of our faith is outraged and blasphemed by war.[38]

---

[36] Charles E. Raven, *War and the Christian*, London: Garland, 1938, p. 21.

[37] *War and the Christian*, p. 21 and see also Charles E. Raven, *Is War Obsolete?*, London: George Allen & Unwin, 1935, p. 39f.

[38] Raven, *War and the Christian*, pp. 48–49.

However, while he often used this Trinitarian formulation, the primary basis for his Christian pacifism appears to have been his Christological and soteriological beliefs. He argued, throughout his writings on the subject, that 'Christ by his Cross presents to us his way of overcoming the sin of the world, and in this form at least the mass of mankind and even of Christians repudiate it'.[39] With G.H.C. Macgregor, Raven claimed that the Gospels, Acts and the Epistles are incontrovertibly pacifist-oriented[40] and that Christ emerges from them as 'the prince of peace'.[41] An adequate understanding of Christology, then, necessitates a pacifist interpretation of Christ. Further, an understanding of soteriology in terms of the 'imitation of Christ', seeing Christ as a representative figure for others and implying 'a real identification of the believer with his Lord', necessitates pacifism for Christian disciples.[42] Given these understandings of Christology and soteriology, he believed that 'the plain fact is that the Church since the First Century and with few exceptions has never, despite its protestations, taken Christ with complete seriousness'.[43]

Had Raven interpreted the New Testament evidence on which he based his Christology differently – as just-war theorists tend to do[44] – his conclusions might have been rather different. Again, had he not based his understanding of soteriology on an 'imitation of Christ', his pacifist conclusions for Christians would not necessarily have followed, even had he maintained his Christological beliefs. So, on other interpretations of soteriology, it would be perfectly possible to argue, that the fact of Christ's pacifism does not necessarily entail pacifism for Christ's disciples. Both features of his theological argument, then, are crucial to his justification of Christian pacifism, whether as direct causes of this pacifism or simply as maintainers of it. In either instance, specifically theological concepts would be given a socially significant role in Raven's overall response to war.

---

[39]   Raven, *The Theological Basis of Christian Pacifism*, p. 21.

[40]   See G.H.C. MacGregor, *The New Testament Basis of Pacifism*, London: James Clarke, 1936.

[41]   See Charles E. Raven, *Lessons of the Prince of Peace*, London: Longmans Green, 1942.

[42]   Raven, *The Theological Basis of Christian Pacifism*, p. 22.

[43]   Ibid.

[44]   E.g. Eberhard Welty, *A Handbook of Christian Social Ethics*, New York: Herder and Herder, 1963, vol. 2, pp. 396–397.

Not surprisingly, then, a case can be made out to the effect that the ethical positions of particular theologians may be influenced directly by their theological concepts. This possibility on its own, however, might appear remarkably uninteresting to the sociologist of knowledge. Werner Stark, for example, would doubtless have argued that such an analysis of Raven belongs properly to microsociology and accordingly cannot constitute a part of a sociology of knowledge.[45] Even if his argument is not accepted, it can be seen that interest in such analysis will be limited only to those already predisposed towards theology.

Much more interesting for sociological theology is the possibility that Raven's theological arguments themselves were socially significant. That is, there is a possibility that, not only was Raven's response to war influenced by theology, but that his theological justification of this response was itself an influence upon others. It is important to study this possibility in terms of the four levels of analysis already suggested; namely theologians, preachers, listeners and outsiders.

As the Regius Professor of Divinity at Cambridge and the author of 25 theological works on a wide variety of subjects, it is difficult to believe that Raven's theological justification of pacifism was not widely known to academic theologians. However unpopular these views and those in favour of the ordination of women might have been among the ecclesiastical hierarchy, his theological justification of them was important, at least within the academic community. William Temple, then Archbishop of York, clearly thought them sufficiently important to be refuted publicly in *The Times* in 1935. Further, on various occasions, Raven used a series of university lectures to promote his theological polemic against war, notably in the Halley Stewart Lecture of 1934 and in the Robert Treat Paine Lectures of 1950, delivered at Boston University, Union Theological Seminary and the University of Chicago. At the time, his views on pacifism may even have been rather better known among academics than his views on other areas within theology.

Undoubtedly, Raven himself thought it important for academics to be concerned intellectually with the issue of pacifism. Against his numerous critics, he maintained, at one point, 'Lord Ponsonby, Lord Russell, Sir Aldous Huxley, Mr Gerald Heard, Mr Middleton Murray and the Bishop of Birmingham are men whose intellectual power is probably greater than that of any group in the

---

[45]   Werner Stark, *The Sociology of Knowledge*, London: Routledge & Kegan Paul, 1958, p. 20f.

public life of Britain ... where they, each from his special angle, have vindicated pacifism, they deserve a fuller answer than the casual comment of ecclesiastics and statesmen'.[46]

Raven also believed that a specifically theological consideration of war might help theology itself to become relevant beyond academic circles. For many years he held 'the particular question of the Christian attitude toward war as the most urgent and the most representative of those problems' concerned with the relationship of belief to practice.[47] He also held that a consideration of the problem might help theology to become more socially significant than it had been for a long time:

> Theologians' ... work has been frustrated by the fact that it is regarded as academic and almost as irrelevant. Their fellow Christians, whose concern is rather to live out the faith as they have received it than to deepen their understanding of its meaning, will only discover a renewed appreciation of it by approaching it along the line of some concrete problem which demands a solution. We have claimed that war is such a problem. To study it would do as much to enlighten and deepen and unify the thought of the Churches as to clear up the particular issue.[48]

Doubtless in order to enable this broadening of theology to take place, Raven deliberately wrote his books on pacifism in a popular style, generally avoiding theological jargon and academic references. He was even invited in 1942 to write the Bishop of London's Lent Book on the theme of peace. A study of the bookshelves of those who were already ministers during the 1930s would suggest that Raven was indeed successful in communicating, at least at this second level. Indeed, he himself, as the author of widely selling books on pacifism and as public speaker and preacher on the subject, was a part of this level of communication and, consequently, a possible influence upon the third level. In addition, his important teaching position at Cambridge would have enabled him to have been in direct contact with the next generation of preachers.

Raven, *War and the Christian*, p. 124.
[47] Raven, *The Theological Basis of Christian Pacifism*, p. 1.
[48] Raven, *War and the Christian*, pp. 182–183.

More importantly, Raven's work on pacifism may well have given the pacifist cause a degree of religious and academic legitimation which it previously lacked at the second, third and even fourth levels. At a time in the 1930s when the prospect of war was increasing, it would have been politically expedient to identify all pacifists as either anarchists or cowards. However, with the support of the cause by people like Raven, these charges became more difficult. He never hesitated to use his experiences as a chaplain in the First World War to refute the second charge and his chair would ostensibly have refuted the first. Just as Clements argues that religious leaders provided legitimation for the Labour Party in New Zealand, so it is possible to argue that Raven and others provided legitimation for pacifism in Britain during the 1930s, even for those not normally associated with the churches.

Overall, a varied pattern of social significance begins to emerge. Without claiming that theology in any way acts as a 'key' variable within modern Britain, a clear possibility arises that it may, at times, be socially significant in shaping attitudes. People outside the churches in the 1930s may never have heard of Raven, let alone actually read his books, but he may nevertheless have made an important contribution to the general legitimation of pacifism at that time.

A very similar argument can be advanced from an analysis of the thoroughgoing pacifist sect, rather than the individual pacifist theologian. Comparing, say, Quakers today with Jehovah's Witnesses, theological considerations do seem to shape their particular responses to war – responses, in turn, that may be significant within society as a whole. Without setting such a claim too high – most people within society are not, after all, thoroughgoing pacifists, or even, perhaps, selective pacifists – a serious possibility can be advanced that theology does act at times as an independent variable.

The response of the Jehovah's Witnesses to war provides a particularly startling example of the way specifically theological considerations may be determinative. Strictly speaking, they are not thoroughgoing pacifists, since, if called upon, they will 'fight for the returning Christ'.[49] Nevertheless, in practice, they have proved to be the most determined draft-resisters of all modern sectarian Christians. So, during the Second World War, of the three groups – Mennonites, Quakers and Jehovah's Witnesses – it was the last group which was the least willing to participate or even to register in the draft and, as a result, some 5,000 served time in prison in

[49]   Bryan Wilson, *Religious Sects*, London: Weidenfeld and Nicolson, 1970, p. 114.

Nazi Germany.[50] While generally rejecting the label of 'pacifism', Jehovah's
Witnesses are, in effect, the most radically pacifist sect in the West.

It seems likely that both their tendency to avoid the label of pacifism and their
actual thoroughgoing pacifism are products of their theological beliefs, particularly
those involving an imminent *parousia*. Although their understanding of the latter
has changed somewhat since their prediction, that the kingdom of God would
begin in 1914, did not materialize in a visible form, they still base their faith on
some imminent cosmic catastrophe. Bryan Wilson argued that they have come to
see 1914 as the beginning of a heavenly and invisible kingdom, in which Christ
and some of the 'anointed class' began to reign:

> Not all of the 144,000 have as yet died, however: some remain on earth, and until
> at least some of these are translated to the heavenly sphere there is an interim,
> in which the world is increasingly experiencing the activities of Satan. Christ
> is at work judging the nations, and the basis for this judgement is the attitude
> of the nations towards the kingdom message and its bearers, that is, Jehovah's
> Witnesses. Those who have rejected the message and persecuted the messengers
> are the goats upon whom judgement will be executed at Armageddon, the great
> war to come ... Millions will die, indeed everyone who opposed Jehovah.
> Thereafter a new heaven with the 144,000 will appear, and a new earth peopled
> by others loyal to Jehovah and by the resurrected dead ... A further judgement at
> the end of the millennium will test the good done by those who previously had
> no chance to hear the message of God.[51]

Wilson suggested that their social involvement was minimal, including their
involvement in human wars, 'less because of injunctions to keep separate from
the world, than because the good Witness is kept busy at Kingdom Hall and in

[50] See Christine E. King, *The Nazi State and the New Religions: Five Case Studies
in Non-Conformity*, New York: Edwin Mellen, 1982; 'Jehovah's Witnesses under Nazism',
in Michael Berenbaum (ed.), *A Mosaic of Victims: Non-Jews Persecuted and Murdered
by the Nazis*, New York: New York University Press, 1990; and 'Responses Outside the
Mainstream Catholic and Protestant Traditions', in C. Rittner, S.D. Smith and I. Steinfeldt
(eds), *The Holocaust and the Christian World*, London: Kuperard, 2000.
[51] Wilson, *Religious Sects*, pp. 112–113.

publicizing the movement'.[52] Undoubtedly, their tightly controlled organization, centring upon a publishing enterprise which enforces doctrinal and practical conformity in its members, is crucial to a sociological understanding of them.[53] Nevertheless, shaped by their strongly held beliefs, it is hardly surprising that Jehovah's Witnesses are unwilling to participate in any way in political wars, or even to have this unwillingness depicted in the political/moral terms of pacifism. On this interpretation, their rejection of war stems, not from a moral rejection of warfare as such, but rather from a theological position which makes all political and 'this worldly' realities irrelevant. Given a radical 'interim ethic', in which present human structures are to be destroyed at any minute, participation in human wars would be pointless, just as it was for first-century Christians.

Such an analysis suggests the clear possibility that, in the case of the Jehovah's Witnesses, theological considerations can act as an independent variable in shaping particular responses to war. In the case of contemporary Quakers this evidence is not so obvious, since other factors in their historical development, notably their comparative acceptance by society at large, may have helped to shape their 'representative' and politically active type of thoroughgoing pacifism.[54] Yet, even with them, it is likely that their theological understanding of individual conscience has shaped their pacifism. It would be difficult for a conscientious Quaker, unlike an Anglican or a Roman Catholic, to accept a particular war as 'just' on the evidence of an outside authority – even those few Quakers who have taken part in wars in the past have tended to conform to my third, rather than to my second, ideal type.

It seems possible also, that it is precisely their emphasis upon individual conscience which has made the Quakers' response to war influential upon those who would not otherwise have been sympathetic to pacifists. In the English context, Bainton argued that 'the Quakers by their allegiance to conscience convinced the government of the rights of conscience, and for the first time were

---

52   Wilson, *Religious Sects*, p. 115.

53   See James A. Beckford, 'The Embryonic Stage of a Religious Sect's Development: The Jehovah's Witnesses', in Michael Hill (ed.), *A Sociological Yearbook of Religion in Britain*, London: SCM Press, 5, 1972, pp. 11–32; and *The Trumpet of Prophecy*, Oxford: Blackwell, 1975.

54   See Bainton, *Christian Attitudes toward War and Peace*, p. 157.

accorded exemption from military service on this ground in 1802'.[55] And Wilson, having suggested that their focus since the mid nineteenth century upon charity was an expression of Quaker conscience, maintained that 'their good work as non-combatants in (First World) War earned them the respect of many who did not share their pacifist principles'.[56]

At least two possible ways emerge in which the Quakers' pacifism may have acted as an independent variable within society. By the nineteenth century they had become politically active and have remained so ever since, exercising an apparent influence disproportionate to their numbers. As a result, on the specific issue of war, they have campaigned, not simply for the legal and political recognition of conscientious objectors, but also for reconciliation between warfaring nations. It is no accident that Quakers have a long involvement with the United Nations in both New York and Geneva and have established a strong reputation for informal and off-the-record diplomatic meetings. In a major study of this long involvement, my colleague Jeremy Carrette has helped to reveal its significance, but also its complexity and ambiguity within the global constraints of the United Nations:

> Religion within globalisation exists inside [a] paradox of inclusion and the centralized systems that structure the inclusion, but part of this inclusion rests on the ability of groups, including religious groups, to be strategic and in this sense we are witnessing a new phenomenon in the study of religion: *religion as a strategic category inside the paradox of global politics*. Religion can be seen as 'strategic' in terms of Foucault's strategic model of power, where power is 'a multiple and mobile field of force relations', something 'never completely stable', as it is not legal or sovereign power, but something 'exercised from innumerable points, in the interplay of nonegalitarian and mobile relations'. In the context of the multiple and mobile sets of force relationships within international institutions like the United Nations, 'religion' is deployed as a discourse to produce a certain re-arrangement of relationships, it facilitates and closes access and engagement between States, between States and NGOs,

[55]   Ibid., p. 161.
[56]   See Wilson, *Religious Sects*, p. 181, although see Peter Brock, *Twentieth-Century Pacifism*, New York: Van Nostrand Reinhold, 1970, p. 20.

and between NGOs themselves, inside the global network of international institutions.[57]

Notwithstanding, explicit political activity may not have been the only way in which religious groups have proved politically influential within society. It seems possible that Quakers also provided an important religious and moral legitimation of pacifism. The rejection of human wars by the Jehovah's Witnesses is apparently too interconnected with their radical sectarian beliefs to be entertained seriously by many other than their own members. That of the Quakers, on the other hand, involves (albeit radically) an element with a rather broader appeal, namely, individual conscience. When this appeal is allied to their observable charitable works, its social significance becomes a real possibility. Sociological theology is, I believe, presented here with a strong possibility that theology, however socially determined in itself, may act at times as an independent variable within society. In the next chapter I shall explore this possibility further, in relation to a single case study.

---

[57]   Jeremy Carrette, 'The Paradox of Globalisation: Quakers, Religious NGOs and the United Nations', in B. Hefner, J. Hutchinson, S. Mels and C. Timmerman (eds), *The Local and the Global in Renegotiating Religious Praxis*, London: Routledge, 2013.

Chapter 2

The Social Significance of the

Honest to God Debate

One of the important tasks of sociological theology is to explore the possibility that theology, even theology in a modern, pluralist society, may at times be socially significant. That is to say, that its influence may sometimes extend beyond the restricted confines of academic theologians and even beyond the confines of the academic community as a whole. This chapter will return to the theological debates about secularization of the 1960s and 1970s explored earlier in Volume 1. However, rather than analysing the social context of theology, it will be concerned instead with the social significance of theology. The focus will also be narrower, analysing a specific debate around Bishop John Robinson's extraordinary and controversial book *Honest to God*.[1] Written in 1963 by a bishop who had already been publicly praised and criticised for defending the publication of D.H. Lawrence's novel *Lady Chatterley's Lover*, it sold many thousands of copies and was extensively debated at the time in many books, periodicals and newspapers – and is still regularly cited in analyses of religious change in modern Britain.[2]

It was a key argument of one of Robinson's most strident theological critics that he, together with Paul van Buren and John Knox, was part and parcel of the secularization process. E.L. Mascall located Robinson in the Protestant school which 'takes as its starting-point the outlook of contemporary secularized man and demands that the traditional faith of Christendom should be completely transformed in order to conform to it'.[3] As seen in Volume 1, Mascall evidently

---

[1] John A.T. Robinson, *Honest to God*, London: SCM Press, 1963.

[2] For example, in Linda Woodhead and Rebecca Catto (eds), *Religion and Change in Modern Britain*, London: Routledge, 2012, it is cited in the Introduction by Woodhead, in chapter 5 by Mark Chapman et al., in chapter 6 by Douglas Davies, and in chapter 7 by Kim Knott and Jolyon Mitchell.

[3] E.L. Mascall, *The Secularisation of Christianity*, London: Libra, 1967, p. 6.

believed this to be a total misunderstanding of the role of theology and in his
judgement Robinson 'completely capitulates to the outlook of the contemporary
world'.[4] Ironically, Mascall's critique of *Honest to God* also provides evidence for
its possible significance. Clearly, he thought that three theological books written
in the same year, *Honest to God*, Paul van Buren's *The Secular Meaning of the
Gospel*[5] and John Knox's *The Church and the Reality of Christ*,[6] were sufficiently
important to warrant a complete book devoted to attacking them. In his preface he
even referred to them as:

> outstanding expressions of a radical and destructive attitude to traditional
> Christianity which has obtained a foothold in many academic circles in the
> United States and the United Kingdom, though until the publication of *Honest to
> God* it was little known to the general public and to the majority of the parochial
> clergy'.[7]

Mascall already had a reputation for producing refutations of contemporary
theological works. In 1962 he wrote a detailed critique, *Up and Down in Adria*,[8]
of the Cambridge symposium *Soundings*[9] and in 1963 he produced a booklet,
Theology and Images[10] largely concerned with refuting A.C. Bridge's *Images of
God*.[11] Nevertheless, he clearly believed that *Honest to God* had proved influential
beyond the confines of academic theology.

For sociological theology it is the very trauma that *Honest to God* created that
makes it interesting. Robinson himself claimed subsequently that he had never
anticipated this trauma:

---

[4]   Mascall, *The Secularisation of Christianity*, p. 7.
[5]   Paul van Buren, *The Secular Meaning of the Gospel*, New York: Macmillan and
London: SCM Press, 1963.
[6]   John Knox, *The Church and the Reality of Christ*, New York: Harper & Row, 1962
and London: Collins, 1963.
[7]   Mascall, *The Secularisation of Christianity*, p. viii.
[8]   E.L. Mascall, *Up and Down in Adria*, London: Faith Press, 1962.
[9]   Alec R. Vidler (ed.), *Soundings*, Cambridge: Cambridge University Press, 1962.
[10]   E.L. Mascall, *Theology and Images*, Oxford: Mowbrays, 1963.
[11]   A.C. Bridge, *Images of God*, London: Hodder & Stoughton, 1960.

The publicity-explosion was neither sought nor expected. If there had been a desire to exploit the market, (a) I should not have given the manuscript to a religious publisher, (b) there would have been a special publicity-campaign to launch it, and (c) I should have written a very different book.[12]

However, a week before publication he did contribute an article to the Sunday newspaper *The Observer*, which the editorial entitled 'Our Image of God Must Go'. He argued later that he wrote this, not to generate publicity for the book, but rather because it provided him with 'a real opportunity outside the normal channels of the Church to engage at a serious level as a Christian in the intellectual debate of our day'.[13] Nevertheless, this overall argument ignores four non-theological features of *Honest to God*, to which I shall return presently and which may help to explain why the book proved so traumatic and possibly so influential.

For whatever reasons *Honest to God* was written (and possibly Robinson himself when he wrote it did not consider too deeply what its effects might be or even for whom he was writing), its immediate repercussions on the theological and ecclesiastical worlds were immense. The then Archbishop of Canterbury, Michael Ramsey, swiftly published a pamphlet, *Images Old and New*,[14] seeking 'to spread reassurance' as Alasdair MacIntyre suggested at the time,[15] and in effect correcting Robinson's doctrinal position. In his Holland Lectures at Oxford in the following year, Ramsey continued on the same theme, but without specifically mentioning *Honest to God*.[16] By 1969 he could write:

Since the stirring of the theological waters some five years ago by Bishop John Robinson's *Honest to God*, theology in England has to a large extent lost what we can now see to have been a long-established insularity. It was perhaps that insularity which made some of us slow to grasp what was happening. It was not that some people called 'new theologians' were inventing theologies

---

[12] John A.T. Robinson in Robinson and David L. Edwards (eds), *The Honest to God Debate*, London: SCM Press, 1963, p. 233.

[13] Robinson and Edwards, *The Honest to God Debate*, p. 234.

[14] A.M. Ramsey, *Images Old and New*, London: SPCK, 1963.

[15] Alasdair MacIntyre, *Against the Self-Images of the Age*, London: Duckworth, 1971, p. 25.

[16] A.M. Ramsey, *Sacred and Secular*, London: Longman, 1964.

of compromise with the secular world: it was rather that they were trying to meet, often in clumsy and muddled ways, pressures and currents already moving powerfully in and beyond Christendom.[17]

The trauma created by *Honest to God* was immediate and widespread. Within weeks of its publication, the Religious Education Press produced O. Fielding Clarke's *For Christ's Sake*, seeking to refute 'Dr Robinson's errors and re-state the Faith in outline'.[18] Clarke himself took time off from his parish and wrote this fierce chapter-by-chapter critique of *Honest to God* in only four weeks. The SCM Press, which published the book on 19 March 1963, managed to bring out a 283-page response entitled *The Honest to God Debate* before the end of the same year. This contained a number of fresh articles concerned with the issues raised by *Honest to God*, 50 letters written to Robinson after its publication and 23 of its many reviews. Indeed theological journals throughout the world reviewed the book. Finally the SCM Press produced a number of subsequent defences by Robinson of his Christian 'orthodoxy', notably his *The New Reformation* in 1965 and *Exploration into God* in 1967 – quite apart from a stream of books by other theologians published by SCM Press and other publishers defending and criticizing *Honest to God*.[19] By the end of the 1960s references to the book were comparatively sparse, but at the time few theological writers passed it unnoticed. Only Richard Dawkins' *The God Delusion*, four decades later, has caused similar theological trauma in modern Britain.[20]

In addition to this trauma, there appeared to be a similar trauma within the non-theological world arising from *Honest to God*. Within a fortnight of publication Michael Ramsey publicly criticized Robinson on television[21] – an unusual step for an Anglican archbishop to take against one of his own bishops. The journalist T.E. Utley asked, 'What should happen to an Anglican bishop who does not believe

---

[17]   A.M. Ramsey, *God, Christ and the World*, London: SCM Press, 1969, pp. 9–10.

[18]   O. Fielding Clark, *For Christ's Sake*, London: Religious Education Press, 1963.

[19]   For example, J.I. Packer, *Keep Yourselves from Idols*, London: Church Book Room Press, 1963, Alan Richardson, *Four Anchors from the Stern*, London: SCM Press, 1963, Clark, *For Christ's Sake*, and Ramsey, *Images Old and New*.

[20]   Richard Dawkins, *The God Delusion*, London: Bantam Press, 2006 and Boston: Houghton Mifflin, 2008.

[21]   Independent Television, 31 March 1963.

in God?', in the *Sunday Telegraph*.[22] C.S. Lewis, E.L. Mascall, Anthony Flew, Sir Julian Huxley, Edward Carpenter and T.R. Milford all contributed articles on the book to *The Observer*. Bryan Green wrote for the *Birmingham Post*, R.P.C. Hanson for *The Irish Times*, Rudolf Bultmann for *Die Zeit* and C.F. Evans spoke on radio. Rarely can there have been so many academic theologians, senior ecclesiastics and others debating about a single book – least of all on the mass media. Writing only months after the publication of *Honest to God*, David Edwards observed:

> The book appears to have sold more quickly than any new book of serious theology in the history of the world. Already over 350,000 copies are in print in Britain, America and Australia, and it is also being published in German, French, Swedish, Dutch, Danish, Italian and Japanese. The discussion has spread even more widely than the readership. Television programmes and sound radio broadcasts, cartoons and satirical jokes, newspaper excerpts and reviews, sermons and Letters to the Editor, swelled the volume of the debate.[23]

The fact that *Honest to God*, unlike most theological or religious works, became a 'best-seller' and that it stimulated over one thousand people to write to Robinson, again indicates that it may have been socially significant. The letters, some of which were reproduced in *The Honest to God Debate* and were then analysed in detail by the sociologist Robert Towler,[24] provided a rich, even if somewhat partisan, source of evidence about the effect of the book on the non-theological public. In addition, Robinson, as a direct result of the trauma created by *Honest to God*, was invited to contribute to a variety of popular newspapers and magazine, including the *Sunday Mirror*, *The Sun*, *TV Times* and *Tit-Bits*. He reached an audience seldom influenced directly by academic theologians.

---

[22]   The *Sunday Telegraph*, 24 March 1963 – for this and subsequent items in this paragraph see Robinson and Edwards, *The Honest to God Debate*, p. 95f.

[23]   Robinson and Edwards, *The Honest to God Debate*, p. 7.

[24]   Robert Towler, *The Need for Certainty: A Sociological Study of Conventional Religion*, London: Routledge & Kegan Paul, 1984.

The Paradox of *Honest to God*

None the less, *Honest to God* also created a paradox. A content analysis of the book suggests features which appear too technical for a non-theological readership and even some of the central ideas within it are not elaborated clearly or succinctly. Robinson's often-repeated claim that he did not intend it to be a 'best-seller', reaching such a wide audience, would seem correct. If *Honest to God* is compared stylistically with some of his more popular writings – such as *But That I Can't Believe*[25] – clear differences emerge.

The contents of *Honest to God* fall naturally under four headings – God, Christ, Prayer and Morality. Three chapters are devoted to the first topic and just one each to the other three. The final chapter, 'Recasting the Mould', repeats some of Robinson's themes, but it too is largely concerned with images of God. It is hardly surprising, then, that much of the subsequent debate among theologians centred upon theistic images and models. Curiously, though, it is precisely this feature of the book which may have proved most difficult for non-theological readers. Such concepts as 'deus ex machina', 'demythologizing', 'existentialism' and 'being' are used without explanation. In addition, he makes frequent reference to Tillich, Bultmann and Bonhoeffer in a manner more designed for theologians than for the general public.

Robinson starts by suggesting that there has been a 'reluctant revolution' in our thinking about God, since, 'in place of a God who is literally or physically "up there" we have accepted, as part of our mental furniture, a God who is spiritually or metaphysically "out there".'[26] In this respect we are different from our fore-fathers, even though 'every one of us lives with some mental picture of a God "out there", a God who "exists" above and beyond the world, a God "to" whom we pray and to whom we "go" when we die'.[27] He argues that these spatial terms are now an 'offence' to many, though he fully realizes that 'to be asked to give up any idea of a Being "out there" at all will appear to be an outright denial of God'.[28] Nevertheless, he maintains that we are being asked to do just this.

---

[25]   John A.T. Robinson, *But That I Can't Believe*, London: SCM Press, 1967.
[26]   Robinson, *Honest to God*, p. 13.
[27]   Ibid., p. 14.
[28]   Ibid., p. 17.

Like Paul Tillich, Robinson believes that traditional proofs for the existence of God are irrelevant, since their result would be merely 'a further piece of existence, that might conceivably not have been there'.[29] So in the second chapter, he argues:

> We must start the other way round. God is, by definition, ultimate reality. And one cannot argue whether ultimate reality exists. One can only ask what ultimate reality is like whether, for instance, in the last analysis what lies at the heart of things and governs their working is to be described in personal or impersonal categories.[30]

So, with Tillich, he prefers to talk about God as 'Being' rather than 'a Being', seeing parallels in Bultmann's programme of 'demythologizing' and Bonhoeffer's castigations of the 'God of religion'. He is aware that this demolition of traditional theism will 'appear to leave many people bereft and "without God in the world"'[31] and attract a charge of atheism to himself, but he still believes it to be necessary in the interests of 'intelligent faith'.

One of the surprising features of *Honest to God* is that the first 44 pages are almost wholly negative and iconoclastic. In them Robinson criticizes a series of traditional images of God and only then does he offer alternative ones. It is possible that this is one of the features that contributed to its overall impact. It is not until the third chapter that he opts unequivocally for Tillich's image of God as 'The Ground of Our Being', arguing that the model of 'depth' is preferable to that of 'height':

> There is no doubt that this simple substitution can make much religious language suddenly appear more relevant. For we are familiar today with depth psychology, and with the idea that ultimate truth is deep and profound. Moreover, while 'spiritual wickedness in high places', and all the mythology of angelic powers which the Biblical writers associate with it, seems to the modern man a fantastic

---

[29] Ibid., p. 29.
[30] Ibid., p. 29.
[31] Ibid., p. 43.

phantasmagoria, similar, equally mythological, language when used by Freud of conflicts in the unconscious appears perfectly acceptable.[32]

Using the concept of 'depth' as his starting-point, Robinson claims, with Tillich, that God is 'the infinite and inexhaustible depth and ground of all being, of our ultimate concern, of what we take seriously without reservation'.[33] Aware that this claim could be mistaken for a Feuerbachian transformation of theology into anthropology, he insists that 'theological statements are indeed affirmations about human existence – but they are affirmations about the ultimate ground and depth of that existence'.[34] Distinguishing this position further from naturalism, he maintains that 'the necessity for the name "God" lies in the fact that our being has depths which naturalism, whether evolutionary, mechanistic, dialectical or humanistic, cannot or will not recognise'.[35]

By comparison with the first three chapters, the fourth, on Christ, received little attention from critics. In structure, though, it is similar to the section on God, since it seeks to disclaim traditional theological images, before offering a Tillichian alternative. It opens with a characteristically stylized account:

> Traditional Christology has worked with a frankly supranaturalist scheme. Popular religion has expressed this mythologically, professional theology metaphysically. For this way of thinking, the Incarnation means that God the Son came down to earth, and was born, lived and died within this world as a man. From 'out there' there graciously entered into the human scene one who was not 'of it' and yet who lived genuinely and completely within it.[36]

Robinson maintains that this traditional interpretation of Christology almost inevitably suggests that 'Jesus was not a man born and bred ... he looked like a man ... he talked like a man, but underneath he was God dressed up – like

---

[32] Ibid., pp. 45–46.
[33] Ibid., p. 46.
[34] Ibid., p. 48.
[35] Ibid., p. 54.
[36] Ibid., p. 64.

Father Christmas.'[37] Here too it is evident that *Honest to God* presents the reader with an unusual mixture of technical theological terms, idiomatic epithets and caricature.

Moving from this negative beginning and having already rejected a purely naturalist interpretation of Christology, Robinson suggests, with echoes of D.M. Baillie,[38] that 'Jesus reveals God by being utterly transparent to him'.[39] With echoes again of Tillich, he continues:

> It is in Jesus, and Jesus alone, that there is nothing of self to be seen, but solely the ultimate, unconditional love of God ... it is as he empties himself not of his Godhead but of himself, of any desire to focus attention on himself, of any craving to be 'on an equality with God', that he reveals God. For it is in making himself nothing, in his utter self-surrender to others in love, that he discloses and lays bare the Ground of man's being in Love.[40]

This combination of elements from Baillie and Tillich, in a reversal of the kenotic theory in Christology, is arguably one of the more original features of *Honest to God*. Yet, it received comparatively little attention from theologians at the time.

The fifth chapter is concerned with prayer and worship, areas in which his views were already well known among theologians.[41] Following his characteristic procedure, he starts with a critical observation:

> Liturgy and worship would, on the face of it, seem to be concerned essentially with what takes place in a consecrated building, with the holy rather than the common, with 'religion' rather than 'life'. They belong to, and indeed virtually constitute, that area or department of experience which appeals to 'the religious type', to those who 'like that sort of thing' or 'get something out of it'.[42]

---

[37] Ibid., p. 66.

[38] D.M. Baillie, *God Was In Christ*, London: Faber and Faber, 1956.

[39] Robinson, *Honest to God*, p. 73.

[40] Ibid., pp. 74–75.

[41] See John A.T. Robinson, *On Being the Church in the World*, London: SCM Press, 1960, and *Liturgy Coming to Life*, London: SCM Press, 1963.

[42] Robinson, *Honest to God*, p. 85.

Too often, he maintains, communion becomes individualistic devotion in which we 'make our communion' with 'the God out there'. He argues that instead communion is essentially a communal event: the function of worship is 'to focus, sharpen and deepen our response to the world and to other people beyond the point of proximate concern (of liking, self-interest, limited commitment, etc.) to that of ultimate concern; to purify and correct our loves in the light of Christ's love; and in him to find the grace and power to be the reconciled and reconciling community'.[43]

On private prayer he is scathing about a type of 'monastic spirituality' which conceives it as a 'turning aside from the business of "the world" to "be with God".'[44] It should be seen rather as a 'penetration through the world to God'.[45] Again, in typically Tillichian terms, he concludes that 'to pray for another is to expose both oneself and him to the common ground of our being; it is to see one's concern for him in terms of ultimate concern, to let God into the relationship'.[46]

The final theme that he considers is that of morality, arguing that 'it is impossible to reassess one's doctrine of God, of how one understands the transcendent, without bringing one's view of morality into the same melting-pot'.[47] There is, however, a crucial difference between this area and that of doctrine, since here, he believes, there has already been a revolution in public opinion. Consequently, 'our only task is to relate it correctly to the previous revolution we have described and to try to discern what should be the Christian attitude to it'.[48] Nevertheless, Robinson still adheres to his method of critical caricature followed by a Tillichian alternative. So, in response to this revolution in morals, he claims:

> There are plenty of voices within the Church greeting it with vociferous dismay. The religious sanctions are losing their strength, the moral landmarks are disappearing beneath the flood, the nation is in danger. This is the end-term of the apostasy from Christianity: the fathers rejected the doctrine, the children

---

43   Ibid., pp. 87–88.
44   Ibid., p. 91.
45   Ibid., p. 97.
46   Ibid., p. 99.
47   Ibid., p. 105.
48   Ibid., p. 105.

have abandoned the morals ... Christianity is identified *tout court* with the old, traditional morality.[49]

Such normative approaches to morality, he believes, distort the teaching of Jesus. The latter 'is saying that love, utterly unconditional love, admits of no accommodation; you cannot define in advance situations in which it can be satisfied with less than complete and unreserved self-giving'.[50] This account of morality in terms of 'situation ethics' is then transcribed into Tillichian terms:

> In ethics this means accepting as the basis of moral judgements the actual concrete relationship in all its particularity, refusing to subordinate it to any universal norm or to treat it merely as a case, but yet, in the depth of that unique relationship, meeting and responding to the claims of the sacred, the holy and the absolutely unconditional. For the Christian it means recognising as the ultimate ground of our being which is thus encountered, and as the basis of every relationship and every decision, the unconditional love of Jesus Christ, 'the man for others'.[51]

Writing at a time when Fletcher's concept of 'situation ethics' was still relatively unknown in Britain, Robinson's views on morality caused considerable debate among theologians and a number of books discussed the 'new morality'.[52] Three years later, however, this attention was deflected to Fletcher himself, with the publication of *Situation Ethics*.[53] But, for a while, the impact of this chapter was almost as great as that of the first three chapters – at least among theologians and preachers.

---

[49]   Ibid., p. 106.

[50]   Ibid., pp. 111–112.

[51]   Ibid., p. 114.

[52]   For example D. Rhymes, *No New Morality*, London: Constable, 1964, cf. Paul Ramsey, *Deeds and Rules in Christian Ethics*, Edinburgh Scottish Journal of Theology Occasional Paper No. 11, 1965 [expanded as *Deeds and Rules in Christian Ethics*, New York: Scribners, 1967]. See also, John A.T. Robinson, *Christian Morals Today*, London: SCM Booklet, 1964.

[53]   Joseph Fletcher, *Situation Ethics*, Philadelphia, PA: Westminster and London: SCM Press, 1966.

In his final chapter he admits that 'it will doubtless seem to some that I have by implication abandoned the Christian faith and practice altogether'.[54] However, he maintains that the changes are essential and that they leave 'the fundamental truth of the Gospel unaffected':[55]

> I believe that unless we are prepared for the kind of revolution of which I have
> spoken it will come to be abandoned. And that will be because it is moulded,
> in the form we know it, by a cast of thought that belongs to a past age—the
> cast of thought which, with their different emphases, Bultmann describes as
> 'mythological', Tillich as 'supranaturalist', and Bonhoeffer as 'religious'.[56]

We must be prepared, he maintains, to let everything 'go into the melting', even 'our most cherished religious categories and moral absolutes' and certainly 'our image of God himself'.[57]

Even this bare summary of the contents of *Honest to God* creates a paradox, which most commentators at the time found difficult to explain. The book relied heavily on technical theologians (notably Tillich) and it used many unexplained theological terms from them – yet it became a 'best seller'. It may, indeed, be doubted whether more than a small minority of those who bought *Honest to God* coped with its stylistic and conceptual difficulties. Whereas it is quite possible to believe that it caused an impact among those specifically trained in theology (who may not all have been thoroughly familiar with Tillich or Fletcher), its impact on the non-theological world was more perplexing.

Sociological theology, then, is faced with a paradox. While it might be accepted that *Honest to God* was socially significant among those with theological training, it is more difficult to assess the likely cognitive effect on those without this training. Even the evidence already suggested of the generalized social significance of the work does not actually dissolve this difficulty. It actually heightens the dilemma. The two sets of evidence – one suggesting that *Honest to God* made an impact well beyond normal theological circles and the other suggesting that stylistically

---

[54]   Robinson, *Honest to God*, p. 123.

[55]   Ibid., p. 124.

[56]   Ibid., p. 123.

[57]   Ibid., p. 124.

and conceptually parts of it might have been incomprehensible outside these circles – appear mutually contradictory. In the face of this apparent paradox it becomes imperative to subject the impact of *Honest to God* to rigorous analysis. More specifically, it is important to assess its social significance in terms of the four levels of analysis suggested earlier, namely: theologians, preachers, listeners and outsiders.

Four Levels of Social Significance

In the light of all the preceding evidence, there can be little doubt that *Honest to God* was socially significant among both theologians and those academics with an interest in theology. Naturally many were highly critical of the work, not a few calling into question Robinson's status as a Christian and as a 'theist' – the youthful Alasdair MacIntyre famously claiming that 'what is striking about Dr Robinson's book is first and foremost that he is an atheist'[58] – but few failed to respond to it in some way. Whatever they thought of its academic merits, most responded to the generalized interest in it by reviewing or commenting upon it. Few theological works can have received such intense inspection within the theological world. Half a century later some theologians might even conclude that its contents are now actually not even contentious. Once it is acknowledged that all theological concepts are analogical or symbolic (as Volume 1 argued), then all Robinson was doing was arguing about the merits of replacing some symbols/analogies with others. He was not replacing non-symbolic with purely symbolic terms (as some appeared to imagine at the time).

As already indicated, two elements in *Honest to God* received particular attention from theologians. The first and by far the most prominent was its concern with images of God: the second was its concern with morality. The latter soon developed into an argument about the merits or demerits of 'situation ethics' and consequently tended to focus instead upon Fletcher, but the former continued to centre upon Robinson for some years, not fading until the end of the decade.

Initially, the theological debate about images of God concentrated upon the cognitive issue of whether or not the Tillichian language proposed by Robinson

---

[58] Robinson and Edwards, *The Honest to God Debate*, p. 215.

could adequately represent Christian belief. Paul van Buren's *The Secular Meaning of the Gospel*, published very shortly after *Honest to God* and owing nothing directly to it, stimulated this debate still further, since here *was* an attempt to translate Christian belief into thoroughly 'secular' terms. Robinson did not wholly accept this radical translation of theistic language into language about 'contagious freedom', but he did welcome it as 'a major contribution' to the debate.[59] Taken together, these two books in particular, stimulated a series of other books, attempting to isolate the key issues of belief involved in the debate.[60]

Before long, however, another issue became dominant in the theological response to *Honest to God*, namely, a focus upon the issue of secularization. Although the term 'secularization' appears very seldom in *Honest to God* itself, it was used by Robinson quite frequently in the subsequent debate and, as seen in Volume 1, became a central issue alike among his critics and defenders. Clearly, his initial argument depended on (a) the belief that there was a process of secularization (or something very much like it) apparent within the West and (b) that Christians should respond positively to it. While few at the time questioned (a), many, like Mascall,[61] were thoroughly opposed to (b).

This first level of analysis presents the fewest problems, especially if 'theology' is regarded primarily as a written discipline. The theological literature of the 1960s shows that *Honest to God* did have an immense effect upon contemporary theology within Britain and indeed upon theology within much of the Western world. Few other works of theology can have achieved such an immediate effect.

Analysis of the social significance of *Honest to God* at the other three levels is not so straightforward. Here, the analysis can no longer rely so directly upon written records, but must, instead, search for other indicators. Since many preachers have received a theological training, it can be assumed that they read *Honest to God* with more understanding than those without such training. At the least, they could have been familiar with some of the unexplained technical theological terms used in the book. There are, indeed, indications that they responded to some of the cognitive issues raised by Robinson and particularly those concerned with images

---

[59]   Ibid., p. 250.
[60]   See Alan Richardson, *Religion in Contemporary Debate*, London: SCM Press, 1966, and David Jenkins, *Guide to the Debate about God*, London: SCM Press, 1966.
[61]   Mascall, *The Secularisation of Christianity*.

of God. Few who worked as ministers at the time can have failed to notice the widespread anxiety expressed by their colleagues over these issues. Bryan Wilson depicted this well when he wrote in 1966:

> The scepticism of modern society has affected the clerical profession profoundly. The attempt to find other levels at which religious propositions are true—that is to say, levels other than the common-sense and literal level—has led to widely diverse clerical interpretations of religion in its contemporary meaning. Clerics have now come to disbelieve in the ultimacy of any answers which they can supply about social questions, as they did earlier about physical questions. As the range of empirical information has increased, acquisition of the knowledge of it and the skills to analyse it and interpret it pass beyond the range of clerical education. The awareness of the relativity of modern knowledge has made the cleric more guarded and less confident in the intellectual content of religion.[62]

This passage contains a number of assumptions that subsequent sociologists have found difficult to accept. Unsurprisingly it is set within the overall context of Wilson's thoroughgoing secularization paradigm, which, as already noted, is now subject to considerable sociological scepticism. Wilson also clearly distinguished between 'common-sense' or 'literal' levels at which religious propositions may be true and 'other' such levels. This was despite, as noted in Volume 1, theologians at the time arguing that no human language can be applied to God univocally.[63] He further contended that ecumenism was increasingly acting as the 'new faith' of the clergy in the absence of theistic beliefs, in an age 'when traditional ideas about God have been radically challenged by bishops of the Church'.[64] Bryan Turner, in contrast, concluded that his understanding of ecumenism was sociologically incomplete.[65]

---

[62] Bryan Wilson, *Religion in Secular Society*, London: C.A. Watts, 1966 and Harmondsworth, Middlesex: Penguin, 1969, p. 96.

[63] E.L. Mascall, *Existence and Analogy*, London: Darton, Longman & Todd, 1949, and John Macquarrie, *God-Talk*, London: SCM Press, 1967.

[64] Wilson, *Religion in Secular Society*, p. 151.

[65] Bryan S. Turner, 'The Sociological Explanation of Ecumenicalism', in C.L. Mitton (ed.), *The Social Sciences and the Churches*, Edinburgh: T&T Clark, 1972, pp. 231–245.

Nevertheless, as a depiction of the clergy in the mid 1960s Bryan Wilson's account may not be too inaccurate. In retrospect, this time proved to be a fairly traumatic one for a number of clergy, as some of the letters from them to Robinson indicated.[66] Cognitive as well as functional, dilemmas did seem to play a part and it is likely that *Honest to God* was a significant variable within this situation. David Edwards, writing shortly after the book's publication, noted that 'many printed comments, and reports of sermons and addresses, emphasized the distress of many Christian believers'.[67] Although a number of radical theological works could have caused this effect among the clergy the very success and wide availability of *Honest to God* makes it an obvious candidate as a key factor within this situation. In contrast, Paul van Buren's *The Secular Meaning of the Gospel* presented the non-academic with semantic difficulties, owing to its frequent use of contemporary philosophy, which, comparatively speaking, *Honest to God* did not.

If this analysis is correct and the cognitive issues raised by *Honest to God* and debated at length by other theologians really did impinge, in part at least, upon the preachers, then it seems possible that they may also have engaged the 'listeners' – a group that includes both those who actually read the book and/or writings about it and those who simply heard the preachers. Mass Observation had established two decades earlier that congregations can be theologically confused.[68] Exploiting this evidence Alasdair MacIntyre ruefully claimed that 'the creed of the English is that there is no God and that it is wise to pray to him from time to time'.[69] Even David Martin, despite his dismissal of the secularization paradigm, argued then that 'the religion of modern Britain is a deistic, moralistic religion-in-general, which combines a fairly high practice of personal prayer with a considerable degree of superstition'.[70] It would take an ingenious survey to show that this cognitive confusion among the listeners was either heightened or diminished by *Honest to God*. The possibility, nevertheless, that it might have had some effect at this level cannot be overruled.

---

[66]   See Robinson and Edwards, *The Honest to God Debate*, p. 48f and Towler, *The Need for Certainty*.

[67]   Robinson and Edwards, *The Honest to God Debate*, p. 48.

[68]   Mass Observation, *Puzzled People: A Study of Popular Attitudes to Religion, Ethics, Progress and Politics in a London Borough*, London: Gollancz, 1947.

[69]   Robinson and Edwards, *The Honest to God Debate*, p. 228.

[70]   David Martin, 'The Secularisation Question', *Theology*, 76:630, Feb. 1973, p. 86.

Nevertheless, the paradox remains. *Honest to God* sold widely among a non-theological public, but it was likely to have been, at least partially, incomprehensible to it. Even the fact that Robinson contributed a number of far simpler articles to 'popular' magazines and newspapers does not resolve this paradox, since it was the book itself that sold so widely. Any sociological consideration of the social significance of *Honest to God* must take this paradox into account.

It is possible, though, that the analysis up to this point has been too cognitive-orientated. From a perspective within the sociologist of knowledge it might be too readily assumed that it is ideas, as ideas, which are socially significant and not ideas as they are in fact presented to the listener. Once analysis focuses upon the latter, four non-theological features of *Honest to God*, require particular attention. Together, they may help to explain both why the book became a 'best-seller' and what its generalized impact may have been.

The first feature is that in *Honest to God* Robinson emphasized his function as a bishop. So, 'it belongs to the office of a bishop ...' are the opening words of the preface.[71] In the first chapter he claims that 'as a bishop I could happily get on with most of my work without ever being forced to discuss such questions':[72] at the end of the chapter he writes that he is 'deliberately writing as an ordinary churchman', not as a professional theologian.[73] From the perspective of publicity, the fact that the writer of the book was a bishop was crucial: all clergy are vulnerable to publicity and bishops even more so. At the same time that Robinson was writing, Bishop Pike was causing an immense stir in the States and soon afterwards the British newspapers were reporting that the Bishop of Munich was suspected of war crimes, the Bishop of Southwell had apparently eloped, the Bishop of Leicester had signed a 'keep the cricket tour' petition in the face of anti-apartheid protests and the Bishop of Coventry had condemned pornography. By emphasizing his function as a bishop, while at the same time writing radical theology, Robinson may well have contributed significantly to its general publicity.

By implication, Wilson appeared to support this suggestion:

---

[71]   Robinson, *Honest to God*, p. 7.

[72]   Ibid., p. 18.

[73]   Ibid., pp. 26–27.

> That some clergy themselves become sceptical, and cease to believe in many
> of the things which laymen believe in as essentials of the faith, or believe in
> them in an entirely different way, can only be a source of confusion and despair
> to those who want to believe in certain, and usually simple, truths. A Bishop
> Barnes of Birmingham in the 1930s and 40s, a Bishop Pike of California, and a
> Bishop Robinson of Woolwich, in the 1960s, are only sources of bewilderment
> to ordinary believers, some of whom are impious enough to wonder why, if
> men think as they do, they continue to take their stipends from Churches which
> commit them, in honesty, to rather different beliefs.[74]

It is interesting to note here that it is the bishops whom Wilson singled out as being socially significant agents of change among laypeople.

Secondly, on more than one occasion in *Honest to God*, Robinson suggests that what he is writing would be regarded by many as 'heretical'. The labels 'heretic' and 'atheist' occur in several parts of the book. So, at the end of the preface he writes that 'what I have tried to say, in a tentative and exploratory way, may seem to be radical, and doubtless to many heretical'.[75] In the section on God, he admits that what he has to say on the subject will be 'resisted as a denial of the Gospel' by ninety- per-cent of the people:[76] in the section on morality, he claims that his views are not 'what men expect the Church to stand for' and that they will be regarded 'as profoundly shocking':[77] and, in the final chapter, he states that some will think he has 'abandoned the Christian faith and practice altogether.'[78] The general effect of hinting so often that he may be a 'heretic' or even an 'atheist' is to make the book highly provocative. A number of people responded by agreeing with these labels as a correct depiction of him.[79]

Thirdly, *Honest to God* is iconoclastic. It has already been shown that each of the four sections – on God, Christ, Prayer and Morality – begins with a demolition of traditional images. In particular, the first of these, in which Robinson seeks to discredit traditional images of God as he understands them, extends to page 44.

---

[74] *Religion in Secular Society*, pp. 97–98.
[75] Robinson, *Honest to God*, p. 10.
[76] Ibid., p. 18.
[77] Ibid., p. 109.
[78] Ibid., p. 123.
[79] Robinson and Edwards, *The Honest to God Debate*, p. 95f.

Even if the specific issues which he is discussing are unclear to the non-theological reader, the fact that he is attempting to break down existing beliefs is perfectly clear.

Fourthly, *Honest to God*, as a work in theology, contains a surprising amount of caricature. His characteristic style in each of the sections is to demolish traditional images in a caricatured form and only then to offer a Tillichian alternative. Writing in the first section on God, he suggests that for most Christians and non-Christians 'he has been more of a Grandfather in heaven, a kindly Old Man who could be pushed into one corner':[80] in the second, he compares the traditional Christ to an 'astronaut': in the third, traditional prayers are termed 'spiritual refills': and in the fourth, traditional morality is said to 'come straight from heaven'. Part of the protest from traditional theologians, such as Mascall, was that their position had been distorted and caricatured.

These four features taken together – an emphasis on episcopacy, a suggestion of 'heresy', of iconoclasm and of caricature – may have served to give *Honest to God* its distinctively polemical and provocative character. Given that the cognitive issues involved in the book would have been blurred for the reader without a theological training by Robinson's frequent use of technical theological terms, it may have been these features which proved socially significant at this level.

This suggestion receives a degree of confirmation from a comparison of *Honest to God* with Robinson's two subsequent works, *The New Reformation?* and *Exploration into God*. Both of these later books are distinctly more eirenic than the first and, although they continue to deal with the same substantive issues, they no longer abound with the four features. So, in *The New Reformation?* Robinson rarely mentions his function as a bishop and no longer suggests that his position will be regarded as 'heretical' or 'atheistic'. Even the opening chapter, with its seemingly iconoclastic title, 'Troubling of the Waters', proves to be eirenic and his concept of 'reformation' turns out to be 'marked as much by evolution as by revolution'.[81] The caricatures of traditional images are also less evident in this later book. In *Exploration into God*, Robinson appears even keener to avoid provocation, arguing now that in *Honest to God* 'I was taking for granted most of

---

[80]   Robinson, *Honest to God*, p. 41.

[81]   John A.T. Robinson, *The New Reformation?*, London: SCM Press, 1965, p. 79.

what I believed'[82] and offering an account of the transcendence of God. Even the chapter titles become eirenic. Instead of a chapter entitled 'The End of Theism?', as in *Honest to God*, the later book has a chapter entitled 'The Displacement Effect of Theism'. In the following chapter on the 'Death of God' theology, Robinson is far more critical of Paul van Buren's *The Secular Meaning of the Gospel* than he was earlier. Significantly, neither of these later books, with their absence of the polemical features of *Honest to God*, became 'best sellers'.

These four features may also have had a certain effect on the fourth level, that of the 'outsiders' (that is, those who neither read any parts of the debate nor heard preachers at the time). Even those who could not name John Robinson or *Honest to God* might still have had some awareness from the widespread media attention that a bishop had been saying provocative things about matters usually accepted by Christians. Robinson's own attempts to communicate in tabloid newspapers and magazines may also have increased this awareness.

Finally, the possibility cannot be ignored that *Honest to God* may have played a part in legitimating existing religious doubt in any of the four levels. It is apparent from some of the letters sent to Robinson after publication, that people, in varying positions and with varying degrees of theological sophistication, felt relief that a bishop had openly expressed doubts on matters of doctrinal orthodoxy. Others, of course, expressed hostility to this expression of doubts, but among those who expressed relief the book appeared to be an important legitimating factor.

The phenomenon of *Honest to God* and the debate that it provoked, presents sociological theology with an exceptionally important, even if rare, case study. It seems clear that the book was socially significant among both theologians and preachers in the mid 1960s. In addition, it seems likely that it was socially significant among congregations and among those acquainted with religious literature at the time. Unusually, it may even have been socially significant among the general public. Its influence varied in content from one group to another, but it would appear to have been widespread. This case study suggests that, at least occasionally, theology, however determined by society, may in turn act as an independent variable within it.

In retrospect, *Honest to God* was also an unusual phenomenon. Its impact was unexpected in the 1960s and has not been replicated since. In the rest of this book

---

[82]   John A.T. Robinson, *Exploration into God*, London: SCM, 1967, p. 14.

I will argue that the social significance of theology is more typically to be located in theological virtues that have been transposed into wider society. This is an argument that will be developed step by step in the chapters that follow.

Chapter 3

Prophecy and the Transposition of Virtues

In Volume 1 it was seen how the paradigm of secularization tended to frame discussion a generation ago about the role of Christianity in shaping British society. Even a brief analysis of contemporary writings in both sociology of religion and theology was sufficient to indicate the importance of this paradigm. Both defenders and critics of the paradigm seemed to agree on its importance. Indeed, more than that, both seemed to accept the same basic starting-point; namely, that, in contemporary, Western society, Christianity is politically insignificant.

Defenders of a thoroughgoing secularization model, like Bryan Wilson in Britain and the young Peter Berger in the United States,[1] tended to argue that there is a general process discernible in Western society whereby all aspects of religion have become increasingly epiphenomenal. Early critics, of course, did not share this viewpoint. Some, like Peter Glasner,[2] questioned whether there really ever was a 'golden age' of religion in Europe, when Christianity was socially significant. Others, like Andrew Greeley,[3] maintained, as seen earlier, that religion remained a remarkably constant phenomenon over the centuries. In contrast, David Martin,[4] while rejecting overall claims about a long-standing process, nevertheless sought to expound a general theory of secularization, outlining the circumstances in which

---

[1]   See Peter L. Berger, *The Social Reality of Religion*, London: Faber and Faber, 1969 [US title, *The Sacred Canopy of Religion*, Garden City, NY: Doubleday, 1967] and Bryan Wilson, *Religion in Secular Society*, London: C.A. Watts, 1966 and Harmondsworth, Middlesex: Penguin, 1969.

[2]   Peter E. Glasner, *The Sociology of Secularisation*, London: Routledge & Kegan Paul, 1977.

[3]   Andrew M. Greeley, *Unsecular Man: The Persistence of Religion*, New York: Schocken Books, 1972 [English title *The Persistence of Religion*, London: SCM Press, 1973].

[4]   See especially David Martin, *A General Theory of Secularization*, Oxford: Blackwell, 1978; *On Secularization: Towards a Revised General Theory*, Aldershot, Hants: Ashgate, 2005; *The Future of Christianity: Reflections on Violence, Democracy, Religion and Secularization*, Farnham, Surrey: Ashgate, 2011.

religious institutions and beliefs do in fact decline, and concluded that Europe is currently confronted with a fragmentation and privatization of Christianity. In effect, the conclusions of these sociologists were remarkably similar despite their real differences over the concept of secularization. Most agreed at the time that, however long this has lasted and however many alternative religious phenomena are present in society, Christianity within Western society is no longer politically significant.

This chapter will argue, in contrast, that although Max Weber, along with Emile Durkheim, did appear to accept that religion was becoming increasingly epiphenomenal in the modern world – both pioneer sociologists of religion are usually seen as secularization theorists – Weber, in particular, also used a rather different paradigm. Instead of viewing religious concepts as simply disappearing under pressure from modernity, he entertained the idea that they still flourished in the modern world albeit not in the form of religious beliefs as such but rather as transposed values or virtues.

Secularization or Transposition?

A number of pieces of evidence seemed to reinforce assumptions about the social and political insignificance of Western religion. There did seem to be a general trend throughout Europe towards a separation of church from state. Few sociologists or political commentators had any serious doubts that Eire and Italy will eventually introduce the sort of distinction between church and state apparent elsewhere. The continued presence of Church of England bishops in the House of Lords or the continued intervention by government into Swedish Church politics did not undermine this confidence. Whether or not this was seen in terms of a secularization paradigm, the general trend seemed obvious.

Again, the statements of contemporary politicians who were known to be practising Christians seemed to support the overall view that Christianity in Western society was now politically insignificant. In Britain it was well known that, despite their public acknowledgements of faith, politicians in the 1960s such as Enoch Powell, Alec Douglas-Home and Quintin Hogg, saw this faith as affecting more their private than their political lives. Perhaps, for this reason, most British politicians at the time seldom made public their private Christian convictions.

Nonetheless, there is another and quite different way of looking at this evidence. This viewpoint takes its initial insight from Weber's concept of the transposition of religious virtues. In Weber's thesis, as noted in Chapter 1, it was virtues which may appear to the theologian as less than central, such as industriousness and asceticism, which were transposed into society. A more thoroughgoing paradigm of transposition might hold, instead, that Western society is embedded in Christian virtues to such an extent that it can scarcely even detect these virtues. According to this view, Christianity has been astonishingly successful in converting Western society– so successful, in fact, that it is difficult to tell Christians apart from non-Christians within it. Again, Weber argued that transposed Christian virtues can persist in society long after their initial institutional basis has been forgotten. So, as seen earlier, the virtues of 'thrift', 'hard-work' and 'honesty', may have been derived originally from theological notions of predestination, sanctification or election (in Weber's view), but they no longer require theological underpinning in the modern world. Such theological roots were important only at the outset. Similarly, it could be argued that other Christian virtues are so well established in Western society that they no longer require support from the churches.

It is important to state this transposition paradigm carefully. It is not necessary to claim that it is the specific teaching of particular European churches which has proved politically significant. Indeed, there is good reason to believe that the particular teachings of many churches on moral or political issues are themselves structured by society, as Volume 2 argued. Rather, the paradigm needs to claim only that certain Western virtues, such as 'justice' and 'peace', have roots in Christianity. Again, the paradigm need not claim that the New Testament gives Christians clear-cut and unambiguous teaching on specific moral issues (it would be difficult to justify such a claim historically). It need only claim that there are certain overall and general (but nonetheless crucial) virtues that are deeply embedded in the Christian belief in a creating, redeeming and sanctifying God.

It might be difficult to isolate such generalized virtues using this paradigm. Yet, if a transposition paradigm is held in anything like a thoroughgoing way, certain rather puzzling phenomena known to sociologists of religion at once became more understandable. Of these, three, in particular, might be singled out.

Firstly, it was usually thought at the time to be extremely difficult to detect the social significance of churchgoing in the West. There was an established correlation between churchgoing and religious beliefs (as one might indeed expect), but secular correlations proved more elusive. Secularization theorists naturally used this as evidence of the epiphenomenality or marginality of churchgoing and of religion in general. However, on a transposition paradigm, this phenomenon was explained in quite a different way. According to this, the distinction between churchgoers and non-churchgoers is inevitably a blurred one, since both groups live in a society that is already embedded in Christian virtues.

Secondly, the tendency of churches (as distinct from sects) to conform to the world was frequently taken as an indication of secularization or, at least as a sign of their political insignificance. To return to the case study used in the first chapter, it was argued that church attitudes towards war tended to differ very little, if at all, from those prevalent in Western society as a whole. Only in the pre-Constantinian church is there a really marked difference between official teaching on war and general public opinion, but arguably Christianity, at this stage, was basically a sectarian form of religion. So, despite the obvious attraction of pacifism in terms of the New Testament, pacifism did not seem to be an option generally open to churches in non-pacifist societies. Even on issues of 'private' morality, such as abortion, it was again possible to detect a strong tendency of churches to conform to the views prevalent in society as a whole. So, although, in Britain at least, as was seen in Volume 2, there was evidence to suggest that the Abortion Act 1968, and the law on divorce before it, were influenced by submissions from the Church of England's Board for Social Responsibility, there was also strong evidence that these submissions had already been profoundly influenced by more general changes of opinion in society at large. Again, this seems to indicate the relative political insignificance of the churches, even in this pertinent area of legislation affecting morality.

However, a transposition paradigm would again suggest a very different perspective. The tendency of churches to conform to society would now be explained by the supposition that this was due to society itself coming to accept a number of key Christian virtues. In a situation in which Christianity had already embedded itself into Western culture and had established its own general virtues at the very heart of Western society, it might come as no surprise to find churches tending to conform to that culture and society.

Thirdly, and somewhat paradoxically, sociologists such as José Casanova,[5] pointed to the disengagement of churches from society – a tendency for churches in Europe and elsewhere to separate themselves from states. In Britain churches have now handed over many of their previously held functions to the state. Welfare agencies, schools and hospitals, belonging to the churches in Victorian times, are now increasingly run by the state. In addition, religious functionaries have handed over many of their roles, in modern society, to the secular professional. The psychiatrist, social worker and social security officer appear to have inherited functions that once might have been thought to belong properly to the clergy. All of these changes are frequently cited as evidence of secularization, or, at the very least, of the marginality of Christian institutions in modern society. Frank Prochaska traces this at length in schooling, philanthropy and nursing – all key areas of activism in Victorian churches – in his book *Christianity and the Social Service in Modern Britain: The Disinherited Spirit*[6] [note the sub-title].

Here again, a transposition paradigm would paint a radically different picture. Now, evidence to the effect that state institutions and professionally trained officials are taking over the tasks of welfare, education and health care from churches, would be seen as the transposition of Christian virtues into society as a whole. The transposition theorist would indeed be encouraged to believe that the Christian virtues of *agape* or 'compassionate care' had become, at least partly, embedded into society. Such evidence encouraged the secular sociologist Paul Halmos to suggest that Christian virtues were still an essential, but largely unacknowledged, feature of 'secular' British counselling in the 1960s:

---

[5]   José Casanova, *Public Religions in the Modern World*, Chicago: University of Chicago Press, 1994.

[6]   Frank Prochaska, *Christianity and the Social Service in Modern Britain: The Disinherited Spirit*, Oxford: Oxford University Press, 2006.

I have tried to show that, *according to the counsellor*, it is not ambivalence but the prevalence of love, which is the ultimate explanatory principle used to control the involvement of the counsellor in the client. The ascetic scrupulousness of self-criticism, and almost a cult of merciless sincerity, are brought to bear on the counsellor's work so that he avoids any kind of self-indulgence, tries not to fulfil therapeutic ambition, or refrains from exploiting his professional function of self-therapy … he relentlessly unmasks his own rationalisations and attempts at claiming virtues and will treat his own indulgences with pitiless candour. On the other hand, he cannot but betray his kindness, concern, and idealism about man in general because of the aspiration … because of his determination to procure more happiness for others.[7]

Doubtless to the surprise of his colleagues at the time, Halmos concluded that this was 'indistinguishable from the moral lessons of Christianity.'[8]

In a similar manner, Adam Dinham and Robert Jackson conclude from their analysis of welfare and education in modern Britain that:

[R]eligion never disappeared, though it was profoundly challenged and changed by both secularizing and pluralizing forces in the post-war period. The spheres of welfare and education reveal that the public realm is not after all the post-religious space which had been imagined, and that Britain is neither simply secular not simply religious but complexly both.[9]

Max Weber and Charles Taylor

Examples could, of course, be multiplied. But perhaps these three are sufficient to indicate that if one starts from a radically different paradigm from that which prevailed generally among sociologists of religion in the 1960s, then the evidence

---

[7] Paul Halmos, *The Faith of the Counsellors*, London: Constable, 1965, pp. 89–90.

[8] Ibid., p. 193.

[9] Adam Dinham and Robert Jackson, 'Religion, Welfare and Education', in Linda Woodhead and Rebecca Catto (eds), *Religion and Change in Modern Britain*, London: Routledge, 2012, p. 290. See also Adam Dinham, *Faith in Social Capital after the Debt Crisis*, London: Palgrave Macmillan, 2012.

appears in a quite new light. This point applies, equally to the theologian, as it does to the sociologist and historian.

It is worth pointing out that features of both epiphenomenalist and transposition paradigms are to be found, at times, in the writings of Max Weber as well as Emile Durkheim. It is odd that, despite his insistence in *The Protestant Ethic and the Spirit of Capitalism* that he was concerned only with the rise of capitalism and not with its continued existence (which could manage perfectly well without its theological roots), Weber, as noted earlier, started with an observation of *contemporary* differences between Catholic and Protestant business-men. Like Durkheim, Weber was, at times, pessimistic about the long-term prospects for religion in Western society and, with this, for the long-term prospects for Western civilization. In so far as this is the case, both sociologists stand in a direct line with secularization theorists and epiphenomenalists of the 1960s. But there are also traces of a transposition paradigm in both of their work. This is most obviously so in Weber's Protestant-ethic thesis, but it is also apparent in his use of the concept of 'charisma'. Durkheim generally played down the social significance of theological ideas as such, as his *Suicide* clearly shows. Yet, throughout his work there is a heavy emphasis upon the importance of religious rituals and institutions for the integration of particular societies. And, in the introduction to *The Elementary Forms of the Religious Life*, he argues that the fundamental categories of thought, such as time, space and cause, are basically religious in origin. Neither sociologist was a thoroughgoing transposition theorist: the overall emphasis in their work was on the past social significance of Christianity in Western society. However, both contrast sharply with those scholars in the 1960s and their heirs today who regard religion in the modern world only as an epiphenomenon.

In their later writings both Bryan Wilson and David Martin (despite their earlier differences on the existence of secularization) arrived at oddly similar conclusions and both at times propounded theses close to Durkheim's original thesis. Wilson came to regard secularization with some of Durkheim's pessimism. Western society has not become a wholly rational and empirically based society; religion is rapidly becoming the prerogative of sectarian movements with no real place in society; and the very integration of Western society, to which

Christianity once contributed, is at risk.[10] Similarly, Martin's later writings have tended to argue that Western Christianity is increasingly characterised by loss, with ephemeral religious forms now filling the vacuum created.[11]

In his major work *A Secular Age* (2007) Charles Taylor has made the contrasts *and* continuities between the different paradigms here clearer. He argues that it is a mistake to conflate Weber's concept of 'disenchantment' (a term that Weber preferred to 'secularization') simply with the decline of religion (even though Weber did as much himself on occasions):

> Disenchantment is the dissolution of the 'enchanted' world, the world of spirits and meaningful causal forces, of wood sprites and relics. Enchantment is essential to some forms of religion; but other forms—especially those of modern Reformed Christianity, both Catholic and Protestant—have been built on its partial or total denial. We cannot just equate the two.[12]

Yet that, of course, is exactly what those fighting 'culture wars' today tend to do. Although Taylor does set out many tensions between modern secularists and Christians on issues of 'faith', science and morality, he repeatedly argues that these tensions are spurious or exaggerated. He depicts as 'closed world structures' scientific and philosophical world-views 'within which the believing option seems strange:'[13]

> We can learn something general about the way closed world structures operate, suffer attack, and defend themselves ... From within itself, the epistemological picture seems unproblematic. It comes across as an obvious discovery we make when we reflect on our perception and acquisition of knowledge. All the great foundational figures: Descartes, Locke, Hume, claimed to be saying what was obvious once one examined experience itself reflectively. Seen from the deconstruction, this is a most massive self-blindness. Rather what happened

---

[10]   See Bryan Wilson, *Contemporary Transformations of Religion*, Oxford: Oxford University Press, 1976.

[11]   See Martin, *On Secularization* and *The Future of Christianity*.

[12]   Charles Taylor, *A Secular Age*, Cambridge, MA: Harvard University Press, 2007, p. 553.

[13]   Ibid., p. 557.

was carved into shape by a powerful theory which posited the primacy of the individual, the neutral, the intra-mental as the locus of certainty. What was driving this theory? Certain 'values', virtues, excellences: those of the independent, disengaged subject, reflexively controlling his own thought-processes … There is an ethic here, of independence, self-control, self-responsibility, of a disengagement which brings control: a stance which requires courage, the refusal of the easy comforts of conformity to authority, of the consolations of the enchanted world.[14]

Taylor argues that secular advocates of closed world structures often caricature the religious as childish, immature and dependent. In the process they fail to recognize that their own position is just as much based upon and shaped by strongly held virtues and even by 'faith' (or, at the very least, opposition to faith – itself shaped by faith):

What seems to accredit the view of the package as epistemologically-driven are all the famous conversion stories, starting with post-Darwinian Victorians but continuing to our day, where people who had a strong faith early in life found that they had reluctantly, even with anguish of the soul, to relinquish it, because 'Darwin has refuted the Bible'. Surely, we want to say, these people in a sense preferred the Christian outlook morally, but had to bow, with whatever degree of inner pain, to the facts. But that's exactly what I'm resisting saying. What happened here was not that a moral outlook bowed to brute facts. Rather we might say that one moral outlook gave way to another. Another model of what was higher triumphed.[15]

Epiphenomenalism and Transposition

Differences between epiphenomenalist and the transposition paradigms can soon become exaggerated and polarized, especially in a Western context of culture wars. Yet the two paradigms are distinct and result in very different outcomes.

---

[14]   Ibid., p. 559.
[15]   Ibid., p. 563.

A more interesting point follows from this. In this I also agree with Charles Taylor that the choice between such paradigms is not simply based upon empirical evidence. In turn this suggests the conclusion that the basic way one assesses the political significance of Western Christianity depends, at least in part, upon an initial non-empirical choice. This conclusion has important implications for both theologians and social scientists.

It was seen in Volume 1 that by the 1970s there was already a widespread recognition among contemporary social scientists (and among physical scientists) that research cannot be entirely divorced from personal values. Notions of the social sciences as value-free enterprises were held less and less frequently. Even a cursory survey of the range of research interests of Western social scientists and the actual research projects they undertook both then and now, or did not or still do not, is sufficient to convince many that values/virtues are manifestly relevant to research. Similarly, among sociologists of religion in the 1970s, there was a growing recognition that this discipline can never be value-free and that the personal and, indeed, religious values/virtues of research-workers are relevant to their research. Were this not the case, the curious lack of interest in the subject between the 1920s and the 1950s, compared with the real interest of the pioneer sociologists and many sociologists since the 1960s, would be difficult to explain. It is hard to avoid the conclusion that it owed something to the dominance of positivism in the 1930s and 1940s.

However, the claim here goes considerably beyond a recognition of value-orientation in the physical and social sciences. More radically, I am claiming that an initial, non-empirical choice shapes the overall way a social scientist assesses the political significance of Western Christianity.

The initial clue to this suggestion lies in the nature of secularization paradigms. One of the most striking features of secularization paradigms and the sort of evidence they use, as was seen at length in Volume 1, is their *reversibility*. Whether the evidence is taken from church attendance statistics, church-state relationships or individual religious or spiritual beliefs, it is never difficult for one sociologist, while still using the same evidence, to reverse the work of another. A careful comparison of Bryan Wilson's *Religion in Secular Society* with Andrew Greeley's *The Persistence of Religion* (whatever their individual merits) demonstrated this point admirably a generation ago, as does a comparison of say Steve Bruce's

Secularization[16] with Grace Davie's *A Sociology of Religion* today.[17] Remarkably, Callum Brown, as a late 'convert' to a theory of secularization, has managed to use evidence forcefully both against and now for secularization.[18]

If this point about reversibility applies to secularization and persistence paradigms, it is likely to be true especially of epiphenomenalist and transposition paradigms, since, in their thoroughgoing forms, they are essentially overall and all-encompassing theories. Even seemingly contradictory evidence is soon encompassed by them, so it is clearly not the evidence alone that determines which of the two types of paradigm is adopted. Both types are adept at handling the same evidence. So, one might imagine that evidence of new religious movements, and seeming vitality in existing movements, would unnerve the thoroughgoing secularization theorist. But, in practice, Berger was rather unusual in being unnerved in this way in his later writings, and indeed, rather premature, in view of the 3,000 year timescale of his secularization paradigm.[19] Similarly, it is the 'invisibility' and generality of the Christian virtues embedded in Western society, in thoroughgoing transposition paradigms, which make them so immune to criticism. It is difficult to see how either type of paradigm could ever be falsified.

There is an obvious objection to this point. It could be claimed that the two types of paradigm are not mutually exclusive, since, as just noted, elements of each can be found in the writings of Weber and Durkheim and even in those of Wilson and Martin. For them it does not appear that the two types of paradigm are overall, all-encompassing and therefore non-empirical theories, but rather, admittedly differing, viewpoints, which can be tested by empirical data.

This point, however, overlooks the bias towards epiphenomenalism in all four sociologists. In practice, it may be difficult to maintain a consistent thoroughgoing epiphenomenalism or a consistent thoroughgoing transposition paradigm. Nevertheless, it is important to note that, if either paradigm is held

---

[16] Steve Bruce, *Secularization: In Defence of an Unfashionable Theory*, Oxford: Oxford University Press, 2011.

[17] Grace Davie, *The Sociology of Religion*, London: Sage, 2007.

[18] Compare Callum Brown, 'Did Urbanisation Secularise Britain?', *Urban History Yearbook*, 1988, pp. 1–14, with his *The Death of Christian Britain*, London: Routledge, 2001.

[19] e.g. Peter L. Berger, 'Second Thoughts on Defining Religion', *Journal for the Scientific Study of Religion*, 13:2, 1974, pp. 125–134; and (ed.), *The Desecularization of the World* Grand Rapids, MI: Eerdmans, 1999.

in a thoroughgoing form, then it can at once be seen that it offers an overall and all-encompassing perspective, in direct conflict with its opposite and generating very different research. Indeed, precisely because they are prerequisites of research into the political significance of Christianity and not products of that research, their basis cannot be wholly empirical. It is for this reason that I would suggest that they depend as much upon choice as upon rational empiricism. It would be extraordinarily difficult to show, for example, that Bryan Wilson's epiphenomenalism (or Steve Bruce's today) was wholly the product of his research – in all his writings on secularization it was presented at the very outset and only then was evidence systematically presented to corroborate it. Further, it is difficult to see how he could have acted otherwise – other than by adopting, just as non-empirically, a transposition paradigm.

The two contrasting paradigms tend to generate different types of research both in the social sciences and in theology. Again, this can be seen most clearly if their thoroughgoing forms are taken, even if few scholars wholly adopt such forms. Epiphenomenalist social scientists will tend to emphasize the socially structured nature of churches' responses to political issues. Since Christianity is regarded by them as an essentially privatized phenomenon, being significant (if at all) for the individual and not for society as a whole, they will tend to see religion in general as the individual's search for 'ultimate concern', 'ultimate meaning' and deliverance from the structural and cultural chaos that surrounds them. Christian institutional structures will be analysed by them in terms of their social determinants and seldom, if ever, in terms of their independent social significance. Whether or not they hold an explicit secularization paradigm, they will not be inclined to the view that modern Christianity in any form – whether in terms of its specific teaching or in terms of the general virtues that it seeks to convey – has any appreciable effect on Western politics. But, from the outset, they are hardly likely to have such an inclination.

Similarly, epiphenomenalist theologians are likely to emphasize the individual and other-worldly nature of Christianity. They are likely to view political theologies, such as Liberation Theology, with unease and to shun any identification of Christian faith with specific, and perhaps even general, political programmes or policies. Their emphasis is typically upon eternity and, if they have any deeply held political beliefs, they are careful to distinguish these from their theological beliefs. From this perspective Edward Norman's controversial 1976 Reith Lectures complained about the 'politicization' of the churches:

> In the world, the Christian seeks to apply the great love of God as well as he can in contemporary terms. And that will actually involve corporate social and political action. But, unlike the secular moralizers whom the Christian activists of the present day so closely resemble, the wise aspirant to eternity will recognize no hope of a better social order in his endeavours, for he knows that the expectations of men are incapable of satisfaction. Before even the goal of one generation is achieved, another sets other goals. 'Take therefore no thought for the morrow', Jesus told his disciples, 'for the morrow shall take thought for the things of itself.' Similarly, Christians are unwise to cling to past models of idealized embodiments of religious order. Conservatives fall into the same error as the progressives, whose politicized Christianity they dislike for political reasons, if they seek to protect a social order of their own preference, of the present or of the past.[20]

In contrast, transposition social scientists and theologians are much more likely to be interested in the political and general moral significance of Christianity. Talcott Parsons (a clear influence upon Robert Putnam who will be discussed in Chapter 6) well illustrated this position. He argued explicitly against a secularization paradigm and against those who maintain that either religion or general moral standards are declining in contemporary Western society. Following Weber, he maintained that the Reformation effected a fundamental moral change among individuals within the West, a change that has, in part, been responsible for the shape of contemporary society. Individuals, once under the strict tutelage of the medieval Catholic Church, had now become religiously autonomous entities. They were responsible, on their own, before God, and God's call to them came without human mediation. As a result, the secular realm was invested with new significance as a field of 'Christian opportunity': in their secular calling individuals were given an assignment to work in the building of the Kingdom of God. In this sense, Talcott Parsons argued that the Reformation represents a Christianization of secular society.

---

[20] Edward Norman, *Christianity and the World Order: The BBC Reith Lectures, 1978*, Oxford: Oxford University Press, 1979, p. 79.

More controversially, Parsons maintained that modern American 'denominational pluralism' also represents a Christianization of society. For him, the denomination is midway between the church and the sect. Like the first it is concerned with society at large, but like the second it is a voluntary association which individuals choose to join and which binds them only by a personal commitment:

> With certain qualifications this can be said to be the case in the United States today and, in somewhat more limited forms, in various other countries. From a religious point of view, this means the discrimination of two layers of religious commitment. One of these is the layer which defines the bases of denominational membership and which differentiates one denomination from another. The other is a common matrix of value-commitment which is broadly shared between denominations, and which forms the basis of the sense in which the society as a whole forms a religiously based moral community.[21]

The connection between the two is vital to Parsons' argument. He saw a close affiliation between denominational pluralism and political democracy. The former is able to institutionalize 'the trust of the individual' which is vital to successful political democracy. It is able to counter those who would question how it is possible for public policy to be determined by the majority of the irresponsible and uninformed: indeed it has been responsible for stimulating both personal responsibility and universal education in society.

Writing more forcefully, as a postmodern theologian, Graham Ward argues that the epiphenomenalist paradigm inherent within liberal secularism is morally deficient:

> Liberalism fostered a hegemonic moral code understood as universal, egalitarian and progressive which defined the character, as well demanding the existence of, secularity. But contained within the cultural logic of liberalism, and therefore secularity, was its own demise. It negotiated the pluralism and difference on the basis of an essential, metaphysical unity: the value of human

---

[21]   Talcott Parsons, *Sociological Theory and Modern Society*, New York: Free Press, 1967.

life. Such humanism was far too frail a foundation. Death camps, genocides and world wars questioned optimistic accounts of being human, while liberalism's commitment to individual rights fostered an increasing social atomism.[22]

While the choice between these two paradigms may not be wholly empirical, it is still a choice which has a profound effect upon research and, more importantly in the present context, one that has obvious relevance to the politicization thesis. The latter can now be seen as only one option and, not at all, as an ineluctable position. A transposition paradigm would suggest, in contrast to the politicization thesis, that if the churches do, at times, seem to be adopting virtues from society at large, rather than offering virtues for that society to follow, this may be because Western society has already been radically christianized and that its apparently secular values are not really, or at least wholly, 'secular'.

If, for a moment, it is assumed that the transposition paradigm is basically correct, as far as the West is concerned, there begins to emerge a new picture of prophecy within the churches. The main function of the churches within Western society would now be seen as their ability, over the centuries, to embed certain general virtues into that society. This is not to say that churches, themselves, would have seen the generation of virtues as their primary function in society and it is certainly not to claim that it is only virtues, rather than beliefs, which lie at the heart of Christianity itself. Rather, given the Christian belief in a creating, redeeming and sanctifying God, certain general virtues (normally thought to be platitudinous, such is the extent of this transposition), like the 'givenness' of human and, indeed, animal life, the presence of purpose and the centrality of love, seem to follow from this. Although these are general virtues and not specific moral requirements, they are nevertheless crucial. Within a society long influenced by churches it may be difficult even to detect these virtues.

It would still be an open question, of course, whether or not general Christian virtues can persist in a society in which churches continue to decline. The possibility that Marxism may contain within it a number of transposed Christian virtues might suggest that these virtues are not as fragile as they might appear to be. Further, even if Western churches were all to continue to decline, it is still extraordinarily difficult to know what effect this might have upon society at large.

---

[22] Graham Ward, *True Religion*, Oxford: Blackwell, 2003, p. 127.

In Sweden, for example, regular churchgoing is as low as anywhere in the West, but there none the less remains a relatively high seasonal conformity and pattern of rites of passage, in addition to an active political role by a number of church leaders. How far one believes that the Swedish people still derive their virtues from Christian traditions may well depend upon whether one adopts a transposition or an epiphenomenalist paradigm.

If it is a function of the churches to embed certain key general virtues into society, it may be a function of the sect, or of the individual prophet within the churches, to proclaim certain moral requirements which are at odds with conventional wisdom. The latter function is more obvious to society than the former. By standing against society on particular moral issues, the sect and the individual prophet can often be highly unpopular. The exemplary pacifism of the Quakers may, at times, be admired (though not emulated) by society at large, but the radical pacifism of the Jehovah's Witnesses, or of particular individuals within the churches, is frequently despised.

I have emphasized the transposition paradigm because the epiphenomenalist paradigm is so widely and so uncritically assumed by others. It does have the advantage, however, of providing a particularly interesting vision of the place of prophecy. In its terms churches, as churches, that is, as bodies attempting to cater for the masses and to maintain close relations with the particular societies within which they are placed, may serve to embed these societies with general virtues, themselves deriving from the Christian belief in a creating, redeeming and sanctifying God. The individual prophet within churches (and within some radical sects) may be able, at times, successfully to challenge and to change specific moral requirements. A transposition paradigm offers fresh perspectives to sociological theology.

Chapter 4

Prophecy and Exclusivism

Understood in Weber's terms the individual prophet and the prophetic sect tend to share a common exclusivism. As an individual, the prophet is often a lonely, iconoclastic figure, little concerned with sustaining a worshipping community, a given tradition or an accepted rite. He, or she, is called to proclaim, and frequently to denounce, and above all to change, other people. For Weber the prophet 'is normally a righteous lay preacher of sovereign independence whose aim is to supplant the traditional ritualistic religious grace of the ecclesiastical type by organizing life on the basis of ultimate ethical principles'.[1] In order to depict the transition from the independent or sectarian prophet to the ecclesial priest Weber devised the concept of the 'routinization of charisma':

> A 'community' or 'congregation' in the specifically religious sense ... does
> not arise in connection with prophecy in the particular sense used here. Nor
> does it arise in connection with every type of prophecy. Primarily, a religious
> community arises in connection with a prophetic movement as a result of
> routinization, i.e., as a result of the process whereby either the prophet himself
> or his disciples secure the permanence of his preaching and the congregation's
> distribution of grace, hence insuring the economic existence of the enterprise
> and those who man it, and thereby monopolizing as well the privileges reserved
> for those [priests] charged with religious functions.[2]

From a perspective within sociological theology, the church and the priest are especially adept at being harbingers of sacred virtues that can be transposed into wider society, whereas the sect and the prophet are more gifted at making strident and sometimes much warranted denunciations of the same society. Church and

---

[1]   Max Weber, *The Sociology of Religion*, London: Methuen, 1965 [1920], p. 78.
[2]   Weber, *The Sociology of Religion*, pp. 60–61.

sect, along with priest and prophet – in tandem and in tension – offer multifaceted Christian responses to society at large.

For the scholar of ancient Judaism, Johannes Lindblom, the prophet is 'a person who, because he is, conscious of having been specially chosen and called, feels forced to perform actions and proclaim ideas which, in a mental state of intense inspiration or real ecstasy, have been indicated to him in the form of divine revelations'.[3] The intense inner conviction of many individual prophets and sects leads them to disregard conventional opinions. Indeed, as 'deviant cognitive minorities' they can be highly judgemental of society at large. Just because the individual priest and the church share the constraints of society, they do not always possess this inner conviction and certainty – or, if they do, they are less likely to attempt to impose it on others, quite regardless of the social disruption that it might cause. In addition, priests who have responsibilities to local churches may be more averse than prophets to the possibility of congregational conflict.[4]

It is precisely this inner conviction or 'mysterious compulsion' (as von Rad termed it) which helps to make both individual and sectarian forms of prophecy so potentially disruptive. As Robert Carroll argued:

> The inevitable subjectivism implied by private inspiration was to become a dominant factor in late seventh-century prophecy and any attempt to delineate the relationship between prophecy and society, or between prophecy and other social authorities, must take full cognizance of this problem … If men may claim to be inspired by God and therefore equate what they say with the words of God then there will be no protection against any number of so inspired persons proclaiming any number of discrete, and even incompatible, messages in society.[5]

---

[3]   J. Lindblom, *Prophecy in Ancient Israel*, Oxford: Blackwell, 1962, p. 46: although see G. von Rad, *Old Testament Theology*, volume 2, Edinburgh: Oliver & Boyd, 1965, p. 62 for a criticism of prophetic 'ecstasy' in Lindblom.

[4]   See Penny Edgell Becker, *Congregations in Conflict*, Cambridge and New York: Cambridge University Press, 1999.

[5]   Robert P. Carroll, *When Prophecy Failed*, London: SCM Press, 1979, p. 14.

An admission of moral ambiguity or multivalency on specific issues belongs more to the priestly and churchly than to the individual prophetic and sectarian functions.

Exclusive Sectarianism

In a context of widespread institutional decline exclusivism might be increasingly attractive to Western Christianity. Whether this decline is configured in terms of a secularization or epiphenomenalist paradigm, sectarian exclusivism is an obvious response. More than anyone else, Bryan Wilson[6] made this connection. It fitted the two major aspects of his work: secularization and sectarianism. He argued that, as institutional churches decline both numerically and in terms of social significance in the West (as distinct from many parts of Africa and South America), so their future survival would be as exclusive sects rather than as inclusive churches. It also fitted the young Peter Berger's analysis,[7] reviewed in Volume 1, of religious believers in the West increasingly becoming 'deviant cognitive minorities' in a context of radical Western secularization. Today, with a widespread resurgence of Pentecostalism in both Western and non-Western countries, alongside an overall decline of churchgoing in many Western countries, this prognosis still has some resonance. Without sharing an intellectual commitment to secularization, it is easy to see why exclusivism seems to prosper in contexts of radical decline. Martyn Percy explains this link as follows:

> [I]t should be recognized that the more marginal and less extensive religion becomes in the public sphere, the more likely it is (consequential, indeed) that intensive forms of religiosity will flourish, including types of fundamentalism, revivalism and the like. Religion, in other words, when un-earthed and de-coupled from social and cultural contexts, has a greater potential to become

6   Bryan Wilson, *Religion in Secular Society*, London: C.A. Watts, 1966, and Harmondsworth, Middlesex: Penguin, 1969 and *Contemporary Transformations of Religion*, Oxford: Oxford University Press, 1976.

7   Peter L. Berger, *A Rumour of Angels*, Garden City, NY: Doubleday, 1969 and Harmondsworth, Middlesex: Penguin, 1970 and *The Heretical Imperative: Contemporary Possibilities of Religious Affirmation*, New York: Anchor, 1979 and London: Collins, 1980.

toxic and self-absorbed. This shift is, at present, detectable in most mainline Christian denominations: the loss of the extensive leads to the heightening of the intensive. That can be beneficial, for a season at least. But unchecked and unchallenged, the pharmacological consequences can be grave. Faith turns in on itself. And churches, here, can then refuse to recognize that their ecclesiology is now a consequence of their marginality, rather than their purity.[8]

Given this analysis the attractions of prophetic exclusivism are obvious. Just as the sect can choose either to withdraw from society altogether (as a number of introversionist sects such as the Exclusive Brethren or the Amish have done) or to confront it directly, so individual prophets who are at odds with society can themselves opt for either withdrawal or radical confrontation. If withdrawal or introversion tends to be regarded as defeatist or even socially irresponsible, radical individual and sectarian prophecy may appear as a more appealing alternative. Even those who hold a transposition paradigm may see the force of this argument, especially if they regard epiphenomenalism as the currently dominant self-perception (however spurious) of many Western Christians.

It is also possible that prophetic exclusivism was the predominant feature of earliest Christianity. In different ways, both Weber and Troeltsch appeared to claim as much. For Weber, the process of 'routinization of charisma' represented the transition from the prophetic message of Jesus to the formation of the early church. The charismatic prophet, Jesus, was followed by the earliest Christians, who quickly modified his message to fast changing circumstances (for example Acts 15), shared financial resources with varying degrees of success (Acts 4:32f) and appointed functionaries (for example Acts 6). In this way, Jesus' prophetic teaching [a characterization rejected, of course, by some scholars[9]] was secured after his death, even if in an inevitably modified and less exclusive form.

For Troeltsch, as noted earlier, the individual mystic, the exclusive sect and the inclusive church are all endemic features of Christianity, even in its earliest

---

[8]   Martyn Percy, *Shaping the Church: The Promise of Implicit Theology*, Farnham, Surrey: Ashgate, 2010, pp. 163–164.

[9]   See Oscar Cullmann, *The Christology of the New Testament*, London: SCM Press, 1959 and C.F.D. Moule, *The Origin of Christology*, Cambridge: Cambridge University Press, 1977.

phase.[10] Under the influence of Bryan Wilson many sociologists of religion in Britain focused upon sects or 'new religious movements' and ignored the mystic type. A few, however, did take note of Troeltsch at this point:

> Mysticism means that the world of ideas which had hardened into formal worship and doctrine is transformed into a purely personal and inward experience; this leads to the formation of groups on a purely personal basis, with no permanent form, which also tend to weaken the significance of forms of worship, doctrine, and the historical element.[11]

'Mysticism' in this definition was variously interpreted by a number of sociologists in the 1970s with most preferring the term 'cult'.[12]

Troeltsch argued that these three types are only evident after the death of Jesus. For him the transition seemed to be marked by a shift from the freedom of Jesus to the constraints of earliest Christianity:

> The Gospel of Jesus was a free personal piety, with a strong impulse towards profound intimacy and spiritual fellowship and communion, but without any tendency towards the organization of a cult, or towards the creation of a religious community. Only when faith in Jesus, the Risen and Exalted Lord, became the central point of worship in a new religious community did the necessity for organization arise.[13]

---

[10] Ernst Troeltsch, *The Social Teaching of the Christian Churches*, volume 2, New York: Harper, 1960 [1912], p. 993.

[11] Troeltsch, *The Social Teaching of the Christian Churches*, volume 2, p. 993.

[12] Cf. Colin Campbell, 'The Cult, the Cultic Milieu and Secularization', in Michael Hill (ed.), *A Sociological Yearbook of Religion in Britain*, London: SCM Press, 1972, pp. 119–136 and J. Milton Yinger, *The Scientific Study of Religion*, New York: Collier-Macmillan, 1970, p. 279f.

[13] Troeltsch, *The Social Teaching of the Christian Churches*, volume 2, p. 993.

The Inclusive Cult

It is possible that in passages like this Troeltsch still reflected a rather nineteenth-century, individualistic picture of the historical Jesus. Geoffrey Nelson, who otherwise followed him quite closely, maintained that 'Christianity in its early stages was a cult in which the Jewish tradition was modified by elements derived from a number of other traditions and particularly from Zoroastrianism and Greek religion'.[14] If, as a number of scholars have argued, concepts like the Son of Man which go back to the 'historical Jesus' have non-Jewish roots, the process of cult formation may have been started by Jesus himself.

Nelson identified three major criteria by which cults can be distinguished from other types of religious groups:

a. Cults are groups based upon mystical, psychic or ecstatic experiences.
b. They represent a fundamental break with the religious tradition of the society in which they arise.
c. They are concerned mainly with the problems of individuals rather than with those of social groups.[15]

For him the cult exists in a different continuum to that of the sect. Whereas the latter may develop into an established sect or into a denomination/church, the cult may either become a more permanent cult (like Spiritualists) or it may develop into a new religion. The last, on this understanding, is presumably what happened within Christianity. A cult founded by Jesus gradually became a new religion.

This theory might help to differentiate earliest Christianity from specifically Jewish sects like the Essenes. Yet it does not supply a very adequate account of the crucial transition here. This might instead be achieved by supposing a shift from cult to sect between the death of Jesus and the emergence of earliest Christianity, suggested powerfully in Roy Wallis' analysis of Scientology.

Wallis argued that the earliest phase of Scientology, then termed Dianetics, can be unambiguously located as a cult. Followers of the movement at this

---

[14]   Geoffrey K. Nelson, 'The Concept of the Cult', *The Sociological Review*, 16:3, 1968, p. 357.
[15]   Ibid., p. 354.

stage typically saw it as providing one of many possible paths to salvation: it produced a synthesis of cultic ideas and beliefs to be found in society in a more general cultic milieu centring upon the teaching of the science fiction writer L. Ron Hubbard; it was loosely organized with few means of enforcing central commands; it was non-exclusive with a high toleration of other practices and beliefs; and its membership changed rapidly. In short, 'an enthusiasm for, or interest in, Dianetics was the only important criterion of membership for most of the following.[16] Even Hubbard was not given the exclusive right to determine doctrine and practice in the movement. All of this conforms closely to Wallis' general description of a cult. For him cults are 'oriented towards the problems of individuals, loosely structured, tolerant, non-exclusive, they make few demands on members, possess no clear distinction between members and non-members, have a rapid turnover of membership, and are transient collectives'.[17]

In the 1950s, however, the movement radically changed. There were serious disagreements between Hubbard and other leaders, disaffections, criticisms from the medical world, and threats of bankruptcy. It was even suggested by 1951 that the movement could manage without Hubbard, who, according to some, was becoming increasingly authoritarian. Further there was increasing opposition to Hubbard's specifically metaphysical, rather than therapeutic, speculations. As a reaction to all of this Hubbard instituted a much tighter control over the movement:

> The boundary between the movement and the world became less fluid. Less tolerance was shown toward nonconformity by members. Greater bureaucratization was implemented to increase control over operations. As criticism was voiced and sanctions introduced against the movement by outside agencies, the movement became increasingly hostile to the surrounding society, its organization became tighter, and expulsions became more frequent.[18]

---

[16] Roy Wallis, *The Road to Total Freedom: A Sociological Analysis of Scientology*, London: Heinemann, 1976 and New York: Columbia University Press, 1977, p. 76.

[17] Ibid., p. 14.

[18] Ibid., p. 251.

Wallis saw this 'sectarianization' as a reaction to the problem of institutional fragility faced by cults like Dianetics, Christian Science and Unity in their early phases:

> Their belief-systems were precarious in that they were liable to selective acceptance and synthesis by seekers recruited often from other cultic groups. Authority within the movement was open to challenge by practitioners, teachers and leaders of local followings. The commitment of members was limited because the doctrine and practice offered was not seen as having any unique salvational efficacy, and hence the loyalty of members was often shared with other groups and practices.[19]

Faced with this situation, Hubbard, Mary Baker Eddy and Charles and Myrtle Fillmore all responded separately by instituting tighter social controls over their movements and, in turn, transforming them into exclusive sects.

For Wallis, then, the sect is an exclusive religious organization in a way that the cult is not. However, both are 'deviant', that is 'deviant in relation to the respectable, the normatively sanctioned, forms of belief prevailing at any time ... deviant in comparison with prevailing indifference, agnosticism, or denominational Christian orthodoxy'.[20] While exclusivism was not used by Wallis as the sole means of distinguishing a sect from a cult or a denomination, it was a central criterion.

Exclusivism was also a central criterion for Weber.[21] For Weber the main differentiating factor between a sect and a church lay in its type of membership. In a sect, membership is characteristically voluntary and exclusive. People typically join a sect through conversion and in the sect there is a comparatively clear-cut distinction between members and non-members and correspondingly little attempt to cater for the masses or to form a relationship with the state. A rigid orthodoxy is usually upheld in a sect and 'heretics' are rigorously excluded. All of these characteristics, for Weber, are logically related to the voluntary and exclusive nature of the sect and are not to be found to the same extent in the church.

---

[19]   Ibid., p. 99.
[20]   Ibid., p. 12.
[21]   Weber, *The Sociology of Religion*, p. 65f.

Further these characteristics (unlike all those of Troeltsch) can equally be applied to non-Christian religious and ideological movements.

Exclusivism in the New Testament

Focusing upon a sociological understanding of exclusivity, it can now be asked whether this analysis can be applied to the New Testament. Can different levels of exclusivism be differentiated in the various layers of tradition and redaction? And if they can, can they be illuminated by the broad cult-to-sect-to-church analysis? It is important to express caution again at this stage. If nothing else, New Testament scholarship over the last one hundred years demonstrates the difficulty of reaching any firm conclusions about the so-called 'historical Jesus'. It is difficult enough to be sure of the so-called 'authentic words' of Jesus or even general concepts like those of the Kingdom of God or the Son of Man: it would not be possible to establish any exact chronology of Jesus' ministry or teaching. So it would be difficult to apply the Wallis cult-to-sect model directly to the life of Jesus himself.

Not just New Testament scholars but Christian theologians generally might also object to the representation of Jesus as a first-century Ron Hubbard or Mary Baker Eddy. There is a real danger of applying insights from an analysis of modern-day, middle-class, intellectualistic movements too literally to Jesus and his immediate followers. As seen in Volume 1, the same point applies to those who make too facile comparisons of New Testament apocalypticism with contemporary millenarianism. The dangers should be obvious.

There is a further point that must be emphasized again. Weber insisted that his church/sect distinctions are 'ideal types'. They are not to be confused with specific empirical examples and in reality they are seldom as clear-cut as the typology might lead the unwary to expect. If there is a cult-to-sect transition apparent within the New Testament, it is a transition which can only be traced in the broadest terms and with considerable hesitancy. It is in this spirit that the following analysis is suggested.

Within the New Testament[22] the predominant tone is exclusivism. Particularly in Paul's writings the typical assumption is that justification/salvation is to be

---

[22]   All verses from NRSV.

found only in Jesus Christ. He insists that 'heretics' must be excluded: 'As we have said before, so now I repeat, if anyone proclaims to you a gospel contrary to what you received, let that one be accursed!' (Gal. 1:9). The writer of Hebrews goes even further: 'For if we wilfully persist in sin after having received the knowledge of the truth, there no longer remains a sacrifice for sins, but a fearful prospect of judgement, and a fury of fire that will consume the adversaries' (Heb. 10:26–27). The logic of much of Paul's theology is that justification/ salvation can only be attained in Jesus Christ:

> Since all have sinned and fall short of the glory of God; they are now justified
> by his grace as a gift, through the redemption that is in Christ Jesus, whom God
> put forward as a sacrifice of atonement by his blood, effective through faith.
> He did this to show his righteousness, because in his divine forbearance he had
> passed over the sins previously committed; it was to prove at the present time
> that he himself is righteous and that he justifies the one who has faith in Jesus.
> (Rom. 3:23–6)

This is Paul's most characteristic argument, that people are justified only by faith, that is faith in Jesus Christ. This exclusivism seems hardly different from that of John: 'Very truly, I tell you, no one can see the kingdom of God without being born from above … Very truly I tell you, no one can enter the kingdom of God without being born of water and Spirit' (John 3:3 and 5).

John Milbank, with characteristic (and profoundly unhelpful) polarization, identifies such exclusivity as of the essence of the Christian narrative:

> For the Christological-ecclesial narrative arises, in the first place, not simply as
> an 'identification' of the divine, but also as a 'reading' and a critique-through-
> practice of all historical human community up to that point … Initially, it defines
> itself as both in continuity and discontinuity with the 'political' societies of
> the antique world. *This account* of history and critique of human society is in
> no sense an appendage to Christianity—on the contrary, it *belongs to its very
> essence*. For first of all, its break with Judaism arises from Christianity's denial
> that the Jewish law is the final key to true human community and salvation. And
> secondly, Christianity's universalist claim that incorporation into the Church is

indispensable for salvation assumes that *other religions and social groupings, however virtuous-seeming, were, in their own terms alone, finally on the path of damnation*. In this fashion a gigantic claim to be able to read, criticize, say what is going on in other human societies, is *absolutely integral to the nature of the Christian Church*, which itself claims to exhibit the exemplary form of human community. For theology to surrender this claim, to allow other discourses – the 'social sciences' for example—carry out yet more fundamental readings, would therefore amount to a denial of theological truth.[23]

What this account misses is that Paul's dominant exclusivism may not actually be consistent. Abraham, living long before the birth of Jesus, is depicted as being justified by faith (Rom. 4 and Gal. 3). And many scholars have pointed to the mysterious words in 1 Corinthians:

> I do not want you to be unaware, brothers and sisters, that our ancestors were all under the cloud, and all passed through the sea, and all were baptized into Moses in the cloud and in the sea, and all ate the same spiritual food, and all drank the same spiritual drink. For they drank from the spiritual rock that followed them, and the rock was Christ. Nevertheless, God was not pleased with most of them, and they were struck down in the wilderness. (1 Cor. 10:1–5)

And yet clearly some of them were accepted by God. Baptism and communion were present in a sense before the birth of Jesus, but then Christ was the rock and was thus present. If this interpretation is correct, then Paul does not totally abandon his exclusivism: Christ is still essential for salvation but not necessarily the post-incarnational Christ.

One of the obvious problems facing Christian exclusivism has been to make sense of the 'saints' of the Old Testament. Were they to be denied salvation simply because they lived before the birth of Jesus? On the face of it, if explicit faith in Jesus Christ is regarded as essential to salvation, then they must be denied salvation. The possibility of Christ's presence in the world before the incarnation

[23] John Milbank, *Theology and Social Theory: Beyond Secular Reason*, Oxford: Blackwell, 2006 (1990), p. 390 [italics added]. I am most grateful to Hugh Rayment-Pickard for locating this quotation since, curiously, the book has no subject index.

is one way out of this dilemma. Another is elusively suggested by the author of Hebrews: 'Yet all these, though they were commended for their faith, did not receive what was promised, since God had provided something better so that they would not, without us, be made perfect' (11: 39–40). A further possibility is suggested by the author of 1 Peter. Early in this 'letter' there is mention of the 'spirit of Christ' working in the Old Testament prophets (1:11), but later it talks of the post-resurrection Jesus Christ proclaiming 'to the spirits in prison' of former times (3:19) and preaching the Gospel: 'For this is the reason the gospel was proclaimed even to the dead, so that, though they had been judged in the flesh as everyone is judged, they might live in the spirit as God does' (4:6).

Despite these various concessions, the overall tone of the New Testament, outside the Synoptic Gospels, is one of exclusivism. This exclusivism is both doctrinal and organizational. As with modern-day sects, exclusivist doctrinal claims go hand-in-hand with strict membership requirements, with rigid distinctions between members and non-members, and with the rigorous exclusion of those who deviate from accepted doctrine or practice. Paul is emphatic: 'Now I appeal to you, brothers and sisters, by the name of our Lord Jesus Christ, that all of you should be in agreement and that there should be no divisions among you, but that you should be united in the same mind and the same purpose' (1 Cor. 1:10), for, after all, 'for in every way you have been enriched in him, in speech and knowledge of every kind – just as the testimony of Christ has been strengthened among you' (1 Cor. 1:5–6). Early Christians must give up living as 'pagans'; they must give up the sexual mores of those who surround them (1 Cor. 5) and their habits of excessive eating and drinking (1 Cor. 11). Indeed, in so far as they have not given up these things 'For this reason many of you are weak and ill, and some have died' (1 Cor. 11:30). Christianity here is clearly more a sect than a cult.

But was this exclusivism characteristic of the teaching of Jesus himself? In his study of attitudes to poverty and riches in the various layers of the Synoptic Gospels, David Mealand argued that it was not:

> A charismatic prophet and healer, with an apocalyptic message about the Reign
> of God, inevitably in certain respects invites comparison with other leaders of
> 'millenarian' movements. Both similarities, and also certain differences, emerge
> from the pursuit of such comparisons ... Jesus seems to have attracted an open

circle of adherents, not all of whom became close followers. The latter certainly left behind both family and possessions and led an itinerant life as associates of the one who proclaimed the new age. Yet though the break with the old life was certainly radical, it did not have the character of exclusivism and even hatred practised by certain modern sectarians. Nor does Jesus seem to have insisted that all his hearers respond in precisely the way his closest followers did, a relatively open circle of adherents, a variety of response was tolerated.[24]

In terms of Wallis' analysis, this movement would appear more cult-like than sect-like.

For Mealand Jesus' message of the Kingdom/Reign of God both reflects the political turbulence of the period and shapes his attitude towards wealth. In the light of his apocalyptic message, all things (including wealth and poverty) become relatively unimportant: the Kingdom of God is characterized by 'feasting and by healing, it is good news for the poor, it brings an end to hunger, sickness, and oppression, an end to Satan's rule'.[25] This millenarian, but not narrowly exclusive, position contrasts sharply with a later Synoptic layer, which Mealand associates with the famine of *c.*AD 48. The woes against the rich and well fed (Lk. 6:24–26), the parable of Dives and Lazarus (Lk. 16:19–31) and the animosity against the rich in Mary's 'song' (Lk. 1:53) are all ascribed to this layer of oral tradition. Together, 'these three passages have in common the theme that in the new age God will reverse, or has already begun to reverse, the good fortune of the prosperous'.[26] He argues that this theology of reversal (which is distinct from the teaching of Jesus) reflects a situation of relative dis-privilege within earliest Christianity and can be compared to the social marginality of other millenarian and apocalyptic sects. The strongest forms of exclusivism are located in this Synoptic layer.

Despite the location of these fiercest attacks on wealth in Luke, Mealand maintains that his own and Matthew's redactions (as distinct from their special sources L and M), in fact reflect a more socially and economically mixed 'church', with a considerably modified hostility to wealth within it. Luke emphasizes the

---

[24]   David Mealand, *Poverty and Expectation in the Gospels*, London: SPCK, 1980, p. 89.

[25]   Ibid., p. 89.

[26]   Ibid., p. 41.

spiritual danger of riches and money which, for him, is silver rather than Mark's copper: 'we also need to note his literary skill, his knowledge of the world, and his obvious affinities with the relatively prosperous classes'.[27] In Matthew the value of money mentioned is higher than either Mark or Luke (for example 10:10), the rich man has to sell only 'possessions' not 'everything' (19:21), he has Jesus blessing the poor in spirit (5:3), Luke's woes are absent, and in short he shows the greatest degree of accommodation to wealth of any of the three evangelists. Mealand concludes that 'some accommodation to the values implicit in a settled community of believers who owned possessions seems to have happened throughout earliest Christianity'.[28]

If David Mealand's careful analysis is to be trusted, a cult-to-sect-to-church model may well make sense of the evidence provided. Jesus' own ministry with the varied followers that surrounded him would form the cult phase. In terms of Nelson's three criteria, the cult of Jesus was focused upon a radically new (criterion 2) possibility and experience (criterion 1) deriving from the inauguration of the Kingdom of God, which demanded from each individual a new and radical response of faith (criterion 3). Like all cults, this movement was relatively open and non-exclusive, even though, in contrast to dominant Jewish orthodoxies, it would have been regarded as deviant. Nelson argued that such cults can become more permanent cults, like modern-day Spiritualists. However, few have followed him in this suggestion. Wilson located Spiritualism as a thaumaturgical sect:[29] Wallis argued that the cult is doctrinally and institutionally fragile: the combination of non-exclusiveness and deviance is one that is difficult to maintain for any length of time. The disruptions within Scientology, Christian Science and Unity show how difficult it is to maintain such a combination. Soon there are leadership struggles, doctrinal debates, new forms of syncretism and difficulties in retaining recruited members. Sectarianization is an obvious response to these threats. And this perhaps is what happened in earliest Christianity immediately after the death of Jesus. The evidence from Paul and the oral tradition of the Synoptic Gospels suggest that exclusivism was strongest in Christianity at this stage. The redactions

---

[27] Ibid., p. 20.

[28] Ibid., p. 92.

[29] Bryan Wilson, 'A Typology of Sects', in Roland Robertson (ed.), *Sociology of Religion*, London: Penguin, 1969, p. 369.

of Luke and particularly Matthew point to a further and later change – this time away from exclusivism. It is possible to argue that this is the start of a sect-to-church process – a process that was only completed with the age of Constantine and the new-found relationship that this brought to Christianity and to Christian theologians such as Ambrose and Augustine. Only in this last age was it possible for Christians fully to adopt the concerns of society at large on issues like war, wealth and poverty.

Again, it should be emphasized that such analysis presents only the broadest picture of earliest Christianity set in ideal typical terms. However, it does offer a general account of Christian exclusivism in specific social contexts. Naturally exclusivism is a relative concept and particular Christians, such as Paul, may be simultaneously exclusive and non-exclusive. Nonetheless the overall bias of each age can be tentatively suggested. That is all that need be claimed here.

Theological Implications

What are the theological implications of this sociological analysis? Here again there is an obvious danger. It is too easy to assume that exclusivism is theologically suspect either because it is less primitive than inclusivism or because its social determinants can be isolated. It might be argued that both of these assumptions rest upon fallacies – the first upon the fallacy of primitivism and the second upon the genetic fallacy. Nevertheless, in this particular instance there are good theological reasons for being suspicious of exclusivism if this sociological analysis is accepted. It is, after all, often assumed by theologians that if something can be reliably shown to belong to the preaching of the 'historical Jesus', then it should be given an especially authoritative status within Christian tradition. It is noticeable, for example, that since the concept of the Kingdom of God has been firmly established by New Testament scholars as belonging to Jesus' central message, theologians have since made considerable use of it. If in addition, the sociologist can convincingly suggest why the earliest Christians adopted a more exclusivist position than that of Jesus, theologians (especially sociological theologians) again may be given additional grounds for regarding Jesus' position as the more authoritative. They may reach this conclusion even while admitting that the cult instituted by Jesus faced the inevitable problem of institutional fragility faced by other cults, depicted, as suggested at the beginning of this chapter, by Weber's concept of the routinization of charisma. Indeed, sociological theologians might go further than this and argue that the sectarian phase of Christianity was an essential part of the growth of Christianity immediately after the death of Christ.

Volume 1 recommended a return to some of the theological insights of F.D. Maurice. Although the object of fierce criticism in his day, a number of distinguished Anglican theologians in the late 1940s and early 1950s, including Alec Vidler and Michael Ramsey, viewed him more positively.[30] Of particular interest here is that Maurice advanced a concept of the church and theology in radical opposition to what he regarded as the exclusive and partisan 'sect' or sectarian movement. He maintained that God has redeemed the whole world, and not just Christian believers, in Christ: that 'mankind stands not in Adam but in Christ':[31] and that, as a result, 'the proper constitution of man is his constitution in Christ'.[32] Having reviewed the divisions of churches in Victorian England, he concluded that:

> These systems, Protestant, Romish, English, seem to me to bear witness of a Divine Order; each to be a miserable, partial, human substitute for it. In every country, therefore, I should desire to see men emancipated from the claims which they have made for themselves, and entering into the freedom of God's Church'.[33]

A doctrine of the Universal Headship and Kingship of Christ (according to which, for instance, baptism is an acknowledgment of a relationship we already have with Christ and not a radical change) was crucial to Maurice's theology. Alec Vidler's verdict on this is worth quoting in full:

---

[30]   See Alec R. Vidler, *Witness to the Light: F.D. Maurice's Message for Today*, New York: Scribner, 1948 and A.M. Ramsey, *F.D. Maurice and the Conflicts of Modern Theology*, Cambridge: Cambridge University Press, 1951.

[31]   From *The Life of Frederick Denison Maurice Chiefly Told in His Own Letters*, London: Macmillan, 1884, volume 2, p. 358.

[32]   F.D. Maurice, *The Church and Family*, London: Macmillan, 1850, p. 46.

[33]   F.D. Maurice, *The Kingdom of Christ, or, Hints on the Principles, Ordinances and Constitution of the Catholic Church: In Letters to a Member of the Society of Friends*, Everyman edition, London: J.M. Dent, 1906 (1837), volume 2, p. 314.

While obviously this doctrine does not lie on the surface of the whole Bible, and while Maurice cannot be acquitted of seeing 'everywhere his favourite ideas' (though this was the last thing he intended to do), yet his main contention is a much stronger one than may appear at first sight to Christians who are accustomed to suppose that Christ is, strictly speaking, the Head only of believers or of the baptized or of the Church as distinguished from the race. The question is whether we can rightly take the affirmations about Christ's relation to the whole order of creation which the Bible ends by making, particularly in the Pauline and Johannine writings, as culminating insights which we are to use in interpreting the whole divine revelation. This is what Maurice did more consistently perhaps than any theologian has yet done. I believe that in principle he was right; but in practice, while he confessed that the universal Headship of Christ was revealed and discovered gradually, he inclined to find direct testimony to it too readily in all parts of the Bible. This was partly due to his unconscious disregard of the canons of historical criticism.[34]

However, as I have just argued, it is possible that in the New Testament it was exclusivism and not inclusivism which was the later development. So Maurice's claims may be stronger than Vidler allowed. Although Maurice is often remembered today as a prophet and political activist, he was predominantly a priestly and inclusive figure, tirelessly opposing sectarianism in any form. It is this aspect of his life which makes him a theologian of such importance here. If he was a Christian prophet, he had little of the exclusivism (however important in times of crisis) so often associated with Christian prophecy.

---

[34] Vidler, *Witness to the Light*, pp. 39–40.

Chapter 5

Prophecy as Praxis

A study of the social significance of theology explores the possibility that theology, even as a product of society, may in turn have an influence upon that society. Theology as a dependent variable within society may also act as an independent variable. Overall, theology is seen as a socially constructed reality – that is, as something that is both socially constructed *and* a social reality. To give a single example, various forms of Marxist theory have maintained that theology is the product and expression of socio-economic divisions within society and, in particular, the expression of the rulers over-and-against the ruled. In these terms theology is seen as a (flawed) social construction. But there is also a possibility that Marx and Engels were themselves unwittingly influenced by the prevailing Hegelian theologies of their day.[1] In addition, Liberation theologians, who appeared particularly influential in parts of Latin America in the 1970s and 1980s, incorporated a Marxist critique actually into their discipline. A complex web of interactions between theology and society emerges: Marxists, themselves possibly shaped by theology, critique theology for being socially structured and theologians, in turn, incorporate Marxism into their discipline and then seek to influence society at large. A study of such complex interaction, together with a concern to understand the social context of theology, lies at the very heart of sociological theology.

It is important not to over-state the 'newness' of the three approaches to theology that have been traced in the three volumes of *Sociological Theology*. Implicitly and, sometimes, even explicitly, critical theologians have often alluded to their particular social context and shown an awareness of the social determinants and significance of their discipline. It is a commonplace of theological polemic to demonstrate how opponents' views are inadequate responses to their social context,

---

[1]   See Roderick Martin, 'Sociology and Theology', in D.E.H. Whitley and R. Martin (eds), *Sociology, Theology and Conflict*, Oxford: Blackwell, 1969.

products of certain social factors, or lead to undesirable social consequences. Further, various forms of Existentialist theology in the 1970s made systematic use of the concept of 'situation in life' [*Sitz im Leben*] or social context – arguing that theology must respond directly to contemporary thought-forms and not simply to those of first-century Christians. In addition, both biblical and doctrinal hermeneutics have shown a considerable awareness of the relation between ideas and beliefs, on the one hand, and social or cultural factors, on the other. Recent historians of Christianity, such as Diarmaid MacCulloch[2] have also shown much interest in the interactions between social and theological factors. A combination of hermeneutics, historical research, apologetics and even theological polemics, has already made considerable use of these three sociological approaches to theology. What theologians have seldom done, though, is to use these approaches systematically or with any reference to the obvious fund of scholarship provided by the sociology of knowledge.

Once these three approaches are studied systematically and rigorously, each raises rather different problems for theologians. As was seen in Volume 1, the first approach, based upon a study of the social context of theology, raises problems more of communication and plausibility than of validity as such. 'Authentic' theology may (as some proponents argue) ignore its social context because it is simply thought to express 'timeless' truths or to use non-negotiable historic terms (as in the creeds). But if so it may simply become unintelligible to many people today. The consequence of ignoring contemporary plausibility structures is for theologians to produce work which may appear increasingly meaningless. Clearly this was a matter that concerned Rudolf Bultmann deeply, even if there is dissent from the analysis of actual plausibility structures that he provided.[3]

---

[2]   Diarmaid MacCulloch, *A History of Christianity: The First Three Thousand Years*, London: Allen Lane, 2009.

[3]   One of the main problems in interpreting Bultmann's position lies in his celebrated claim that 'myth should be interpreted not cosmologically, but anthropologically, or better still, existentially' when he has already defined 'mythology' as 'the use of imagery to express the other worldly in terms of this world and the divine in terms of human life' (Rudolf Bultmann, 'New Testament and Mythology', in H.W. Bartsch (ed.), *Kerygma and Myth*, London: SPCK, 1953, p. 10). He makes the claim precisely because he believes it to be demanded by the scientific view-point of twentieth-century people. A number of the contributors to *Kerygma and Myth*, including Thielicke and Schumann, criticized this claim at the time: G. Vaughan Jones, *Christology and Myth in the New Testament*, London: Allen & Unwin, 1956; H.P. Owen, *Keygma and Myth and Revelation and Existence*, Cardiff:

This also animates many who are developing contextual theologies in the Global South or postmodern theologies in the North. While it is obviously possible for theologians to ignore their social context, many do not. They might agree instead with Graham Ward that: 'To understand not simply where theology is today, but its direction in the future, its vocation, it must assess its cultural context.'[4]

The second approach, based on a study of the social determinants of theology, does, at first, appear to raise the problem of validity in a critical way. The systematic attempt to explain theological ideas as products of particular social structures, does seem to be an attempt, by the sociologist, to falsify them, or, at least, to support a relativist position. Even when a distinction is made, between 'explaining' something and 'explaining it away' and a further distinction is made between the 'origins' and 'validity' of ideas, a problem of validation remains if not for the sociologist, at least for the theologian. As Karl Mannheim – a sociologist overlooked by most theologians, with the important exceptions of Gregory Baum, Douglas Davies and Dan Frank[5] – argued, the social source of ideas is usually thought to be relevant to their truth or falsity, whether or not a formal logical relationship exists.[6] So, as maintained at length in Volume 2, if we successfully demonstrate a disreputable source for something, we usually distrust it thereafter – genetic fallacy or no genetic fallacy. And this despite a disconcerting element within some Christian theology which almost glories in disreputable origins. For Paul the *skandalon* created, for Jews and Gentiles, by the origins of Christianity in the Cross, was almost something to boast about. And for theologians like Kierkegaard, Christianity was considered to be both outrageous and nevertheless true. Further, various types of Mystical theology have delighted in paradoxes verging on outright inconsistencies.

University of Wales, 1957; and John Macquarrie, *The Scope of Demythologizing*, London: SCM Press, 1960, all criticized Bultmann's position.

4   Graham Ward, 'Theology and Postmodernism', *Theology*, 100: 794, 1997, p. 439. See also Graham Ward, *True Religion*, Oxford: Blackwell, 2003, p. 139.

5   Gregory Baum, *Religion and Alienation: A Theological Reading of Sociology*, New York: Paulist Press, 1975 [reprinted Ottawa: Novalis, 2006] and *The Social Imperative: Essays on the Critical Issues that Confront the Christian Churches*, New York: Paulist Press, 1979; Douglas J. Davies, *Meaning and Salvation in Religious Studies*, Leiden: E.J. Brill, 1984; and Dan Frank, *The Word and the World: Religion After the Sociology of Knowledge*, London: Continuum, 2007.

6   See Karl Mannheim, *Ideology and Utopia*, London: Routledge & Kegan, 1936.

Yet, there is still an aspect of this sociological approach to theology which does concern its validity. If, for example, a Marxist critique of the discipline is adopted, whereby it is seen as an expression of the ruling class, and confirmation for this is gathered from the middle-class bias of most Western churches today, then it might become more difficult to trust its 'universality'. Or again, if it is evident that the churches' pronouncements on ethical issues such as abortion and euthanasia tend to follow more than lead public opinion (as Volume 2 in part suggested), it might become more difficult wholly to trust them in the future.

In this last situation, theologians are faced with a number of options. They may question either the particular findings or the methodological bias of the sociologist. Alternatively, they may return to a complete separation between origins and validity, claiming that, whatever the social source of their theological notions, they are still valid. However, if they resort to none of these options they may be persuaded to revise their claims or their ideas. In the process, they would be affording sociological analysis a more central role than is usual in the validation of theological notions, since it is such analysis which provides them with the initial suspicion of the invalidity of the notions. This is not to claim that sociological analysis can directly discredit particular theological positions. Such a claim would result in the sort of confusion of sociological and theological concepts criticized in earlier volumes. Rather, it is to claim, more modestly, that sociological analysis may, at times, raise theological suspicions.

Alfredo Fierro took this as the initial starting point for his political theology. He was deeply critical of José Porfirio Miranda's approach to Christian-Marxist dialogue,[7] arguing that, in the end, he 'engages in an apologetics of coincidence and convergence … the result – or rather, the aim which governs his work from the very start – is to make Marx nothing less than a prophet beholden to biblical tradition'.[8] For Fierro, it was simply not sufficient to demonstrate a convergence between biblical and Marxist concepts; 'it is hardly surprising that one might find ideas from the Bible in Marx or any other Western thinker. It only confirms what we have known for a long time: that biblical thought has penetrated deeply into

---

[7]   José Porfirio Miranda, *Marx and the Bible*, Maryknoll, NY: Orbis, 1974.

[8]   Alfredo Fierro, *The Militant Gospel*, Maryknoll, NY: Orbis and London: SCM Press, 1977, p. 373.

Western civilization and left a real mark on it.'[9] Rather, the question he sought to face is, 'assuming the Marxist theory as correct, is any faith or theology possible at all?'[10] This is an explicitly methodological position. He was not seeking to sanctify Marxist theory as such: instead, he believed that it is the job of the theologian, in any age, to explore contemporary theories (whether Marxist, Freudian, Existentialist, or whatever) to see whether or not faith or theology is possible on their basis. In his attempt to answer this specific question, he suggested a starting point for Christians and Marxists alike, founded on the Marxist principle of analysing 'social relationships as being conditioned or determined by the economic base'.[11]

Fierro's work is rich with insights and has many resonances with the theoretical position here, some of the most important are contained in the following quotation:

> The first and primary thesis of a historical-materialist theology entails the adoption of Marxist theory and maintains that ideas and beliefs are determined or conditioned by the economic base, by the production relationships in a given society. This applies to religious ideas and beliefs as well. Even in this initial thesis, however, one may see an irreducible opposition arising between believers and Marxists. Are they strictly determined by the economic base or only conditioned by it? Orthodox Marxists ought to maintain that ideas and beliefs are rigorously determined by the economic structure whereas orthodox Christians could not maintain that; Christians could only say that religious ideas and beliefs are at most conditioned by socioeconomic factors.[12]

He argued, however, that this apparent opposition is based on an out-dated understanding of the relationship between cause and effect. In fact, 'modern thought is abandoning the etiological approach that looks for cause and effect relationships; it is now more interested in investigating relationships and correspondences between different phenomena'.[13] A number of contemporary

---

9   Ibid., p. 373.
10 Ibid., p. 375.
11 Ibid., p. 377.
12 Ibid., pp. 378–379.
13 Ibid., p. 379.

sociologists[14] were indeed critical of what they considered to be a pre-Humean understanding of causality. The theologian is asked only to concede that there is a relationship between 'purely' theological ideas and social structures and that the latter constrain the former. Once this point is conceded, then Fierro's analysis follows. Given that he was concerned with the social determinants of theological ideas from an explicitly Marxist perspective, he maintained that theologians can never avoid social determination, they can only choose by what kind of social determinants their ideas are to be fashioned. Like many others influenced by South American Liberation theology in the 1970s, Fierro concluded that genuine theology must always side with the oppressed and with the working classes. He admitted that all ideas (one's own, as well as those of one's opponents) are socially determined or constrained: no one can escape this. He avoided the mistake of some exponents of Liberation theology in imagining that it is simply 'bourgeois' Western theology which is socially structured. As a result he avoided the scathing criticism of much Liberation theology by Alistair Kee (who two decades earlier had done more than almost anyone else to introduce South American Liberation theologians to the West)[15] when he argued that it had failed to take seriously Marx's *social* critique of religious institutions.[16] Fierro did indeed take this critique seriously and maintained that the individual cannot escape social determination but can opt for one kind of social determination rather than another.

This specific solution was obviously directly related to Fierros's adoption of a Marxist perspective and, as such, was highly relevant to the contemporary Marxist-Christian dialogue. A more general point, though, also emerges from his analysis. He maintained that an understanding of the socially structured nature of theology should lead to less absolutist theological claims in the future: 'if we accept the hypothesis of historical materialism, we can only have a theology that is not all transcendent vis-à-vis the realm of other human ideas'.[17] At the very least,

---

[14] Cf. John Rex, *Key Problems of Sociological Theory*, London: Routledge & Kegan Paul, 1961, and Bernard Barber, 'Toward a New View of the Sociology of Knowledge', in Lewis A. Coser (ed.), *The Idea of Social Structure*, San Diego, CA: Harcourt Brace Jovanovich, 1975.

[15] Alistair Kee, *A Reader in Political Theology*, London: SCM Press, 1974.

[16] Alistair Kee, *Marx and the Failure of Liberation Theology*, Philadelphia, PA, and London: Trinity Press International and SCM Press, 1990, p. 260.

[17] Fierro, *The Militant Gospel*, p. 382. cf. Werner Stark, *The Sociology of Knowledge*, London: Routledge & Kegan Paul, 1956, pp. 26f.

a sociology of knowledge (whether Marxist or not) might help, on this basis, to generate a degree of theological humility.

However, it is the third approach, based upon a study of the social significance of theology, which offers the theologian the most serious problems of validation. What appears to the sociologist as the social significance of theology, appears to the theologian as its social importance. There is an inescapable evaluative element in the latter's response to this phenomenon which the former usually attempts to avoid. The claim that will be developed now, from a specifically theological perspective, is that an adequate assessment of the validity of particular theological notions should take into account their potential or actual social effects. Further, if these effects appear to be at variance with deeply embedded Christian virtues (often themselves held in tension within Christian tradition), the theologian is given grounds for distrusting their validity. If accepted, this peculiarly social criterion for assessing the validity of theological notions has radical implications for theology at large.

Graham Howes points to the danger of such a claim:

> Gill's somewhat facile elision between the truth claims of a theology and its potentially meliorative secular consequences or his highly reductionist presumption that theology's social significance is contingent on its ability to act as a social determinant.[18]

I would not want to make such a claim in this facile form. I see it in more negative terms as akin to the 'suspicion' (whether theological or sociological) expressed in the quotation from David Martin in the introduction to this volume. As will be seen in the final chapter, forms of theology that have proved so damaging, for example, in the context of global AIDS should, I believe, raise suspicions about their validity. From this it follows that responsible theology ought to take account of its intended *and* unintended social effects. Similarly, in her important new book *Global Justice, Christology and Christian Ethics*, Lisa Sowle Cahill argues (in contrast to Graham Howes) that:

---

[18] Graham Howes, 'A Response to Dan Frank', in Dan Frank, *The Word and the World: Religion After the Sociology of Knowledge*, London: Continuum, 2007, p. 89.

> Bad theologies can engender practices that have a negative effect on the
> community's relation to God; social effects that are patently out of line with
> the gospel are very reliable symptoms of inadequate or unfaithful theologies.[19]

Faith Tested by Practice

The claim that the potential or actual social effects of particular theological notions
are relevant to their validity, points to a deep rift within much Western intellectual
thought. Despite the fact that philosophy and the emerging social sciences were
scarcely differentiated until the late nineteenth century, the prevailing wisdom
within the West today suggests that, the study of 'ideas', as 'ideas', belongs largely
to the discipline of philosophy and the study of human behaviour belongs to the
social sciences. In general, social scientists have tended to avoid epistemological
questions, whereas philosophers have tended to overlook the socially structured
nature of ideas. Given this sharp division between the study of 'ideas' and the study
of 'behaviour', immediate hostility must be expected for any attempt to suggest a
relationship between the social effects and validity of theological notions.

There is, however, a radical alternative to this prevailing wisdom, suggested by
Marxist thinkers. In various ways they have tended to reject the study of 'ideas',
simply as 'ideas', and unrelated to empirical 'behaviour' and have attempted to
offer, instead, a synthesis of the two. Among Marxist writers, the division between
philosophers and social scientists is not nearly so apparent as it is among non-
Marxist intellectuals. Further, although there are very sharp divisions among
Marxists themselves, there might be widespread agreement that 'ideas' can be
fully understood only in relation to 'behaviour' and vice versa. For the Marxist,
the problem with Western philosophy is that it is overly cognitive and, all too
often, chooses to ignore empirical factors and determinants, such as class, power-
structures and economic-structures. The problem with much Western social
science, on the other hand, is that, from the perspective of the Marxist, it tries (and
fails) to be 'value free' and ignores the moral and political context within which
it operates and shapes its research. So, Marxist philosophers will tend to carry a

---

[19] Lisa Sowle Cahill, *Global Justice, Christology and Christian Ethics*, New York and
Cambridge: Cambridge University Press, 2013, chapter 1.

concern for socio-political structures actually into their philosophy and Marxist social scientists will filter their empirical research through a self-conscious philosophical/ideological commitment.

The germ of this radically different orientation, as suggested in Volume 2, can be traced back at least to Karl Marx and Frederick Engels' *The German Ideology* of 1844. In this extended polemic against the prevailing Hegelian and Young Hegelian forms of theology and philosophy, the two authors sought to show the basis of 'ideas' and consciousness in class structures and material behaviour. They contended that, despite its stress on the social significance of ideas, Hegelianism was itself ideology, reflecting a spurious division between mental and material behaviour and, in turn, an equally spurious division between the privileged rulers and the non-privileged ruled. As noted earlier, there is much debate, of course, about the exact import of their term 'ideology' and whether, or not, they explained its origins solely in terms of economic sub-structures. What is interesting here is that they contended that 'ideas' which are left unrelated to 'actions' are vacuous and that even the socially concerned Feuerbach ignored the social basis of ideas.

The following quotation from *The German Ideology* well illustrates the opposing perspectives of the Hegelians and Marx and Engels:

> In direct contrast to German philosophy which descends from heaven to earth, here we ascend from earth to heaven. That is to say, we do not set out from what men say, imagine, conceive, nor from men as narrated, thought of, imagined, conceived, in order to arrive at men in the flesh. We set out from real, active men, and on the basis of their real life-process we demonstrate the development of the ideological reflexes and echoes of this life-process. The phantoms formed in the human brain are also, necessarily, sublimates of their material life-process, which is empirically verifiable and bound to material premises.[20]

The blend of empirical and philosophical elements and the correlation between 'actions' and the validity of 'ideas', evident in this passage, are quite alien to much Western philosophy. Yet they may have more resonance for theology. Some have comprehensively adopted a Marxist critique of knowledge and society into their

---

[20] Karl Marx and Frederick Engels, *The German Ideology*, edited by C.J. Arthur, London: Lawrence & Wishart, 1970 (1846), p. 47.

theologies: some have even used this critique to assess the validity of particular theological positions. Yet with the slow demise of Liberation theology and rapid collapse of political Marxism this critique may no longer be thought to supply a relevant analysis of the societies within which theologians now operate. Although an explicit correlation between Marxist and Christian thought would have undoubted usefulness in certain contexts – indeed it has been attempted on several occasions over the last 30 years – it is doubtful if it would receive widespread support in the present Western context.

Whatever the merits or demerits of the Marxist perspective within philosophy or the social sciences, it is arguable that its insistence upon the inseparability of 'ideas' and 'practice' [the term 'praxis' has often been used to signify this inseparability] is still peculiarly pertinent to Christianity. Without a whole-scale commitment to the Marxist critique of society, it is possible to maintain that 'faith' and 'praxis' will be badly misunderstood within Christian theology if they are treated separately. For Christians, 'beliefs' are not usually statements merely about 'the way things are', that is, they are not simply cognitive. Credal statements, for example, are not just recitations of religious knowledge or opinion: when used within the liturgical context they are expressions of religious commitment. As Talcott Parsons observed, 'acceptance of a religious belief is ... a commitment to its implementation in action in a sense in which acceptance of a philosophical belief is not ... religious ideas may be speculative in the philosophical sense, but the attitude towards them is not speculative in the sense that "well, I wonder if it would make sense to look at it this way?"'.[21] At the very least, some degree of correlation between 'faith' and 'praxis' would appear essential within Christian theology, in a way that it might not be elsewhere. Indeed, I prefer to use the term 'faith', in this context, to 'belief', precisely because an element of commitment is implicit within it. In addition, it avoids some of the philosophical and sociological difficulties attached to the concept of 'belief'.[22] The term 'praxis', on the other hand, is intentionally wide – covering both intended and unintended modes of behaviour. Prophecy belongs more to the former than the latter.

---

[21] Talcott Parsons, *The Social System*, Glencoe, IL: The Free Press and London: Routledge & Kegan Paul, 1951, p. 367.
[22] See Abby Day, *Believing in Belonging*, Oxford: Oxford University Press, 2011.

Once this possibility is allowed – that the social effects of theological notions might be relevant to their validity – then the reason for much of the polemic within the history of Christian theology becomes evident. The Christological and Trinitarian controversies that took place within the Early Church were not fired simply by a desire for correct 'religious knowledge'. In part, the struggles before Chalcedon were politically and culturally based, reflecting the balance of power and difference of milieu between East and West. But they were also fired by the fear that distorted Christian faith would lead to distorted practice. If this were not the case, then the extraordinary degree of bitterness caused over a single Greek letter in the *homoousios/homoiousios* debate would be without adequate explanation. At the heart of this debate and many another between, say, Docetists, Arians, Apollinarians, lay the fear that if Christ was only 'like' God or only 'like' humans, then he could not have effected humanity's redemption and, in turn, humanity's sinful nature could not have been changed. A Christology that expressed anything less than the incarnation of God in the world was thought, at Chalcedon, to be socially ineffective. A docetic Christology denied that Christ ever became a human being, whereas an adoptionist Christology denied that he was ever fully God. The result of either was thought to be the same: the incarnation would have been ineffective and humankind would have been left unredeemed.

A double link, then, can be seen in the Early Church's correlation of faith and praxis. Wrong faith was to be feared, both because it had the immediate social effect of 'anarchy' and 'immorality', and because it involved the eschatological risk of eternal damnation. Just as orthodoxy and orthopraxis were deemed to go hand-in-hand, so conversely did 'heresy', 'anarchy', 'immorality' and 'damnation'. In the medieval church, too, and in the bitter controversies engendered by the Reformation, the same correlations are to be found. Religious tolerance, regarded as a desirable virtue, is a comparatively modern phenomenon and is possible only when 'heresy' is no longer widely feared. In ages of religious intolerance much depended upon accurate theology. In his remarkable Gifford Lectures, *The Face of God* (to which I will return at the end of this chapter), the philosopher Roger Scruton, venturing for once into theological territory, captures this correlation well. For him it is a distinctive, creative, but sometimes troubling, feature:

> By signing up to doctrine you are incorporated into [a] community. And this
> incorporation is regularly reaffirmed through sacred rites that signify, in some
> way, the collective relation of the community to its God … I think it is this
> fact about religion, far more than any apparent conflict between its doctrines
> and the theories of science, which explains the sense that somehow religion
> and science are at odds with each other. If a belief offers membership then it
> has to be protected in some way—the destiny of a human community has been
> bound up with it, and the defence of the belief is a defence of the community.
> This explains the concept of heresy, and why heretics are so severely treated in
> traditional religions. It explains why heretics are more fiercely persecuted the
> smaller their deviation from orthodoxy—deviate far enough and you are not part
> of the community, so that your beliefs can be ignored. Deviate by an inch and
> you threaten the community from within.[23]

Within some of the more radical sects today 'heresy' is still perceived as a major
threat. Movements, like those of the Jehovah's Witnesses and the Scientologists,
go to great lengths in devising social mechanisms for controlling 'heretical' views.
In the case of the Scientologists this meant, as has been seen in the previous
chapter, changing from a somewhat diffuse counselling movement or 'cult'[24] to a
strictly controlled, bureaucratic sect. In the instance of the Jehovah's Witnesses,
'orthodoxy' is only maintained at the expense of a high loss of members.[25] Yet in
either movement 'heresy', if allowed, would entail, not merely a change of faith,
but also a change of praxis. Once dissuaded from their ardent millenarianism,
Jehovah's Witnesses might lose much of their enthusiasm for proselytism and,
once allowed to experiment with differing counselling techniques, Scientologists
might lose much of their commitment to the techniques and metaphysical beliefs
of the movement as a whole. In both sectarian movements, the social effects of
'heresy' are to be feared: a rigid orthodoxy is offered as a means to control these
effects.

---

[23]   Roger Scruton, *The Face of God*, London: Continuum, 2012, pp. 16–17.
[24]   See Roy Wallis, *The Road to Total Freedom: A Sociological Analysis of Scientology*,
London: Heinemann, 1976 and New York: Columbia University Press, 1977.
[25]   See James A. Beckford, *The Trumpet Call of Prophecy*, Oxford: Blackwell, 1975.

An emphasis upon the social effects of faith was also to be found, as just mentioned, in certain types of Existentialist theology in the 1970s. Here, the emphasis was less upon the evil effects of 'heresy', than upon the beneficial effects of the Gospel narratives. The Gospels are to be trusted, not because the events they describe are historically accurate, even less because the church claims that they are to be trusted, but rather because they still have the power to change people. It is the Gospel narratives regarded as proclamation that are seen as salvific. Various theologians have held this position in the last one hundred years – ranging from the proponents of 'symbolic Christology', through followers of Bultmann, to some more recent exponents of the Gospels as 'story'. They have in common, a disinterest in the 'historical Jesus' as seriously affecting Christian faith today, a tendency to distrust metaphysics and an emphasis upon the present social effects of the Gospels.

A rather different emphasis upon the social effects of faith was to be found in Liberation theology. Closer to the traditional understanding of 'heresy' than the emphasis of Existentialist theology, exponents tended to point to the harmful social effects of opposing viewpoints. So, they often claimed a close correlation between Western theology and Western imperialism and colonialism (or sometimes just between Western theology and Western male chauvinism). This was often linked to a positive emphasis upon the 'liberating' social effects of Liberation theology itself. While a Marxist critique of society was by no means essential to this approach to theology, it was in reality often adopted within it.

A strong emphasis upon the connection between faith and praxis has again been one of the chief characteristics of Political theology. As Moltmann insisted: 'the new criterion of theology and faith resides in praxis'.[26] For Gutierrez, this emphasis was captured by the phrase 'theology as critical reflection on praxis'.[27] A study of praxis for him, was relevant to the actual verification of theology:

> 'To do the truth', as the Gospel says … acquires a precise and concrete meaning
> in terms of the importance of action in Christian life. Faith in a God who loves us
> and calls us to the gift of full communion with him and brotherhood among men

---

[26] Jürgen Moltmann, 'Gott in der Revolution', quoted by Fierro, *The Militant Gospel*, p. 396.

[27] Gustavo Gutierrez, *A Theology of Liberation*, London: SCM Press, 1974, pp. 6f.

not only is not foreign to the transformation of the world; it leads necessarily to the building up of that brotherhood and communion in history. Moreover, only by doing this truth will our faith be 'verified', in the etymological sense of the word. From this notion has recently been derived the term orthopraxis, which still disturbs the sensitivities of some. The intention, however, is not to deny the meaning of orthodoxy, understood as a proclamation of and reflection on statements considered to be true. Rather, the goal is to balance and even to reject the primacy and almost exclusiveness which doctrine has enjoyed in Christian life and above all to modify the emphasis, often obsessive, upon the attainment of an orthodoxy which is often nothing more than fidelity to an obsolete tradition or a debatable interpretation. In a more positive vein, the intention is to recognize the work and importance of concrete behaviour, of deeds, of action, of praxis in the Christian life.[28]

This passage demonstrates well the emphasis upon praxis in both Liberation and Political theology. Even in the 1970s there was a growing amount of internal criticism within the movement and real methodological differences soon emerged.[29] But most might have agreed upon the centrality of praxis over faith. As Segundo argued, for Liberation theologians 'faith … is not a universal, atemporal, pithy body of content summing up divine revelation', but rather 'the possibility of fully and conscientiously carrying out the ideological task on which the real-life liberation of human beings depends'.[30]

Strongly influenced by the writings of Jacques Derrida – at a time when interest in Liberation theology was already beginning to wane – Graham Ward traces another correlation between faith and praxis:

[T]heological discourse typifies the nature of all discourse, for all discourse pursues and promotes 'at least the trace of a prior word', a word which is 'this primordial promise.' Derrida writes that without 'this divine promise

---

[28]   Gutierrez, *A Theology of Liberation*, p. 10.

[29]   See especially José Miguez Bonino, *Revolutionary Theology Comes of Age*, London: SPCK, 1975, [US title: *Doing Theology in a Revolutionary Situation*, Minneapolis, MN: Fortress, 1975] and Fierro, *The Militant Gospel*.

[30]   Juan Luis Segundo, *The Liberation of Theology*, Maryknoll, NY: Orbis and London: Macmillan, 1977, p. 122.

which is also an injunction' there 'will only be conventional rhetoric ... It will suffice to doubt this promise ... in order to unfold ... the field of rhetoricity.'[31] Theological discourse articulates the theology of discourse itself. The economy of signification *is* this economy of faith. Faith is not understood as a leap in the dark. It is not simply a matter for human choice. There is a quasi-transcendental promise that is give. Faith is, then, *both* gift and personal commitment. But there is no principle of faith evident prior to and outside the act of faith itself in Christian utterance/testimony. Faith is *both* Christian praxis and its condition.[32]

Of course, the fact that a correlation between faith and praxis has been made within Christian theology, does not of itself demonstrate that it ought to be made. Still less does it demonstrate that the social effects of theological notions are relevant to their validity. This is especially the case when it is admitted that so much of this correlation has been made on a now thoroughly anachronistic understanding of 'heresy' (even if it was still evident in some versions of Liberation theology).[33] Few may wish to return to the attacks against 'heresy' and the fiery theological polemics that have bedevilled so much Christian history. Many might now regard as distortions past correlations of opposing theological convictions with 'anarchy', 'immorality' and 'eternal damnation'. They might also find it shocking when John Milbank appears to give voice to these correlations. It is, nonetheless, still possible that previous attempts to link faith and praxis (however distorted) were pointing to an all-too-often ignored correlation.

This correlation is clearly present in parts of the New Testament. The mysterious, eschatological parable of the sheep and the goats lays emphasis upon both the positive and the negative social effects of faith: 'Truly I tell you, just as you did it to one of the least of these who are members of my family, you did it to me' and 'Truly I tell you, just as you did not do it to one of the least of these, you did not do it to me' (Mt. 25:40 and 45). The parable denies neither the importance of faith nor its eschatological consequences, yet it makes a clear

---

[31] Quotations from Jacques Derrida, *Psyché: Inventions de l'autre*, Paris: Editions Galilée, 1987, pp. 548–549 and 556.

[32] Graham Ward, *Barth, Derrida and the Language of Theology*, Cambridge: Cambridge University Press, 1995, p. 251.

[33] Bonino, *Revolutionary Theology Comes of Age* makes important criticisms of this feature of some Liberation theology.

connection between faith and behaviour. Again, there is the frequent mention by Paul of the 'fruit of the Spirit' and of the changes effected by our life 'in Christ' – all of which are discernible in this life. And the Johannine Epistles constantly connect faith with its social effects: 'Little children, let us love, not in word or speech, but in truth and action' and 'Those who say, "I love God", and hate their brothers or sisters, are liars; for those who do not love a brother or sister whom they have seen, cannot love God whom they have not seen' (1 John 3:18 and 4:20). James 2 is clearly not alone in connecting faith with praxis.

This connection is again supported by those interpretations of the Synoptic Gospels which hold together the parables and miracles of Jesus. Both find a common purpose as proclamations and even demonstrations of the Kingdom of God: 'But if it is by the finger of God that I cast out the demons, then the kingdom of God has come to you' (Lk. 11:20). Further, the whole Passion story in these Gospels becomes, not just an expression of Jesus' faith, but a demonstration of this faith. For Matthew, in particular, as his constant use of Old Testament 'proof texts' indicates, the Passion events served to verify the faith that lay behind them. Here faith was tested, and indeed vindicated, by praxis.

The specific connection here, between the social effects and the validity of particular theological notions must be qualified in a number of ways.

First, it should be emphasized, again, that this belongs properly to sociological theological. From the perspective of the sociologist of religion, there can be no legitimate jump from the social effects of faith to the validity of that faith. Durkheim's celebrated claim that 'there are no religions which are false ... all are true in their own fashion',[34] was, it is important to note, a specifically sociological claim. He expressed the conviction that 'it is inadmissible that systems of ideas like religions, which have so considerable a place in history, and to which, in all times, men have come to receive the energy which they must have to live, should be made up of a tissue of illusions'.[35] For Durkheim, religious belief and ritual were 'true', not because he himself was a religious believer (he was not), but because, as a sociologist, he observed that it was a social reality exercising a crucial social function. Similarly, the sociological identification of theology with

---

[34] Emile Durkheim, *The Elementary Forms of the Religious Life*, London: George Allen & Unwin, 1976 [1915], p. 3.

[35] Durkheim, *The Elementary Forms*, p. 69.

theodicy[36] affords theology a crucial social function: since theodicy is an omni-present cultural phenomenon, theology is, by definition, an omni-present social reality. Nevertheless, in neither instance does the sociologist, as a sociologist, wish to claim that religion or theology really reflects 'the way things are', or that particular expressions of faith 'do justice to God'. The claim is only that religion is an understandable and sincere (and, perhaps, effective) human response to genuine human problems. The claim of sociological theology, in contrast, does wish to go further: the theologian is concerned to assess how far particular theological notions adequately reflect the object of worship and [for the explicitly Christian theologian] the virtues held in tension within Christian tradition.

Secondly, this proposal does not replace the other methods of assessing theological notions. One of the criticisms frequently made of Bultmann's theology was that, despite his prodigious biblical scholarship, his whole emphasis was upon the present-day effects of Christian faith. He showed little interest in historical 'checks' for those effects and offered little reason to believe that they were the same today as they always had been.[37] In contrast, sociological theology need not question the admissibility of historical and philosophical means of assessing particular theological positions. It need claim only that social means have been wrongly neglected.

Thirdly, only provisional suspicion or attraction can be gleaned from a study of the social effects of theological positions. There are two sides to this crucial claim, one positive and the other negative. Negatively, if it can be shown that certain theological notions, as perceived by others, lead to social effects that appear inconsistent with the virtues held in tension within Christian tradition, then the theologian is given provisional warning that, either they, or the way they are understood, may be false. Naturally, particular theological notions may have different social effects in different social contexts. For example, Matthew 27:25 (the so-called Christ-Killer text: 'Then the people as a whole answered, "His blood be on us and on our children!"') has quite different connotations – and possibly effects – today, after the Nazi holocaust, to those intended by the Gospel writer. Theological notions may, indeed, have several effects upon societies.

---

[36]   E.g. by Peter L. Berger *The Social Reality of Religion*, London: Faber and Faber, 1969 [US title, *The Sacred Canopy of Religion*, Garden City, NY: Doubleday, 1967].

[37]   See further the critics in *Kerygma and Myth* and elsewhere, cited in n. 5 above.

Again, it may not always be easy to be sure of the virtues held in tension within Christian tradition. Modern understandings of the multivalency of biblical tradition make this particularly difficult.[38] Nonetheless, without having to resort to even more arbitrary external criteria or values, a concern for inner coherence is usually thought to be a proper part of the theologian's task.

Positively, it is tempting to verify theological notions by the simple pragmatic principle of whether or not they 'work'.[39] Many people perhaps may validate their particular expressions of faith by some such principle, not by their supposed 'empirical fit',[40] or by the additional belief that they will be 'eschatologically verified'.[41] Such a straightforward theological (as distinct from general philosophical) pragmatism has obvious attractions: the social effects of theological notions which accord with Christian faith and practice (and in this sense 'work'), would act as 'proof' of the validity of these notions. Unfortunately, expressions of faith that 'work' may still be false. So, the faith of the Jehovah's Witness, that God is to bring the world to an end in the next few years, has undoubted benefits. Individual so persuaded are given a clear incentive to strive hard for others, to concentrate exclusively upon the Kingdom of God and to live devoted and faithful lives. In terms of many other Christian denominations these features, taken on their own, might seem admirable. An exclusive use of social effects to assess the validity of theological notions – without a parallel assessment of their fit with the virtues in tension gleaned from Christian tradition and a critical analysis of the way God is thought to act by past Christian thinkers – may lead to some curious results.[42] Social means of assessing theological notions can offer at best only provisional attraction or suspicion.

Fourthly, an obvious objection to this proposal is that theologians cannot be held responsible for the social effects of their notions. For example, if Weber is correct and there really was a connection between the theological notions of

---

[38]   Cf. James D.G. Dunn, *Unity and Diversity in the New Testament*, London: SCM Press, 1977 and John Barton (ed.), *The Cambridge Companion to Biblical Interpretation*, Cambridge: Cambridge University Press, 1998.

[39]   Cf. Gutierrez, *A Theology of Liberation*, p. 10f.

[40]   See I.T. Ramsey, *Religious Language*, London: SCM Press, 1957.

[41]   See John Hick, 'Theology and Verification', in Hick (ed.), *The Existence of God*, London: Macmillan, 1964.

[42]   Cf. Fierro, *The Militant Gospel*, pp. 392f.

Calvin, as popularly perceived, and the moral ideas necessary for the spirit of Capitalism at its inception in the West,[43] Calvin cannot himself be held accountable. According to this view, theologians should be held accountable only for the ideas they have proposed and not for the ideas others perceive them to have proposed. So, the research finding that some particularistic expressions of Christology and soteriology appear to be strongly correlated with anti-semitism[44] should not necessarily worry their exponents.

Naturally it may be difficult actually to demonstrate a link between certain types of practice and particular expressions of faith. From a sociological perspective, measuring the social significance of particular theological positions is undoubtedly difficult though by no means impossible. However, from a theological perspective, the concept of 'accountability' in this objection involves ethical, rather than theological, considerations. Yet, if theologians are concerned to communicate, then, as Volume 1 argued at length, they should take seriously the social context within which they operate. What is now claimed is that their concern for this context should also lead them to study the ways in which their ideas are perceived by others and the potential and actual effects these ideas might then have upon them. A crucial part of the theological task might then involve a systematic attempt to assess the possible social effects of all theological ideas and positions.

Faith and General Virtues

Theologians have typically been concerned more to examine the social implications of theology than to measure its social effects. There is now very widespread agreement that Christianity does have moral, social and even political implications. Chapter 7 will look at evidence that theological conservatives have a tendency to emphasize the moral implications of Christian faith for individuals,

---

[43]   See Max Weber, *The Protestant Ethic and the 'Spirit' of Capitalism*, New York: Scribner, 1958 [1905].

[44]   See Charles Y. Glock and Rodney Stark, *Christian Beliefs and Anti-Semitism*, New York: Harper, 1966 and Richard L. Gorsuch and Daniel Aleshire, 'Christian Faith and Prejudice: Review of Research', *Journal for the Scientific Study of Religion*, 13:3, 1974, pp. 281–307.

whereas more radical Christians characteristically place greater emphasis upon the political implications of faith. On overall virtues, however, there appears to be far more commonality between conservatives and radicals – just as there was between Edward Norman and his British critics a generation ago. There are even important commonalities between the virtues held alike by many secularists and Christians. In a Western context such virtues can even appear platitudinous. But in terms of a transposition paradigm this is only to be expected.

Again, there is nothing new about theological disagreements over the extent to which faith necessarily involves praxis. The relationship of theology to political, moral and social realities has occupied theologians at least since the time of Augustine. It was also clearly a matter of considerable importance at the time of the Reformation. In more recent theology, it was the source of much of the discord between Brunner and Barth. For Brunner, fairly detailed social and political implications could be derived from the Christian doctrine of creation.[45] Barth, in contrast, remained comparatively apolitical in his theological writings, despite his personal political involvement and even though, in later life, his position shifted. In Liberation theology this disagreement was taken still further.

My own position is closest, perhaps, to some of the discussions in Europe that resulted from the political upheavals of the 1930s and early 1940s. These events served particularly to focus the issue of the social, political and moral implications of Christian faith. Especially important were the discussions influenced by the Universal Christian Council for Life and Work. In 1937, this Council became one of the two founding bodies of the World Council of Churches and was committed to the view that Christianity is a carrier of virtues that are not derived directly from reason but that are nevertheless still relevant to national politics. This view is clearly present in the writings of the two giants among church-leaders of this time, namely William Temple and John Baillie.

In his writing on Christianity and the social order, Temple argued as follows:

> The method of the Church's impact upon society at large should be twofold. The Church must announce Christian principles and point out where the existing social order at any time is in conflict with them. It must then pass on to Christian citizens, acting in their civic capacity, the task of re-shaping the existing order

---

[45]   E.g. see Emil Brunner, *Justice and the Social Order*, Leicester: Lutterworth, 1945.

in closer conformity to the principles. For at this point technical knowledge may be required and judgements of practical expediency are always required. If a bridge is to be built, the Church may remind the engineer that it is his obligation to provide a really safe bridge; but it is not entitled to tell him whether, in fact, his design meets this requirement … In just the same way the Church may tell the politician what ends the social order should promote; but it must leave to the politician the devising of the precise means to those ends.[46]

Temple was under no illusion that this position is vulnerable, both from within and without, the church:

The Church is likely to be attacked from both sides if it does its duty. It will be told that it has become 'political' when in fact it has been careful only to state principles and point to breaches of them; and it will be told by advocates of particular policies that it is futile because it does not support these. If it is faithful to its commission it will ignore both sets of complaints, and continue so far as it can to influence all citizens and permeate all parties.[47]

Temple typically located the influence of the church, as the church in society, in the area of general principles – or 'virtues' as they are usually termed today. He was emphatic that the church, as such, cannot support particular political programmes. But the latter can, and indeed should, be supported by individual Christians. In response to the contemporary social problems, Temple proceeded to elaborate a fairly extensive political programme. At the same time, he insisted that others may be more politically competent than he to criticize this programme and to suggest another and that it is not meant to be a programme which all Christians ought to support. For him 'there neither is nor can be any such programme'.[48] For Temple, then, prophecy belongs to the churches only in relation to general principles or virtues: particularized prophecy is an individual phenomenon.

---

[46] William Temple, *Christianity and the Social Order*, London: Pelican, 1956 [re-published, London: SPCK, 1976], p. 50.

[47] Temple, *Christianity and the Social Order*, p. 51.

[48] Ibid., p. 121.

A very similar position is to be found in the reports of the Church of Scotland's war-time commission, chaired by John Baillie. Like Temple, the members of this commission showed themselves to be well aware of the double criticism to which the politically active church is subject. But they maintained that it rests upon a mistake:

> Religion is not merely one department of life alongside of politics, nor is the Church merely one corporation among others like the State or the League of Nations or the trade union. What we have rather to understand is that in the framing of every one of our practical decisions, and not least of our decisions concerning the social, economic, and political ordering of our earthly society, two disparate kinds of knowledge are always called into play. We have always to draw on our knowledge of moral and spiritual principles, and we have always to draw also on what we can only call our departmental knowledge in some particular and specialised field.[49]

Like Temple, they insisted that the proclamation of moral and spiritual virtues belongs to the function of the church. They also insisted that, since the church cannot normally take stands on departmental (or 'technical' as Temple calls it) knowledge, it 'is never in a position to identify itself completely with any particular political, economic, industrial, educational, scientific, or other programme'.[50] On the other hand, the individual Christian has a duty to be involved in such programmes and to seek to influence them in the light of Christian virtues, especially in a society still, at least nominally, Christian.

Again like Temple, the commission did take the risk of making more specific pronouncements. To enable it to do this, it adopted the notion of 'middle axioms'.[51] For the commission, middle axioms are 'secondary and more specialised principles

---

[49] John Baillie (ed.), *God's Will for Church and Nation: Reprinted from the Reports of the Commission for the Interpretation of God's Will in the Present Crisis as Presented to the General Assembly of the Church of Scotland During the War Years*, London: SCM Press, 1946, p. 36.

[50] Baillie, *God's Will for Church and Nation*, p. 37.

[51] Ronald Preston, 'Vision and Utopia', a letter in *Theology*, 81:684, 1978 and Peter Hinchliff, 'Religion and Politics: The Harsh Reality', in Haddon Willmer (ed.), *Christian Faith and Political Hopes: A Reply to E.R. Norman*, London: Epworth, 1979.

which exhibit the relevance of the ruling principles to the particular field of action in which guidance is needed ... They are not such as to be appropriate to every time and place and situation, but they are offered as legitimate and necessary applications of the Christian rule of faith and life to the special circumstances in which we now stand.'[52] These intermediate principles involve a degree of risk and are situational in a way that the general principles or virtues derived from the Gospels are not. Yet they are necessary in order to link these virtues with particular situations.

There is a crucial difference between the positions of Temple and the Baillie Commission. Writing as an individual, Temple was prepared to risk political suggestions which, he admitted, that as the then chairman of the Convocation of York, he would not ask, or even allow, this church body to endorse. The commission, on the other hand, through its use of middle axioms felt able to make concrete (albeit fallible) suggestions as a corporate body. It may come as no surprise to discover that the Church of Scotland's General Assembly, at least immediately following the Second World War, tended to make more detailed and specific moral, social and political pronouncements than the corresponding Church of England bodies.

For both Temple and the Baillie Commission the main hesitation about the church making specific moral, social and political pronouncements lay in the incompetence of theologians, as theologians, or Christians, simply as Christians, to arbitrate on matters concerning technical or departmental knowledge. For them, politics, like engineering or shoe-making, involves technical competences not to be found in the Bible. In so far as general virtues are involved in politics, engineering or shoe-making, theologians can contribute *as theologians*. Unless they are to interfere in matters that are quite beyond their competence, *that* must usually be the extent of their contribution.

There are indeed many instances of the churches, in the past, interfering in scientific and political matters which would thoroughly embarrass many Christians today. Nonetheless, a distinction between general principles/virtues and technical knowledge can be made too readily. Obviously, the practicalities of politics involve very considerable legislative, constitutional and administrative skills. They also continuously involve moral virtues, even when these virtues are

---

[52]   Baillie, *God's Will for Church and Nation*, p. 45.

invisible to those actually engaged in politics (virtues which, as already argued, in terms of a transposition paradigm, may derive originally from Christian tradition). But political decision-making also involves many different sorts of specifically political commitments, no doubt relevant to virtues, but not derived directly from them. These political commitments divide Christians, as much as non-Christians and are not necessarily dependent upon technical knowledge. And because they so thoroughly divide Christians, they tend to make any attempt by particular churches to take sides and to make specific political pronouncements, look partisan. Given the spread of political loyalties among Christians, it may be particular commitments, more than technical knowledge, which divide them on political issues.

A second reason, not so obvious to Temple or the Baillie Commission, for wishing to restrict church pronouncements lies in the socially constrained nature of so many of these pronouncements on specific social, moral and political issues. In Volume 2 it was seen that churches have a tendency to reflect and not simply shape public moral perceptions – even when they imagine that they are arbitrating quite independently. Despite H. Richard Niebuhr's celebrated American study, *The Social Sources of Denominationalism*,[53] being available for over a decade, neither Temple nor the Baillie Commission showed much awareness of this point. So, the Baillie Commission, having stated that the church cannot be identified with particular programmes, conceded, at one point:

> There will indeed be cases in which either the moral issues concerned are of so overriding a character or the weight of expert opinion on the technical issues is so united that the Church, confidently judging that dissent is more likely to proceed from the lack of a proper devotion to the true spiritual ends involved rather than from honest uncertainty as to the means best suited to their attainment, may in practice throw its full weight into the support of a particular policy.[54]

There is an important point, but it is a dangerous one. The moral situation in Hitler's Germany or Apartheid South Africa surely required that the stand of

---

[53]   H. Richard Niebuhr, *The Social Sources of Denominationalism*, New York: Henry Holt, 1929.

[54]   Baillie, *God's Will for Church and Nation*, p. 37.

churches at the time ought to have been clear. Yet, apart from such situations, it is precisely when churches have felt that they had the weight of expert opinion behind them, that they have all too often demonstrated their fallibility. The debates with Galileo or Darwin are obvious examples of this and it is doubtful whether the weight of expert opinion would have been on the side of someone like Josephine Butler at the time of her campaigns against the Contagious Diseases Acts in the nineteenth century. The 'weight of expert opinion' may sometimes be as much socially structured as the particular proclamations of churches.

Virtues, too, can be rationalized, ignored or confused. For example, Edward Norman criticized the then Bishop of Worcester's defence of a report on the 'closed shop' in industry. The latter had claimed that 'tolerant attitudes, flexibility and compassion' are Christian virtues that should be transfused into society. In a telling (even if characteristically acid) response, Norman argued:

> Now 'tolerance', 'flexibility' and 'compassion' are not distinctively Christian virtues, though two of them are arguably classical pagan ones, nor does an examination of the history of Christianity suggest that the Church is the most suitable agency to secure their application. And anyway, whatever the pedigree of these concepts, the fact is that their real virtue is entirely dependent upon the ideas to which they are made to relate; and that is something which alters according to circumstance and the general prescriptions of the prevailing ideology. The Bishop's patronage of these selected qualities turns out to be sponsorship of the content of contemporary liberalism.[55]

His point is important, especially if it is combined with the major contention of Reinhold Niebuhr that individual Christian virtues apply only awkwardly to institutions.[56] Even the most thoroughgoing transposition paradigm should not assume uncritically that currently fashionable virtues necessarily derive from Christian tradition. It is also questionable whether the Church of England could seriously have had 'a position' on an issue such as the closed shop. But, to claim that churches, throughout history, must have exemplified the virtues they believe

---

[55] Edward Norman, *Christianity and the World Order*, Oxford: Oxford University Press, 1979, p. 8.

[56] Reinhold Niebuhr, *Moral Man and Immoral Society*, New York: Scribner, 1934.

to be implied in Christian tradition, themselves, before they proclaim them to others, might simply reduce them to silence. Nor does it necessarily follow that virtue 'is entirely dependent upon the ideas to which they are made to relate'. Nonetheless, Norman's overall critical point remains: particular *perceptions* of Christian virtues are not immune from social constraints.

Whether or not Temple was always aware of this point, he was clear in his own mind that the principles/virtues of a Christian social order which he put forward – freedom, fellowship and service – are all 'derived from the still more fundamental Christian postulates that Man is a child of God and is destined for a life of eternal fellowship with Him'.[57] To put this point more technically, Temple was convinced, and sought to demonstrate, that there is a logical relationship between the Christian doctrines of creation, redemption and sanctification and the general principles/ virtues of freedom, fellowship and service. As a result, he believed that it was the duty of the churches to proclaim these virtues to society at large, even at the risk of criticism, and that it was the duty of individual Christians to try to relate these virtues to their own particular technical knowledge in relation to the social problems confronting them.

The position suggested here can, perhaps, be best seen in the context of a concrete example. Again, the issue of pacifism provides a good illustration. In the 1930s (as Chapter 1 indicated), Temple and Raven stood on opposite sides in the debate about pacifism in the Church of England. The former even accused the latter of being 'heretical in tendency' and it is quite clear that Raven himself believed that both the New Testament and Christian doctrine supported a pacifist position. The conflict between these two theologians appears to be a classic conflict of Christian prophecy. What could easily be missed in this situation is that the two men would certainly have shared a common conviction that Christians ought to be peace-makers and that war itself is inherently evil. Both Raven and Temple would also have agreed that the virtues of peace-making and war-aversion are inherent in Christian tradition. Not only does the New Testament specifically commend 'peace-makers', but the doctrines of creation, redemption and sanctification imply a policy towards fellow human beings which is at odds with the warlike and, since Augustine, there has been a long tradition of theologians drawing an analogy between earthly peace and the heavenly peace.

---

[57]   Temple, *Christianity and the Social Order*, p. 74.

Rather, the disagreement between the two lay in the *way* in which they believed that Christians ought to be peace-makers. Raven, once he became a pacifist, maintained that the way to keep peace was for others to become pacifists. But, of course, others have concluded (Temple among them) that the way to keep peace is to offer resistance, defence and deterrence against evil-doers. Undoubtedly, these different positions do contain genuine moral differences, but they also contain differences of political judgement. So, some pacifists have maintained,[58] that non-violent forms of resisting evil can be more effective than the use of violence and war. Non-pacifists have seldom been impressed with this argument. Yet, the difference between them here is one of judgement more than belief.

In the debate about war, it seems difficult or even impossible for churches, as churches, to adopt a thoroughgoing pacifist position – however much they might sympathize with the pacifist cause and with the pacifist orientation of so much of the New Testament. Yet, churches can seek to embed the virtues of peace-making into society at large, together with the virtues of forgiveness and reconciliation. In so doing, they may well be attacked, both by the ardent militarist and by the thoroughgoing pacifist. More hurtfully, they may also be accused, by those who live in a society in which these Christian virtues have already been transposed, of voicing platitudes. However, individual Christians can more readily go beyond this position. They can seek to relate these virtues to the particularities which surround them. They must expect to disagree, at times, with their fellow Christians and even perhaps with their own churches. It is they who are faced with the task of trying to relate their various political, moral and technical ideas to Christian virtues. In Chapter 8 I will argue that such a strategy can make sense of what a theologian *as a theologian* might be able to contribute in the public forum of health care ethics today – suggesting that virtues connected with healing can, with effort, be foraged from the Gospels and then be applied normatively to complex dilemmas in bioethics.

Despite his public criticism of Raven's pacifism, it is possible that Temple would not have wished to see a church in which pacifism was absent. In other contexts he argued that it was right that dissentient minority views on political issues should be represented in the church. As an example, he cited the then

---

[58]   Cf. United Reformed Church, *Non-Violent Action*, London: SCM Press, 1973; and Glen Stassen (ed.), *Just Peacemaking*, Cleveland, OH: Pilgrim Press, 1999.

Bishop of Gloucester who, unlike the other Church of England bishops, was highly critical of the League of Nations, believing that it lured people into the false sense of security that resulted in the Second World War. He reminded the church that the majority may sometimes be wrong and that in any case 'even though a large majority of Christians hold a particular view, the dissentient minority may well be equally loyal to Christ and equally entitled to be recognized as loyal members of His Church'.[59]

However, there is a danger in this analysis. It might be assumed, too readily, that there is a common Christian conviction about 'peace-making'. Here, too, Liberation theologians provided a point of contrast. Bonino, for example, argued that there are really two understandings of 'peace' in Christian theology, the first a priestly understanding and the second a prophetic one:

> The first one equates peace with order, lack of conflict, harmonious integration – one would almost say 'ecological balance in nature and society' ... It dominates the Greco-Roman conception of peace and has shaped the theological tradition since Augustine. The other view of peace is typically represented by the prophets, but can be shown, I think, to be the predominant one in the Bible. Peace is a dynamic process through which justice is established amid the tensions of history ... an ever renewed task, and a fruit of active love. It is quite evident that the possibility of conflict will be differently viewed in these two conceptions. For the first it will be in itself negative, a rupture in harmony; for the second it may be a positive manifestation of the situation which requires righting. Violence in the more specific sense of physical compulsion or destruction may be accepted or rejected in either of the two views, but acceptance or rejection will be viewed in a different way. In the first it will be judged in terms of order; in the second, in terms of the struggle for justice.[60]

Bonino appeared to identify the first understanding of 'peace' as the one predominant in Western theology and the second as the essentially biblical one adopted by South American Liberation theology. No doubt, he would have viewed

---

[59]   Temple, *Christianity and the Social Order*, p. 28.
[60]   Bonino, *Revolutionary Theology Comes of Age*, p. 116.

the Life and Work movement's attempt to distinguish virtues as a typically Western piece of abstraction and as symptomatic of a divorce between faith and practice.

Yet, there is a hint, in this quotation, that there were moral differences among Liberation theologians themselves. There is an obvious division between those who were prepared to sanction violence in the context of revolutionary struggle and those who were not.[61] It is not simply that they perceived the empirical situation differently – one group deciding that violence would prove more effective and the other not. It would seem that they had already decided, in advance of a situation, that violence was either permissible or not. It is difficult to avoid the conclusion that this was a decision in principle. Of course, there is an important point in Bonino's claim. It must never be imagined that the virtues of 'love', 'peace' and 'justice' always carry the same meaning for all Christians in widely different social contexts. When he came to summarize his own position he maintained dogmatically that, 'there is no divine war, there is no specifically Christian struggle … there is no room for crusades, for sacred wars'.[62] This reads very much like a statement of general principle.

Altruism Rediscovered

The next two chapters will be concerned with the theologically significant issue of 'social capital'. The focus in them will be especially upon the virtue of altruism and some of its manifestations in specific (and changing) attitudes and behaviour. Continuing themes traced in Volume 2, it will become apparent that altruism can be found both among the religiously active and those who are not. There are clear continuities (as a transposition paradigm would predict) between the virtues held by religious and secular individuals. Yet, it will also be seen that evidence of altruism is *significantly and directionally* (albeit not exclusively) correlated with regular churchgoing: the more that people go to church, the more altruistic they appear to be. Interestingly, it is this aspect of the religiously active that Roger Scruton finds most important in his attempt to locate 'the face of God' in the

---

[61] See further Alistair Kee (ed.), *Reader in Political Theology*, London: SCM Press, 1974.

[62] Bonino, *Revolutionary Theology Comes of Age*, p. 124.

world. He is well aware that some socio-biologists explain altruism simply as a product of (cooperative) animal and human evolution rather than of moral reasoning or persuasion. However he argues that such explanations typically employ a 'minimalist concept of altruism':

> according to which an organism acts altruistically if it benefits another organism at a cost to itself. The concept applies equally to the soldier ant marching into the flames that threaten the anthill, and the officer who throws himself onto the live grenade that threatens his platoon. The concept of altruism, so understood, cannot explain, or even recognize, the distinction between the two cases. Yet the ant marches instinctively towards the flames, unable either to understand what it is doing or to fear the results of it, while the officer lays down his life for his friends.[63]

For him it is 'intentionality' that marks the crucial difference here between the ant and the human. He might have added that, ironically, had the officer himself been trained in socio-biology and had decided from this training that altruism really is just a residual product of evolution, he might then have concluded that he was no longer morally bound by it (just as many committed to socio-biology also conclude[64] that they are no longer bound by religion despite the benefits that it might once have given human beings). On this basis an officer well-schooled in socio-biology might simply resist an evolutionary impulse to save his platoon.

While overlooking this particular possibility, Roger Scruton argues that modern 'consumer society' simply blunts our capacity for sacrifice. Pornography 'defaces' (literally) love, fast-food destroys the rituals of communal eating, functional architecture removes decoration and beauty and easy entertainment just distracts us. As a result 'moments of sacred awe' have become rare in the modern world. Yet, however rare, in his lyrical conclusion he does detect some such moments:

> So what and where is the face of God for the one who believes in his real presence among us? The answer is that we encounter this presence everywhere, in all that

---

[63]   Scruton, *The Face of God*, p. 26.

[64]   See, for example, Daniel Dennett, *Breaking the Spell: Religion as a Natural Phenomenon*, New York: Viking and London: Allen Lane, 2006.

suffers and renounces for another's sake. Things with a face are illuminated by the subjectivity that shines in them, and which spreads around them a halo of prohibitions. When someone enters the moment of sacrifice, throwing away what is most precious, even life itself, for the sake of another, then we encounter the supreme moment of gift. This is an act in which the I appears completely. It is also a revelation. In sacrifice and renunciation the I makes its own being a gift, and thereby shows us that being *is* a gift. In the moment of sacrifice people come face to face with God, who is present too in those places where sorrow has left its mark or 'prayer has been valid'.[65]

The relation between faith and practice, properly understood, is manifestly complex. A fundamental issue in sociological theology is to distinguish carefully between the social effects and the social implications of particular theological notions and then to trace the connections between the two. To return to this difficult distinction, it is evident that there is, at times, a radical difference between the supposed implications of particular notions for theologians themselves and the effects or significance these notions might then have upon society at large. The two are distinct but not entirely unconnected and sociological theology needs to be responsive to both.

In his writings David Martin has long acknowledged that the boundaries between theology and sociology are permeable. Although the starting points for the two disciplines (each variously understood) are different, their language, themes and concepts frequently overlap. Once again he uses a musical metaphor to express this:

[T]he relations between theology and sociology are such as hold between varieties of ordinary discourse, and may therefore be bedevilled by the extraordinary and uncontrolled richness of language … The problem of relating two discourses rooted in ordinary language does not end here. The ordinary writing of ordinary language mixes modes almost as rapidly as music changes keys. A piece of

---

65   Scruton, *The Face of God*, p. 177.

writing, which in its general tenor is mostly sociological or mostly theological, may veer rapidly through several other kinds of logic and modality.[66]

Staying with the language of modality, sociological theology may be seen as a discipline that consciously works in a number of keys. In one key it seeks to unpack the social implications of varying theological notions. This is primarily a theological task. In another key it seeks to use social data, techniques and theories, in order to compile a picture of the actual, possible and potential social effects of notions. This is primarily a sociological undertaking. In a different key again it seeks to compare emerging patterns of virtues held in tension within Christian tradition to see whether they raise suspicions about their validity (along with philosophical and historical means of assessment). This is also a primarily theological task, as is the key of re-assessing the social implications of these notions. As in music these 'keys' interweave and, even when they seem to reach a resolution, it is a resolution that always waits in humility for better music beyond.

In the chapters that follow I will deliberately use a mixture of quantitative, quasi-quantitative and qualitative sociological methods alongside a theological mode steeped in virtue ethics. In the next chapter I will argue that claims made about 'social capital' are particularly interesting for sociological theology but that they need to be tested empirically. In the following chapter I seek to do just that, looking at a range of quantitative data, some already published but others entirely new. The great strength of such quantitative data is that they allow correlations to be tested rigorously, publicly and in manner that can then be re-tested by others. But, of course, quantitative data are not to everyone's taste. So I conclude this section with a verbal summary of some of my main findings. In Chapter 8 I adopt an approach somewhere between quantitative and qualitative data, echoing quasi-quantitative research on interviews that tests for the regularity of concepts used (except that I am testing not interviews but healing stories from the Synoptic Gospels). In the final chapter my approach is purely qualitative, constructing and comparing ideal typologies that suggest resonances between 'leprosy' within different parts of the Bible and the global challenge of AIDS in the modern world. Throughout these differing methodological modes my central concern is

---

[66] David Martin, *Reflections on Sociology and Theology*, Oxford: Clarendon Press, 1996, pp. 23–24.

to locate religious virtues that may have both social significance *and* theological implications.

PART II
Social Capital

Chapter 6

Theology and Social Capital

The ongoing debate about religion and social capital has been noted in passing in both of the previous volumes. Now it must be explored more deeply since it is crucial to an analysis of the social significance of theology. At its most robust, the concept of *social* (as distinct from economic, human or physical) capital suggests that human well-being is uniquely 'enriched' by communal networks of shared beliefs and practices, including those of faith traditions. Conversely, the loss of such communal networks, even those of faith traditions, will result in 'impoverished' human well-being. Some political communitarians might agree with the broad parameters of both of these statements, but would omit any reference to faith traditions. For them communal networks of shared beliefs and practices can function with or without faith communities. However, within the growing literature on social capital, most proponents include some reference to faith communities and a number regard faith communities as crucial to social capital, linking an apparent diminution of social capital to the evident erosion of faith communities in many Western countries.

Although, as he acknowledges, the term 'social capital' has been used variously since at least 1916, Robert Putnam's widely read *Bowling Alone*[1] has dominated recent research on this topic. Unlike, say, Pierre Bourdieu, who used the concept of 'social capital' in the 1980s, Putnam's writing is usually clear and, like the earlier work of James Coleman, it is based in quantitative statistics. However, unlike Bourdieu and Coleman, he likes to use populist images to promote his theories. His image of 'bowling alone' is intended to capture a significant social change in much of the Western world in the second half of the twentieth century – a shift away from long-established social networks. Once Americans played bowls in leagues, usually after work, but now they tend to bowl alone or with their close

---

[1]   Robert D. Putnam, *Bowling Alone: The Collapse and Revival of American Community*, New York: Simon & Schuster, 2000.

friends and families. It is a populist image sometimes used to depict a gradual shift from public, corporate worship to private, individualized spirituality in Britain over the last century. It can also be used to depict a shift away from religious and civic forms of marriage in much of the Western world and from active political membership, and even voting at all, in many democratic countries. For Putnam such shifts involve a diminution of the added value that 'social capital' offers:

> By analogy with notions of physical capital and human capital—tools and training that enhance individual productivity—the core idea of social capital theory is that social networks have value. Just as the screwdriver (physical capital) or a college education (human capital) can increase productivity (both individual and collective), so too social contacts affect the productivity of individuals and groups. Whereas physical capital refers to physical objects and human capital refers to properties of individuals, social capital refers to connections among individuals—social networks and the norms of reciprocity and trustworthiness that arise from them. In that sense 'social capital' is closely related to what some have called 'civic virtue'. The difference is that 'social capital' calls attention to the fact that civic virtue is most powerful when embedded in a dense network of reciprocal social relations. A society of many virtuous but isolated individuals is not necessarily rich in social capital.[2]

There are some important features in this quotation. Social capital can have an individual or collective effect. However it is most 'powerful' when it is collective. Social capital can be seen in functional terms as being concerned with 'productivity', but it also appears to have moral content since it is concerned with 'civic virtue'. In addition, a society of many virtuous individuals is not necessarily 'rich in social capital'. As the book proceeds it becomes evident that Putnam, for the most part, regards social capital to be beneficial and its loss as something to be regretted. For him social capital is both a 'private good' and a 'public good', involving mutual obligations and reciprocity.[3] Nevertheless, he has an early sharp reminder that this is not always so:

---

2   Ibid., pp. 18–19.
3   Ibid., p. 20.

Networks and associated norms of reciprocity are generally good for those inside the network, but the external effects of social capital are by no means always positive. It was social capital, for example, that enabled Timothy McVeigh to bomb the Alfred P. Murrah Federal Building in Oklahoma City. McVeigh's network of friends, bound together by a norm of reciprocity, enabled him to do what he could not have done alone ... Social capital, in short, can be directed toward malevolent, antisocial purposes, just like any other form of capital ... Therefore it is important to ask how the positive consequences of social capital—mutual support, cooperation, trust, institutional effectiveness—can be maximized and then negative manifestations—sectarianism, ethnocentrism, corruption—minimized.[4]

In a later chapter he discusses 'the dark side of social capital', but he does not return to the awkward McVeigh example. He discusses, instead, whether a diminution in social capital has been accompanied by an increase in toleration in American society (he argues that it has but that the two are unrelated) and whether there is a relationship between strong social capital and social inequality (always difficult for those churches that are in effect segregated on ethnic, as seen in York in Volume 2, on social class lines). Running through all of these examples are obvious moral presumptions about what is 'good' (mutual support, cooperation, trust, reciprocity, institutional effectiveness, tolerance, equality) and what is 'bad' (sectarianism, ethnocentrism, corruption, intolerance, inequality). As a socio-political scientist he can specify (up to a point) how such goods or virtues can be maximized and such bads minimized, but not how this distinction can be morally justified in the first place. Even his crucial distinction between 'bonding' and 'bridging' forms of social capital does not finally enable him to make such a justification, since (in the same parenthesis above) 'mutual support' appears to be bonding and 'tolerance' to be bridging. The problem is quite simply that sometimes Putnam treats bonding as bad (for example McVeigh) and other times as good (for example because it contributes to productivity).

Lucy Lee, in an otherwise excellent analysis of religious trends revealed by recent British Social Attitudes data, unintentionally displays a very similar problem. Her analysis is fully consonant with the cultural paradigm of churchgoing championed

---

4   Ibid., pp. 21–22.

in Volume 1. This paradigm starts from the sociological presumption that religious beliefs and values are shaped through religious socialization (formal or informal). Of course they may, in turn, shape religious practices and organizations, but they do need initially to be culturally embedded in human beings. This paradigm looks for a causal relationship between forms of religious beliefs and values, on the one hand, and specific types of religious belonging. A cultural paradigm expects to find that, unless religious socialization is actively fostered by parents across generations (which has not happened substantially in Britain over the last six decades with the demise of Sunday schools and child church attendance), then Christian beliefs and practices will become increasingly attenuated among the young. Lucy Lee focuses upon annual religious affiliation and attendance BSA data (rather than upon belief which features more rarely in BSA questionnaires) and finds just such attenuation. Between 1983 and 2010 those not 'belonging to a particular religion' increased from 31 to 50 per cent. By 2010 there was a very sharp contrast between young and old: with 64 per cent of those aged 18–24 stating that they have no religion, compared with 28 per cent of those aged 65 or over. (In contrast, Geoffrey Gorer, using a very similar question to BSA, found an overall rate of 23 per cent in 1950 with only very slight differences between generations.)[5]

She also argues that this is a cohort difference (that is, due to a shift in culture) and not a life-cycle difference (that is, people getting more religious as they grow older). Counting against a life-cycle difference is evidence that those with no religion remained non-religious over time: '30 per cent of those born between 1936 and 1945 did not follow a religion in 1983 (when they were aged 28–47 years), compared with 31 per cent in 2010 (when they were 65–74 years).'[6] Significantly, 94 per cent of those not following a religion in 2010 had also been brought up with no religion. Her overall point remains largely intact despite missing one piece of evidence. From the outset BSA data has shown that up to two-thirds of the youngest respondents (18–24 years) did not follow a religion. Yet, over a generation they did slightly modify this position. So in 1983–84 61 per cent of the youngest group gave the no-religion response, but by 2010

---

[5]   Geoffrey Gorer, *Exploring English Character*, London: Cresset Press, 1955: see further Table 3 in my *Churchgoing and Christian Ethics*, Cambridge: Cambridge University Press, 1999, p. 88.

[6]   Lucy Lee, 'Religion' in *British Social Attitudes 28th Report*, London: Sage, 2011, p. 181.

this cohort (now aged 45–54) recorded 51 per cent. Similarly, in 1994 no-religion was 66 per cent for the youngest group, reducing to 60 per cent for those aged 35–44 in 2010. This suggests that there *is* a life-cycle difference (perhaps when people themselves become parents) albeit in a context of a much stronger cohort difference.

Finally she summarizes (without any reference to the now contentious secularization paradigm):

> Britain is becoming less religious, with the numbers who affiliate with a religion or attend religious services experiencing a long-term decline. And this trend seems set to continue; not only as older, more religious generations are replaced by younger, less religious ones, but also as the younger generations increasingly opt not to bring up their children in a religion—a factor shown to strongly link with religious affiliation and attendance later in life.[7]

This is all consonant with a cultural paradigm that sees churchgoing decline as less a result of secularization (although secularization may be one of its consequences) than an inability of most churches to achieve 'generational replacement'. However, having reached this judicious conclusion, Lucy Lee briefly addresses the issue of social capital:

> What does this decline mean for society and social policy more generally? On the one hand, we can expect to see a continued increase in liberal attitudes towards a range of issues such as abortion, homosexuality, same-sex marriage, and euthanasia, as the influence of considerations grounded in religion declines. Moreover, we may see an increased reluctance, particularly among the younger age groups, for matters of faith to enter the social and public spheres at all.[8]

Here she is less sure-footed. The complex evidence used in Volume 2 is simply bypassed. Arguably bishops in the Church of England *were* instrumental in the 1960s in effecting changes in English and Welsh law on induced abortion and on decriminalizing homosexuality and suicide (as well as capital punishment) despite

---

[7] Ibid., p. 182.
[8] Ibid., p. 183.

some later recriminations. In addition, as was suggested earlier, there is clear evidence of differences between Catholic authorities that typically opposed many of these changes at the outset and practising lay Catholics in a number of Western countries who supported them. Her conclusions here appear too polarized. In terms of social capital they are also too selective.

Her selectivity about 'liberal attitudes' can be illustrated from research carried out on the social attitudes of Australian churchgoers in the 1980s. The sociologists Gary Bouma and Beverley Dixon[9] compared four groups whose stated churchgoing was as follows: those who went to church at least once a month; those who went every two or three months; those who went less regularly; and those who never went. Their views on abortion, homosexuality and euthanasia closely matched Lee's assumptions: 51 per cent of the monthly churchgoers stated that abortion is never justified; 26 per cent of those attending every two or three months; 26 per cent also of those attending less regularly; and just 17 per cent of those who never attended. So, 30 years later, with a substantial decrease in church attendance there today (as in Britain) it might be safely predicted that opposition to abortion will have diminished (even without churchgoers themselves reducing their opposition). A similar pattern was evident for those who thought that homosexuality is never justified (57 per cent; 40 per cent; 39 per cent; and 31 per cent) and that euthanasia is never justified (43 per cent; 17 per cent; 16 per cent; and 17 per cent). But what about other forms of 'liberalization'? The same survey showed that there were similar differences about those who thought that lying in your own interest is never justified (64 per cent; 41 per cent; 43 per cent; and 38 per cent), that buying something you know is stolen is never justified (82 per cent; 66 per cent; 69 per cent; and 68 per cent), that avoiding transport fares is never justified (71 per cent; 54 per cent; 55 per cent; 54 per cent) and that cheating on taxes is never justified (65 per cent; 36 per cent; 46 per cent; and 41 per cent).

There is also nothing in Lucy Lee's conclusions about the evidence, to be reviewed in the next chapter, that various expressions of altruism are strongly linked to religious activism. In sharp contrast, Robert Putnam had begun to notice

---

[9]   Gary D. Bouma and Beverley R. Dixon, *The Religious Factor in Australian Life*, MARC, Australia: World Vision and Zadok Centre, 1986.

this in *Bowling Alone*, reaching a very different conclusion about the social consequences of a decline in churchgoing:

> Let us summarize what we have learned about the religious entry in America's social capital ledger. First, religion is today, as it has traditionally been, a central fount of American community life and health. Faith-based organizations serve civic life both directly, by providing social support to their members and social services to the wider community, and indirectly, by nurturing civic skills, inculcating moral values, encouraging altruism, and fostering civic recruitment among church people. Second, the broad oscillations in religious participation during the twentieth century mirror trends in secular civil life—flowering during the first six decades of the century and especially in the two decades after World War II, but then fading over the last three of four decades ... For the most part younger generations ... are less involved both in religious and in secular activities than were their predecessors at the same age ... Americans are going to church less often than we did three or four decades ago, and the churches we go to are less engaged with the wider community.[10]

The particular altruistic features of churchgoing noticed in *Bowling Alone* are volunteering and philanthropy. A sharp contrast is drawn between church members, 75–80 per cent of whom give to charity and 50–60 per cent volunteer, and non-members, only 55–60 per cent of whom give and 30–35 volunteer. Even when giving and volunteering specifically within churches is excluded, 'active involvement in religious organizations is among the strongest predictors of both philanthropy and volunteering'.[11]

Yet he detects a major problem emerging in the United States despite its resilient religious life. Giving and volunteering in the wider community ('bridging' forms of social capital) are stronger among Protestants than they are among Catholics and, within Protestantism, it is among the mainline denominations that they are strongest. In contrast, giving and volunteering are more church-focused among evangelicals, who are stronger at 'bonding' than they are at 'bridging'. Yet it is the mainline Protestant denominations in the United States that are particularly

---

[10] Putnam, *Bowling Alone*, p. 79.

[11] Ibid., p. 67.

experiencing decline. So, if the next generation is disaffecting from these denominations – becoming either more secular or more evangelical – then the 'bridging' forms of giving and volunteering within the wider community are likely to diminish.

The narrative provided in *Bowling Alone* does seem to fit my account of sociological theology surprisingly well. It sees churches as both dependent and independent social variables. It acknowledges institutional decline without accepting the thoroughgoing secularization paradigm. It recognizes frankly the 'dark side' of social capital. It outlines a civic role for churches that does not make strident claims about their prophetic function. It also matches very well Margaret Harris' detailed and careful organizational study of Christian and Jewish congregations in England during the 1990s:

> It seems, then, that English congregations may indeed provide many of the benefits anticipated by earlier writers on civil society including the development of citizenship skills, fostering of voluntarism, promoting social cohesion and responding to social problems. However, the case studies provided little evidence that congregations are directly involved in promoting social change, informing public policy or acting in a 'prophetic' role. Such work *was* mentioned by several interviewees but usually in the context of a concern that it was always crowded out by the imperative to respond to immediate needs of members and local communities.[12]

Yet *Bowling Alone* has also faced some serious criticisms.[13] Some have argued that the concept of 'social capital' is neither novel nor well defined. Although Putnam dates its use to 1916, social engagement and impact have been concerns of economists and political theorists for much longer than that. Even Putnam varies his depictions, sometimes using the term social capital (offering varying definitions over time) and, on other occasions, some other term. A lack of a clear and stable definition then produces difficulties in determining, let alone measuring,

---

[12]   Margaret Harris, *Organizing God's Work: Challenges for Churches and Synagogues*, Basingstoke, Hants: Macmillan and New York: St. Martin's Press, 1998, p. 199.

[13]   For these see Stephen Baron, John Field and Tom Schuller (eds), *Social Capital: Critical Perspectives*, Oxford: Oxford University Press, 2000; and John Field, *Social Capital*, London and New York: Routledge, 2003.

the scope of social capital. His reasoning can also be surprisingly circular with social capital becoming both a depiction and an explanation. In addition, as noted already, there does seem to be a normative/prescriptive feature underpinning his narrative, which makes his work attractive to some politicians but confusing to his social scientific colleagues.

Yet, while acknowledging these criticisms, *Bowling Alone* has still proved stimulating to those interested in its religious and theological implications.[14] In this context, though, it raises additional questions. Is it 'religious' capital that is socially significant or 'spiritual' or even 'sacred' capital? Some theorists see the latter as the broader or more generic phenomenon or even as an increasingly distinctive part of modern culture. In a powerful analysis of child abuse in residential schools in Ireland a generation ago – again with a normative/prescriptive feature underpinning it – Gordon Lynch argues that sacred forms and hierarchies, that had once contributed strongly to post-independence Irish identity, also shaped scandalous denials by Catholic leaders and politicians alike of extensive abuse perpetrated by members of religious orders. After setting out evidence to support this, he concludes:

> There are, of course, no straightforward happy endings, and the public scandal of the residential school system in Ireland has become entangled in controversy over the process of redress, and allegations of profiteering by organizations keen to get a commission from survivors' compensation packages. But this case demonstrates not only that sacred forms have the potential *both to legitimate and challenge* practices that blight human lives, but that the relative power of sacred forms is also subject to the choices of human agents, and the ever-changing social, cultural, and political contexts in which they live.[15]

---

[14]   See Corwin Smidt (ed.), *Religion as Social Capital: Producing the Common Good*, Waco, TX: Baylor University Press, 2004; Robert Furbey, Adam Dinham, Richard Farnell, Doreen Finneron, and Guy Wilkinson, *Faith as Social Capital: Connecting or Dividing?*, Bristol: Policy Press, 2006; Chris Baker and Jonathan Miles-Watson, 'Faith and Traditional Capitals: Defining the Public Scope of Spiritual and Religious Capital: A Literature Review', *Implicit Religion*, 13:1, 2010, pp. 17–69; and Adam Dinham, *Faith in Social Capital after the Debt Crisis*, London: Palgrave Macmillan, 2012.

[15]   Gordon Lynch, *The Sacred in the Modern World: A Cultural Sociological Approach*, Oxford: Oxford University Press, 2012, p. 86 [italics added].

Putnam's main focus a decade later, in *American Grace*[16] written with David Campbell, is still upon participation in organized forms of religion (which, after all, are more accessible than privatized spirituality to quantitative analysis). Other theorists have been critical of international religious comparisons sometimes made by exponents of social capital. How is it possible to control and then compare variables accurately for whole countries on the basis of their supposed dominant forms of religion? Of course the same problem faced Max Weber in his bold attempt to track the influence of the so-called 'Protestant ethic' across different nations. *American Grace* avoids this problem too. It is emphatically depicting the current religious situation in the United States and it is not even particularly well informed about similar research conducted elsewhere in the Western world (which the next chapter will try to correct). Despite these limitations *American Grace* offers a much richer account of religiously derived social capital, set into a broad context of successive religious changes in America, than *Bowling Alone*.

American Grace argues that religion in the United States has become increasingly polarized in recent decades. As a response to the 'sexually libertine Sixties' conservative religion grew in size, prominence and political significance. This, in turn, produced a backlash, especially among the young who became religiously disaffected. Moderate denominations shrank in size and religious and secular Americans held increasingly divergent worldviews. Yet, thanks to the long-established American tradition of 'religious bridging' this polarization has seldom led to deep conflict. This for Putnam and Campbell is the American 'grace':

> Although differences in levels of religious diversity by religious traditions are interesting and important, one should not miss the forest for the trees. *Most Americans are intimately acquainted with people of other faiths.* This, we argue, is the most important reason that Americans can combine religious devotion and diversity … We are suggesting that having a religiously diverse social network leads to a more positive assessment of specific religious groups … One place to find such a rationale is in the literature on social capital, by which we mean the

---

[16]   Robert D. Putnam and David E. Campbell, *American Grace: How Religion Divides and Unites Us*, New York: Simon & Schuster, 2010.

norms of trust and reciprocity that arise out of our social networks ... bridging is vital for the smooth functioning of a diverse society.[17]

The chapter specifically on 'Religion and Good Neighborliness' is set into this broad narrative. It concludes that:

> Religious Americans are generally better neighbours and more active citizens, though they are less staunch supporters of civil liberties than secular Americans. Moreover, religious Americans are more satisfied with their lives. As we have seen, however, theology and piety have very little to do with this religious edge in neighborliness and happiness. Instead it is religion's network of morally freighted personal connections, coupled with an inclination toward altruism, that explains both the good neighbourliness and the life satisfaction of religious Americans.[18]

I promised in earlier volumes to return to this conclusion about the social insignificance of theology in this important context. However, it is worth recalling just how it was reached. On the basis of two large surveys of cohorts measured in 2006 and 2007, Putnam and Campbell compile what they term 'an index of religious social networks'. This is based upon the number of close friends weekly churchgoers have in their congregation, their level of participation in small groups in their congregation and the frequency of their talking about religion with family and friends. Using this index they conclude that religious social networks are a powerful predictor of good neighbourliness in the form of volunteering for secular causes, giving to secular causes, membership of civic groups, working on community projects, collaborating on community problems, working for social reform, attending club meetings, serving as organizational leaders, voting in local elections, and attending public meetings.[19]

As has been seen, *Bowling Alone* examined differences between church members and non-members, finding large differences between them on giving and volunteering in the wider community. *American Grace*, in contrast, examines

---

[17]   Ibid., pp. 526–527.
[18]   Ibid., p. 492.
[19]   Ibid., p. 472.

differences between weekly churchgoers and those who attend rarely or never [unlike the data reported in the next chapter it largely ignores monthly and occasional churchgoers], but finds very similar differences on giving and volunteering in the wider community. So, whereas only 6 per cent of weekly churchgoers reported that they had made no charitable donations in the last year, this rose to 32 per cent among nonchurchgoers. Similarly, 40 per cent of weekly churchgoers said that they had volunteered to help the poor or elderly and 36 per cent to help school or youth programmes, but this dropped to 15 per cent among nonchurchgoers for both forms of volunteering. Once again, *American Grace*, notes that such altruistic action is somewhat more typical of mainline Protestant denominations than others. In addition, *American Grace* also detects the differences on civic activity mentioned in the previous paragraph. The authors admit that it is difficult to prove causality (rather than just correlation), but they suggest that comparing the 2006 and 2007 samples there is some evidence that individuals who changed their level of churchgoing in that year (up or down) also changed their levels of donating and volunteering accordingly.

Putnam and Campbell then test the theological beliefs of their respondents on God, eschatology, salvation and biblical inerrancy. Could these beliefs account for different levels of good neighbourliness? Somewhat flippantly they report:

> Most Americans have firm [seemingly arcane] theological commitments that they believe may determine their eternal fate. It is therefore reasonable to expect that those commitments might be part of the explanation for the distinctive social behaviour of religious Americans. In fact, however, we can find no effect whatsoever of those theological views on the religious edge in good neighbourliness. Certainly, each of the twenty-five different measures is in itself correlated with religiosity (as measured by church attendance, for example). However, controlling for frequency of church attendance, not one of them is correlated with the measures of good neighbourliness ... It is tempting to think that religious people are better neighbours because of their fear of God or their hope of salvation or their reading of the Good Word, but we find no evidence for those conjectures.[20]

---

[20] Ibid., p. 467.

In *Churchgoing and Christian Ethics* I too reported, on the basis of qualitative interviews with regular churchgoers in Kent conducted by Tom Frame in 1997, that they did not make explicit faith connections with their local volunteering until prompted to do so. I concluded that 'voluntary service appears typically to be an unspoken part of churchgoing culture'.[21] However, there is a crucial difference between 'churchgoing culture' which might itself be influenced by theological factors and 'religious social networks' which might or might not (depending upon whether it is 'religious' or 'social' that is emphasized). It is possible that *American Grace* overlooks some rather important evidence at this point.

The most obvious piece of evidence is contained in both *Bowling Alone* and *American Grace*, namely that Protestant mainline denominations in the United States *are* more actively concerned than others with the wider community. The theological influence here may not be specifically mediated through particular beliefs about eschatology or salvation (which are often quite pluralistic within these denominations). They may accord more with the nuanced approach taken by Robert Wuthnow:

> In the final analysis, congregations are at the heart of American religion and thus play a central role in service provision, and yet they are neither the primary location of such provision, at least as far as formal programs are concerned, nor can service provision be understood solely in terms of congregational analysis. Congregations are more like the staging grounds for service provision than like actual service providers. They mobilize the people, support them spiritually, remind them of their moral responsibilities, and reinforce them their commitments by putting them in contact with like-minded believers.[22]

Wuthnow even supplies a plausible account of why churchgoers sometimes appear so reluctant to connect their local volunteering with faith:

[21]   Robin Gill, *Churchgoing and Christian Ethics*, Cambridge: Cambridge University Press, 1999, p. 176.
[22]   Robert Wuthnow, *Saving America? Faith-Based Services and the Future of Civil Society*, Princeton and Oxford: Princeton University Press, 2004, p. 63.

From listening to scores of volunteers describing their motives for becoming involved, the one thing I can say with certainty is that having a story to account for one's volunteering is important *and* these stories generally disclose complex self-reflections about how and why a person became involved in volunteering. In religious contexts, people often suggest motives that sound utilitarian, such as saying that they just enjoy working with children or that serving soup or building houses is a refreshing change of pace from selling software or life insurance … When they mention religious motives, they are often somewhat embarrassed by these connections, downplaying them or … balancing them with statements that sound more self-interested … [But] what they receive by being part of a religious group is the opportunity to talk about what they have done and to receive encouragement. They sometimes pray for the people they are helping and hear others pray for them and, above all, they have opportunities to tell their stories.[23]

If Putnam and Campbell had looked beyond the United States (and even there not all researchers have agreed with their conclusions)[24] they would have noticed that this (understated) connection between mainline Protestant denominations and volunteering is characteristic of other Western countries.[25] The large Australian *National Church Life Survey* of 1991 provides interesting evidence here. Since this was a survey of churchgoers alone, the results cannot be compared readily with levels of voluntary service in the rest of society (although there is other Australian evidence which can be).[26] Instead it provides an important comparison of different levels of involvement within Anglican and Free churches. Overall 27 per cent of churchgoers in the survey were 'involved in wider community care/welfare/social action'. However it was churchgoers within the more theologically liberal denominations who were most involved. Within the Uniting Church the

---

[23]   Wuthnow, *Saving America?*, pp. 131–132.

[24]   See John Wilson and Thomas Janoski, 'The Contribution of Religion to Volunteer Work', *Sociology of Religion*, 56:2, 1995, pp. 137–152.

[25]   P-Y. Lam, 'Religion and Civil Culture: A Cross-National Study of Voluntary Association Membership', *Journal for the Scientific Study of Religion*, 45:2, 2006, pp. 177–193.

[26]   See Peter Bentley and Philip J. Hughes, *Australian Life and the Christian Faith: Facts and Figures*, Kew, Victoria, Australia: Christian Research Association, 1998, p. 66.

level of involvement rose to 36 per cent and within the Anglican Church it was 32 per cent. In contrast, it was just 12 per cent in the highly conservative Westminster Presbyterian Church, 13 per cent in the Foursquare Gospel Church, and 15 per cent in the Assemblies of God, the Christian Revival Crusade and the Church of the Nazarene.

Using data from the United Kingdom, the next chapter will also suggest that there is evidence that specifically theological differences between biblical literalists and non-literalists do shape their altruistic attitudes quite differently. In contrast, the only difference between these two groups noticed by Putnam and Campbell is that non-literalist regular churchgoers are 'generally more trusting than secular people' whereas the literalists are less so.[27] There could be more social significance to this theological difference than they acknowledge.

---

[27] Putnam and Campbell, *American Grace*, p. 468.

Chapter 7

Altruism among Churchgoers

It was argued in Volume 1 that sociologists of religion involved in the debate about secularization a generation ago tended to make sweeping historical claims (on both sides of the debate) using weak empirical data in contradictory ways. More than that, they typically made claims about religious change or long-term persistence on the basis of static data about religious involvement. As a result I became increasingly convinced that *longitudinal* historical data was needed if this debate were really to be improved. It was this conviction that drove my own research in the sociology of religion during the 1980s and early 1990s, focused upon attempting to collect and analyse churchgoing census data (starting in the 1830s), and that resulted in my book *The Myth of the Empty Church* (1993).

About a year after its publication I received an unexpected visit from the American social demographer Kirk Hadaway and sociologist of religion Penny Long Marler. They had not only read *The Myth of the Empty Church* carefully, they had made extensive notes on my sources. In passing they also asked me why I had not used data from questionnaire surveys on religious attitudes, beliefs and stated practices. My response was that I had assumed that, because survey questions changed over time, reliable longitudinal data could not be drawn from them. However they showed me that this assumption was inaccurate; Gallup Polls, in particular, tended to ask unchanged questions over many decades. The eventual result of this conversation was our joint paper, which for the first time systematically mapped longitudinal religious beliefs in Britain.[1] This, in turn, was followed by my book *Churchgoing and Christian Ethics* which suggested that there is abundant evidence – largely ignored by other sociologists of religion at the time – that increasing levels of churchgoing are correlated with distinctive

---

[1]   Robin Gill, C. Kirk Hadaway and Penny Long Marler, 'Is Religious Belief Declining in Britain?', *Journal for the Scientific Study of Religion*, 37:3, 1998, pp. 507–516.

moral virtues and stated moral behaviour. In the light of the ongoing debate about religion and social capital in the previous chapter, it is time to revisit and update this evidence, and suggest how it might relate specifically to social capital.

Earlier Correlations

In *Churchgoing and Christian Ethics* I did note two important instances of sociologists of religion who had already noticed this correlation and mapped it as a *process* (that is, the more frequently individuals go to church the more likely they are to have altruistic moral convictions). The previous chapter referred to one of these, the work of Gary Bouma and Beverley Dixon in Australia during the 1980s.[2] Alongside this Australian research, the work of Leslie Francis and William Kay in the 1990s, especially in their *Teenage Religion and Values*,[3] was particularly important. Using a sample of just over 13,000 British young people aged 13 to 15, they showed that, among early teenagers at least, there are many differences of religious and moral belief between churchgoers and non-churchgoers. They divided their sample into the following levels of church attendance: those who attend 'nearly every week' (11 per cent of the sample), those who attend 'sometimes' (35 per cent), and those who 'never' attend (54 per cent). Included in this survey were responses to a wide variety of moral and social attitude statements, most of which show significant correlations with churchgoing.

A number of statements in the Francis-Kay survey test altruistic attitudes, showing clear differences between the three groups of: weekly churchgoers; occasional churchgoers; and non-churchgoers. Responses to the following statements demonstrate this:

'I am concerned about the poverty of the Third World' (79 per cent; 67 per cent; 51 per cent).

---

[2]   Gary D. Bouma and Beverley R. Dixon, *The Religious Factor in Australian Life*, Kew, Victoria, Australia: World Vision and Zadok Centre, 1986.

[3]   Leslie J. Francis and William K. Kay, *Teenage Religion and Values*, Leominster, Herefordshire: Gracewing Fowler Wright, 1995.

'I am concerned about the risk of pollution to the environment' (74 per cent; 73 per cent; 59 per cent).

'I am concerned about the risk of nuclear war' (69 per cent; 68 per cent; 59 per cent).

'There are too many black people living in this country' (11 per cent; 16 per cent; 24 per cent).

'I think that immigration into Britain should be restricted' (27 per cent; 32 per cent; 34 per cent).

'There is nothing I can do to solve the world's problems' (15 per cent; 21 per cent; 30 per cent).

It is sometimes claimed that Christians/churchgoers are less concerned about the environment and more racist than others. The evidence here does not seem to support this. If anything the opposite may be the case. It could be that the greater environmental and racial awareness of many congregations was already fostering a culture which was distinct from society at large. Francis and Kay seemed to support such a cultural interpretation at this point:

> Churchgoers, of whichever denominational group, demonstrate far fewer racist attitudes than non-churchgoers. Whatever else may be said about the church, it is apparent that it is an international and multi-racial community or collection of communities with social opinions, in many respects, quite separate from those of the surrounding society.[4]

Perhaps less surprisingly, teenage churchgoers are more inclined to condemn pornography and television violence than others. The responses to the statement 'Pornography is too readily available' (41 per cent; 33 per cent; 28 per cent) and 'There is too much violence on television' (27 per cent; 21 per cent; 15 per cent) show this. These differences may also reflect a greater concern

---

[4]   Ibid., p. 218.

among churchgoers for the vulnerable. These British teenage churchgoers, like the adults in Australia, are more inclined to believe that 'Abortion is wrong' (50 per cent; 36 per cent; 35 per cent) and 'Divorce is wrong' (27 per cent; 20 per cent; 19 per cent). Here too it seems that on most sexual issues churchgoers are more inclined to hold 'conventional' beliefs than non-churchgoers. Nevertheless, remarkably, only a minority of teenagers support these beliefs even among weekly churchgoers. In response to 'Contraception is wrong' only one in twenty agree, even among churchgoing Roman Catholics. Evidently young Roman Catholics make distinctions within official Catholic teaching, since two-thirds of them still think abortion to be wrong. Since abortion arguably involves the taking of life of one who is vulnerable, whereas (hormonal) contraception does not, this difference may owe more to altruism than to convention. Indeed, only 22 per cent of Roman Catholic churchgoers believe that 'It is wrong to have sexual intercourse outside marriage', 32 per cent that 'It is wrong to have sexual intercourse under the legal age', and 35 per cent that 'Homosexuality is wrong'. From a perspective of official Roman Catholicism this is scarcely a 'conventional' group.

These findings on altruistic attitudes suggest, as the authors noted, that 'church attendance is associated with ... a greater sense of concern on a wide range of issues and a greater sense of being able to make a positive contribution to world problems'.[5] There were some obvious gaps in their data as well as some fairly crude measures. For example, although the attitudes of the young people were tested, their stated behaviour was not. There was no attempt to discover whether or not they belong to other caring organizations or groups or about whether or not they are involved in voluntary work within the community. And some of the attitude measures, such as that on racism, lacked sophistication. Despite these weaknesses, Francis and Kay provided important early evidence about a progressive connection between altruism and religious practice.

The young churchgoers also seem to have a stronger sense of moral order. On each of the individualist moral situations presented to them, weekly churchgoers differ from others, being distinctly less inclined to moral relativism:

---

[5]   Ibid., p. 80.

There is nothing wrong in …

playing truant from school (10 per cent; 14 per cent; 22 per cent)

buying alcoholic drinks under the legal age (27 per cent; 35 per cent; 44 per cent)

buying cigarettes under the legal age (16 per cent; 23 per cent; 31 per cent)

writing graffiti wherever you like (10 per cent; 13 per cent; 19 per cent)

cycling after dark without lights (8 per cent; 11 per cent; 20 per cent)

travelling without a ticket (11 per cent; 15 per cent; 23 per cent)

shop-lifting (3 per cent; 5 per cent; 9 per cent).

Francis and Kay concluded:

> Certainly churchgoing is associated with respect for rules and law which implies that the nature of teenage religion, fostered by churchgoing has an element within it conducive to legal or moral restraint. We may be correct in seeing teenage religion as a manifestation of a desire for order or, alternatively, a recognition of an order whose existence depends on God … Those who attend church weekly have a clearer idea of right and wrong than do non-attenders.[6]

There is a judicious choice of words in this conclusion which leaves the issue of causation ambiguous. On the one hand, this sense of order is 'fostered by churchgoing', but on the other religion may be a response to 'a desire for order'. Using regression analysis on the data it is possible to establish that the variables here are significantly correlated. Francis and Kay used this form of statistical analysis carefully at every point in their study, establishing in the process that there is a causal link, in one direction or the other, between belief/values and churchgoing. It should also have been possible to use a specifically directional form of analysis to test whether or not a step-by-step increase in churchgoing is matched by a corresponding increase in belief/values. If more distinctions had been made than the three levels of churchgoing offered by Francis and Kay, then it should have been possible to apply such a directional test more rigorously. It became clear to me at the time that both forms of statistical analysis needed to be used.

---

[6]   Ibid., pp. 110–111.

Churchgoing and Volunteering

In the previous chapter it was noted that volunteering in the wider community was seen as a crucial feature of religious social capital. In *Bowling Alone* Robert Putnam paid attention to the correlation between adult church membership and volunteering and, more recently in *American Grace*, between church attendance and volunteering. However, both of these correlations had already been noted in research elsewhere. As seen already, Australian research that had already made this connection in the 1980s.

The two sets of European Value System Study Group (EVSSG) surveys[7] in the early 1980s and 1990s also both noted a number of significant differences between adult churchgoers and non-churchgoers across Europe. In the 1980s across Europe 19 per cent of the whole sample was involved in voluntary work of one sort or another (EVSSG defined 'voluntary work' very broadly). Among non-churchgoing Catholics this level dropped to 12 per cent, rising to 28 per cent among weekly churchgoing Catholics. However, among Protestants this difference was even more marked, with 10 per cent of non-churchgoing Protestants in contrast to 58 per cent of weekly churchgoing Protestants. The British 1981 EVSSG data showed a very similar pattern, with 19 per cent of the whole sample in contrast to 50 per cent of weekly churchgoers. The British 1990 EVSSG comparable figures were 23 per cent and 48 per cent respectively. So regular churchgoers in Britain, and more widely in Europe, were two or three times more likely than other people to be involved in some form of voluntary service. Even when specifically church related voluntary service was taken out of the analysis, it still appeared that churchgoing was a highly significant variable. In other words, it was already clear that churchgoers were disproportionately involved in secular forms of voluntary service in the community. Comparing a churchgoer with a non-churchgoer who had no belief in God, the former was some three times more likely to be involved in voluntary service than the latter.

---

[7]   See Jan Kerkhofs, 'Between "Christendom" and "Christianity"', *Journal of Empirical Theology*, 1:2, 1988, pp. 88–101. For specifically British EVSSG data see Mark Abrams, David Gerard and Noel Timms (eds), *Values and Social Change in Britain: Studies in the Contemporary Values of Modern Society*, London: Macmillan, 1985, and Noel Timms, *Family and Citizenship: Values in Contemporary Britain*, Aldershot, Hants: Dartmouth, 1992.

Churchgoing and Christian Ethics (1999) tested these correlations afresh using 1980s and 1990s data from British Household Panel Survey (BHPS) and British Social Attitudes (BSA). Now I am also testing data from BSA 2000s, European Social Survey (ESS) 2002, and English Church Census 2005.[8] BHPS data allow a series of detailed comparisons of the active membership of religious and other caring groups. The churchgoing rates of members of voluntary service groups are more than double those of the population at large. Members of religious groups are more than three times as likely as non-members to be involved in voluntary service. They are also disproportionately involved in all of the other caring groups – such as community groups, environmental groups, Scouts and Guides – as well as in self-help groups – such as tenants groups, parents associations, pensioners groups and political parties.

Using BHPS data for 1995, members of religious groups were more than three times as likely to be members of voluntary service groups than others. So, whereas 3.9 per cent of those who did not mention being members of a religious group stated that they were members of a voluntary service group, this rose to 13.6 per cent among members of a religious group. The latter were also about twice as likely to belong to a parents association (7.3 per cent as distinct from 3.5 per cent), a community group (3.3 per cent as distinct from 1.5 per cent), a tenants group (19.8 per cent as distinct from 9.7 per cent), an environmental group (6.3 per cent as distinct from 3.6 per cent), and the Scouts or Guides (1.6 per cent as distinct from 0.9 per cent). And they were three times as likely to belong to a political party (7.8 per cent as distinct from 2.6 per cent) or to a pensioners group (2.4 per cent as distinct from 0.9 per cent).

The membership of both religious and voluntary service groups consisted of twice as many women as men. So perhaps women are simply more religious and caring than men. Perhaps in part they are, yet the ratio of religious members to non-members in the voluntary groups was similar among men (11.9 per cent to 3.3 per cent) as among women (14 per cent to 4.5 per cent). Indeed, 29 per cent

---

[8]   The data used here (for *BSA*, *BHPS*, *ESS* and *English Church Census*) were made available through Data Archive. The data were originally collected by the ESRC Research Centre on Micro-social Change at the University of Essex. Neither the original collectors of the data nor the Archive bear any responsibility for the analyses or interpretations presented here.

of the men who were members of a voluntary service group also belonged to a religious group (among women this rose to 39 per cent).

Overall a very high 27 per cent of members of voluntary service groups reported that they were weekly churchgoers (in the sample as a whole it was 11 per cent) and 42 per cent went at least once a month (it was 18 per cent in the whole sample). And 35 per cent of them were members of a religious group, as distinct from 13 per cent of the whole sample. Naturally this means that a majority of members of a voluntary group, or those active within one (they were very largely the same people), were not members of a religious group or regular churchgoers. It is important not to claim too much at this point. So, without knowing more about the detailed background of volunteers, it would be an exaggeration to claim that without actively (or formerly) religious helpers voluntary service work would collapse in Britain. The most that can be claimed is that there does seem to be a strong relationship between voluntary service and some forms of religious membership. Only a third of volunteers reported that they never went to church at all, whereas in the whole sample they amounted to two thirds. On all of these measures those involved in voluntary service groups were disproportionately religious.

Another, more technical, way of testing this relationship is to do linear regression analysis on the membership of all of the different caring and leisure groups. The results suggest that membership of women's institutes and voluntary service groups are the most closely linked to membership of religious groups. They also suggest that membership of community, religious, women's institutes, and environmental groups are most closely linked to voluntary service groups. It might be thought that women's institutes are rather different from the caring groups and that perhaps this particular relationship owes more to the predominantly female character of both the religious and voluntary service groups. However, it may well be that there is a more directly causal relationship as well. Many women's institutes meet in church properties and have regular talks on voluntary service in the community. They may also act as informal recruiting places both for church membership and for more active voluntary service.

The groups that are least related to religious membership, in these regression tests, are the leisure groups. Membership of a social group or a sports group is negatively associated with membership of a religious group. Using linear regression on the 1994 question about moral standards, it also appears that members of these two groups differ sharply from members of religious groups. Membership of a sports group does seem to be more closely related to membership of a voluntary service group, but membership of a social group does not.

Taken together all of this suggests that there are clusters of caring groups within which membership of religious groups is a highly significant factor. Of course the relationship between the groups is complex and there is much evidence of overlapping concerns and membership. These are not entirely separate enclaves and causality is unlikely to be in a single direction. For members of some of these caring groups other factors appear more important than religious belonging. For example, membership of environmental groups is more closely related to membership of voluntary service and political groups than to religious groups. 14.4 per cent of voluntary service members belong to environmental groups as distinct from 3.4 per cent of non-members, and 13.7 per cent of those belonging to a political party do as distinct from 3.4 per cent of those not belonging. These are stronger relationships than those already noted with religious membership.

While this is so, the actual membership of political groups (3.1 per cent of the whole sample) and voluntary service groups (4.9 per cent) is very much smaller than that of religious groups (12.7 per cent). As a result only 12 per cent of the members of environmental groups also belong to a political party and 19 per cent to a voluntary service group. In contrast 21 per cent belong to a religious group and 30 per cent of active environmentalists report that they go to church at least once a month – a higher level of support for environmental issues among the religious than is sometimes maintained. The only groups in BHPS which are as large, or larger, than religious groups are trade union, social and sports groups – and none of these is strongly associated with caring groups. In this respect religious groups are unique. The net result is that a sizeable section of each caring group is also religious. So, if the active membership of each of the groups is examined, 54 per cent of those active in the women's institutes also attend church at least once a month, 42 per cent of those in voluntary service and women's groups, 38 per cent of those in political parties, 33 per cent of those in parents associations and community groups, and 32 per cent of those active in tenants/residents groups. Anglicans are much more likely than Roman Catholics to be active in political parties and environmental groups, whereas Roman Catholics are more likely to be active in trade union groups. Among those active in voluntary service groups the balance between churchgoers in the Anglican, Roman Catholic and Free Churches is fairly even. While few caring groups might actually collapse without the active participation of churchgoers, all would be seriously affected.

British Social Attitudes data add further evidence to this profile of churchgoers. In all of the BSA evidence cited here data for four distinct levels of churchgoing are reported, and tested statistically for directionality,[9] in the following order: respondents who go to church at least once a week; those who go at least once a month; those who go less often; and those who never or almost never go to church. BSA respondents in 1994 were shown a card listing nine different options and were asked, 'Are you currently a member of any of these?: Tenants'/residents' association; Parent-teachers association; Board of school governors/school board; A political party; Parish or town council; Neighbourhood council/forum; Neighbourhood watch scheme; Local conservation or environmental group; Other local community or voluntary group'. A strongly significant directional pattern emerges in the four levels of churchgoing among those who responded that they were a member of a community/voluntary group (15 per cent; 17 per cent; 8 per cent; 3 per cent). If those aged 35–59 are isolated, an even clearer directional pattern is apparent (20 per cent; 19 per cent; 11 per cent; 5 per cent). In both instances only 3 per cent of those who gave a no-religion response were members of such a group. So, to express this difference at its sharpest, a middle-aged weekly churchgoer here was four times more likely to be a member of a community or voluntary group than a middle-aged non-churchgoer and almost seven times more likely than someone in the no-religion category.

The groups mentioned in this BSA question are different from those in BHPS (for example, the latter includes sports and social groups). Nevertheless there is a similar pattern, suggesting that churchgoing is strongly related to voluntary service. In BSA, as in BHPS, members of the voluntary groups are twice as likely to go regularly to church as the population at large. In both BSA and BHPS 27 per cent of these members are weekly churchgoers and 46 per cent in the first and 42 per cent in the second go at least once a month. Membership of the other groups taken together

---

[9]   Somers' ordinal by ordinal directional test in SPSS has been used on all BSA directional data in this chapter with significance between .000 and .006 (and just .000 for the much larger BHPS and ESS samples).

also shows that churchgoers are more heavily involved than other people. Among those in BSA who report that they are members of none of the nine groups listed, there is a significant pattern of churchgoing directionality (70 per cent; 76 per cent; 83 per cent; 86 per cent). Again, as was noted in BHPS data, the involvement of churchgoers in environmental groups is higher than is sometimes portrayed. In this instance membership can be tested across two BSA surveys. Amalgamating data from BSA 1993 and 1994, churchgoers appear to be at least as likely to be members of an environmental group as non-churchgoers (8 per cent; 9 per cent; 7 per cent; 5 per cent: and no-religion 7 per cent).

It is important once again not to exaggerate differences between churchgoers and other people. Most of the British respondents involved in voluntary service do not go to church regularly and most of those who go regularly to church are not involved in non-church voluntary service. Furthermore, although regular churchgoers in BSA 1993 were more inclined to agree that 'everyone has a duty to volunteer', a proportion of non-churchgoers did too (46 per cent; 27 per cent; 39 per cent; 31 per cent: and no-religion 27 per cent). Nonetheless, a surprisingly high proportion of voluntary workers do go to church and churchgoers themselves are far more likely than other people to become voluntary workers. Linear regression analysis indicates that frequency of churchgoing in BSA 1994 is a highly significant variable in predicting voluntary service (as it is in BHPS) – it is as significant as age and tertiary qualifications and more significant than gender, income or schooling.

Using more recent data from the British Government's Citizenship Survey some campaigning groups[10] have argued that differences in volunteering between religious and non-religious people have now all but disappeared. Unfortunately this survey tends to rely upon the weakest of religious indicators, namely affiliation (Q: 'What is your religion even if you are not currently practising?'). When a distinction is added with a follow-up, albeit largely undefined, question (Q: 'Do you consider that you are actively practising your religion?'), significant differences emerge at least among Christian respondents: now it found that 'non-practising Christians; practising and non-practising Hindus, Muslims and Sikhs; those of "other" religions who are non-practising, and those with no religion (compared to practising Christians)' were 'less likely to participate regularly

---

[10] http://www.humanism.org.uk/news/view/899 [accessed: 9 October 2012].

(that is, at least once a month) in formal volunteering', just as were those with few or no educational qualifications.[11] However, it also found that most respondents – whether they self-identified with a religion or not – gave as their motivation for such volunteering the response 'I wanted to improve things/help people (62 per cent). Only a minority responded that 'It's part of my religious belief to help people' (17 per cent).

What about Europe as a whole? Is there recent evidence to corroborate the findings of EVSG in the 1980s and 1990s? Two new sources are particularly important here. The first is Wave 1 of ESS in 2002. This offers a substantial basis for quantitative analysis of some 40,000 respondents from 20 European countries. It tests regularity of churchgoing in comparable ways to BSA (albeit with 19 rather than 10 per cent of weekly churchgoers and 29 rather than 16 per cent when monthly churchgoers are added, with fewer people saying they never go to church – 31 rather than 56 per cent) and attitudes towards, and participation in, voluntary organizations. The second source of recent evidence is the Welfare and Religion in a European Perspective (WREP) project which offers qualitative data that helps to give more nuance to the broad ESS evidence. With case studies focused upon towns in Sweden, Norway, Finland, Germany, England, France, Italy and Greece, WREP has (among other objectives) mapped differing forms and roles of volunteering within churches.

The sharpest difference between churchgoers and non-churchgoers in ESS is on attitudes towards voluntary organizations. Each of the following shows statistically significant directionality. Asked about their importance, weekly churchgoers are twice as emphatic as respondents who never go to church that voluntary organizations are 'extremely' important (8.7 per cent; 7.0 per cent; 5.8 per cent; 4.3 per cent). Asked how important they consider it is 'for a person to be active in a voluntary organisation' in order 'to be a good citizen', weekly churchgoers are more than twice as supportive (11.2 per cent; 9.4 per cent; 6.6 per cent; 5.0 per cent). Compared with BHPS the voluntary organizations mentioned in ESS lack specificity (doubtless because it is difficult to establish categories that fit every European context). Volunteering for political, social or hobby organizations shows no consistent directional statistical significance

---

[11]   http://www.communities.gov.uk/documents/statistics/pdf/1547056.pdf [accessed: 13 September 2012], para 2.22.

related to churchgoing. But the relatively small percentage of respondents who undertake voluntary work in 'an organisation for humanitarian aid, human rights, minorities or immigrants' does (2.2 per cent; 2.2 per cent; 1.5 per cent; 1.4 per cent). Given the sheer size of the ESS sample (weighted for the relative sizes of national populations), it is perhaps not surprising that the data for all three of these questions show clear directional statistical significance. This suggests that without the presence of churchgoers across 20 different European countries, including Britain (and in the absence of any other cultural means of replacing them), altruistic beliefs and practices connected with voluntary work might not actually vanish – a transposition paradigm suggests otherwise – but it could be emasculated. As in Australia and the United States so in Europe.

But what about the balance between voluntary action and state provision around Europe? WREP is helpful and nuanced in addressing this question. It sees religious organizations as both dependent and independent variables within the varying socio-political contexts of Europe. Within England, Anders Bäckström and Grace Davie suggest, 'responsibility is taken by the state for basic social issues such as health, education and social care, although independent agencies are also given considerable scope'. Within Germany and France, for example, 'the state has responsibility for the social welfare framework, while voluntary bodies of various kinds (including large numbers of paid professionals) play a defining role'. Within Sweden, Norway and Finland the state is given 'overall responsibility for general social welfare, while voluntary organisations provide only complementary services'.[12]

Anders Bäckström and Grace Davie argue that theological factors have, at least in part, shaped these different responses:

> Indeed, an important starting point for the study as a whole lies in the fact
> that the majority churches of Europe—as theologically-motivated carriers of
> values—are related to the different welfare models that have emerged across
> the continent. Specific theologies quite clearly lead in different directions,
> bearing in mind the multiplicity of factors that must be taken into account in

---

[12] Anders Bäckström and Grace Davie, 'The WREP Project: Genesis, Structure and Scope', in Anders Bäckström, Grace Davie, Ninna Edgarth and Per Pettersson (eds), *Welfare and Religion in 21st Century Europe*, Volume 1, Farnham, Surrey: Ashgate, 2010, p. 4.

these evidently complex processes. In England, for example, the Church of England has very largely withdrawn from the provision of welfare as such, but retains a critical voice … In the Nordic countries, the Lutheran folk-churches have embraced the doctrine of the 'two kingdoms'—a body of teaching which ascribes much more positively a particular role to the state in the organization of welfare. In Italy, and to some extent in Germany and France, Catholic social teaching has been influential in a different way, this time through the concept of subsidiarity—a notion which implies that welfare, just like everything else, should be delivered at the lowest effective level of society … In Greece, the church has become increasingly observant of social issues through a renewed understanding of the church as *diakonia*.[13]

Unsurprisingly, the levels and forms of religious volunteering in the wider community vary from one of these contexts to another. But even in Sweden – with such a strong state responsibility for social welfare – volunteering is increasingly important: 'volunteer work in social care and welfare organizations appears to have increased in the past ten years in a number of countries, notably in Sweden, perhaps in response to the current situation of the welfare state'.[14]

From the 450 interviewees in the case studies of the WREP project, it emerges that 'almost none' take the position that churches should neither 'speak out in public debate' nor 'take on practical social work'. Almost all accept that churches should at least 'take on practical social work', despite ongoing tensions with social work that is delivered by paid professionals, even if churches in some contexts refrain from public debate:

An excellent illustration can be found in the unequivocal response of a Greek interviewee who declares: 'Should is the wrong word: there is no should about it … Church and social service are one and the same, indistinguishable' … Likewise a German interviewee says: 'The church needs to have social activities. Otherwise it is no longer a church.'[15]

---

[13] Ibid., p. 5.

[14] Bäckström, Davie, Edgarth and Per Pettersson (eds), *Welfare and Religion*, p. 37.

[15] Per Pettersson, 'Majority Churches as Agents of European Welfare', in Anders Bäckström, Grace Davie, Ninna Edgarth and Per Pettersson (eds), *Welfare and Religion in 21st Century Europe*, Volume 2, Farnham, Surrey: Ashgate, 2011, p. 39.

Churchgoing and Christian Ethics argued that such evidence illustrates both the fragility of the Christian life and its distinctiveness. Voluntary service in the community always offers an impossible challenge for churchgoers and lays them open to the damaging criticism of hypocrisy. There is no limit to the voluntary service that could be given since human need is so unbounded. As the plight of the urban destitute increases within Europe, so opportunities for voluntary service become ever more pressing for those with eyes to see and ears to hear. The parable of the sheep and the goats becomes an ever sharper critique of the actual lives of Christians in Europe and elsewhere. It can hardly be surprising that Christians are so often accused of hypocrisy – the demands of faith are so high and the capacity of the faithful so limited. At the same time churchgoers do seem to be more likely to serve than other people. This ambivalence is aptly expressed in this Synoptic story:

> A dispute also arose among them as to which one of them was to be regarded as the greatest. But he said to them, 'The kings of the Gentiles lord it over them; and those in authority over them are called benefactors. But not so with you; rather the greatest among you must become like the youngest, and the leader like one who serves. For who is greater, the one who is at the table or the one who serves? Is it not the one at the table? But I am among you as one who serves.[16]

Altruistic Attitudes and Motivation

BHPS and BSA also provide a wealth of data about altruistic attitudes and motivation. Often these are strongly linked to age and gender. Nevertheless there is much evidence that churchgoing is also an important factor. Those who go regularly to church do appear to be more honest and altruistic in their attitudes than other people. Here, too, the distinctiveness of churchgoers is relative rather than absolute.

In BHPS, when asked directly about 'declining moral standards', respondents in 1994 were shown a card with four options on it – 'great deal', 'fair amount', 'not very much', and 'not at all' – with the instruction to give the answer

---

[16]   Luke 22:24–27 (NRSV).

'that comes closest to how concerned you are'. In the sample as a whole 49 per cent opted for 'a great deal', 36 per cent for 'a fair amount', 13 per cent for 'not very much', and 3 per cent for 'not at all'. Yet among weekly churchgoers in 1994 the level of concern was very considerably higher: 71 per cent of them responded 'a great deal' and just 1 per cent 'not at all'. Testing the data against five different levels of churchgoing, there was again a significant directional relationship: a 'great deal' of concern was expressed by 71 per cent of weekly churchgoers; 61 per cent monthly; 54 per cent occasional; 44 per cent 'practically never'; and 48 per cent 'weddings etc'. This directionality was present in all age-groups, but overall levels increased with age and among women. Differences can be seen clearly comparing the 16–24 age-group (35 per cent; 35 per cent; 18 per cent; 19 per cent; 17 per cent) with the 65+ age-group (85 per cent; 82 per cent; 75 per cent; 62 per cent; 75 per cent). However in all but the youngest age-group a majority of weekly churchgoers expressed a 'great deal' of concern, as did a majority of weekly churchgoing men (64 per cent).

While this does provide evidence for a directional link between churchgoing and moral concern, it does not establish altruistic attitudes as such. Evidence for this can be drawn from the responses to other questions. Immediately following the question about moral standards, the adults surveyed were given a list of five qualities and asked: 'If you had to choose, which quality on this list would you pick as the most important for a child to learn to prepare him or her for life?'. Combining the first and second choices of respondents, 64 per cent chose 'think for self', 53 per cent 'help others', 46 per cent 'work hard', 29 per cent 'obey parents', and 7 per cent 'well liked'. However, the 'help others' option again showed evidence of a significant directional relationship to churchgoing: it was given as the first or second choice by 59 per cent of weekly churchgoers, 56 per cent monthly, 55 per cent occasional, 52 per cent 'practically never', and 50 per cent 'weddings etc.' Once again this shows that differences between churchgoers and non-churchgoers are relative not absolute. Many share similar concerns, even though churchgoers tend to hold these concerns more strongly.

A similar pattern is evident in the youth sample (11–15 years). Respondents were asked about a number of areas in which 'young people can get into trouble for doing' whether they were 'extremely serious, very serious, fairly serious, or not very serious'. The six areas were stealing money, young people swearing, smoking, telling lies to parents, playing truant and taking drugs. Having answered they were then asked: 'I am going to read all six things again. Please wait until I have read them all, before you answer, and then tick the box of the thing you think is the most serious of all'. Taking drugs and stealing money were the most serious for all groups, yet the relative proportions differed. So, whereas 84 per cent of non-churchgoers ticked drugs and 10 per cent stealing, among weekly churchgoers this changed to 67 per cent and 18 per cent. And 14 per cent of the weekly churchgoers ticked 'telling lies to parents', in contrast to just 5 per cent of non-churchgoers. It certainly cannot be claimed that the non-churchgoing young people in the sample lacked a sense of wrongdoing. Here too differences between churchgoers and non-churchgoers were relative – a majority in both groups agreed about wrongdoing.

Another question to adults in 1994 provides evidence of altruistic attitudes. Those surveyed were asked to respond to the statement that, 'Adult children have an obligation to look after their elderly parents.' 35 per cent of the whole sample agreed or strongly agreed and 32 per cent disagreed or strongly disagreed, with 33 per cent neither agreeing nor disagreeing. Taking the agree/strongly agree category, a significant directional relationship to churchgoing can be found: 47 per cent of weekly churchgoers; 35 per cent monthly; 34 per cent occasional; 35 per cent 'practically never'; and 32 per cent 'weddings etc.' On this item the youngest age-groups showed the sharpest differences, especially the 16–24 age-group (55 per cent; 44 per cent; 35 per cent; 34 per cent; 33 per cent) and the 25–34 age-group (57 per cent; 36 per cent; 32 per cent; 28 per cent; 31 per cent). Yet among older people, the 65+ age-group, the pattern was more mixed (42 per cent; 37 per cent; 28 per cent; 42 per cent; 35 per cent). Curiously both the young and the elderly responses may enshrine altruistic tendencies – the young for believing that elderly parents should be cared for and the elderly for not wishing to be a burden upon their children. A rather sophisticated pattern of altruism begins to emerge. Altruistic attitudes do seem to be directionally related to differing regularities of churchgoing. They may also be related to the different perspectives that age brings. This evidence is impressive because of the sheer size of the BHPS sample.

In the analysis of BHPS data two further areas of altruism are interesting, namely advice to the young to 'help others' and to look after elderly parents. Both show a

significant directionality with churchgoing. BSA data provide two similar pieces
of evidence. In BSA 1989 respondents were asked to identify the 'most important
factor in choosing a new job', suggesting 'to help others' as one of the options.
Respondents were given three separate choices altogether. Adding these together,
there is a clear difference between churchgoers and non-churchgoers among those
choosing 'to help others' as an option (28 per cent; 23 per cent; 16 per cent; 6 per
cent). Similarly in BSA 1983 clear differences are apparent between churchgoers
and non-churchgoers among those who agreed that 'children should look after aged
parents' (55 per cent; 42 per cent; 42 per cent; 39 per cent). As found in BHPS, it
is those aged 18–34 who showed the strongest directionality on this issue (57 per
cent; 26 per cent; 36 per cent; 34 per cent). The elderly themselves – perhaps for
just as altruistic reasons – were more reluctant to agree to this.

Clearly there are continuities as well as discontinuities here between
churchgoers and non-churchgoers. Continuity is very evident, for example, in
the proportions of adult churchgoers and non-churchgoers who in BSA 1986
agreed that 'parents should teach children unselfishness' (78 per cent; 71 per cent;
77 per cent; 79 per cent: and no-religion 75 per cent). Again, in the same survey
most people agreed that 'faithfulness is very important for marriage' (93 per cent;
88 per cent; 87 per cent; 89 per cent: and no-religion 82 per cent). Some values
do seem to be shared widely across society on such personal issues, even though
small differences between churchgoers and non-churchgoers can still be detected.

This last point is a strong feature of BSA questions that have recurred over
the years on personal honesty. At the end of reviewing BSA 1984 and 1987 data,
Michael Johnston concluded:

> 'Moral traditionalism' remains a firm feature of British life. And while sections
> of the population differ, sometimes to a marked degree, in how they feel they
> would act in ethically challenging situations, they still seem to agree upon the
> *relative* seriousness of a range of 'rule-breaking' behaviours. Moreover, there is
> even less variation between subgroups in the ways they respond to the actions of

others – judgements which contribute to the 'civic' aspects of the culture. Taken together, the evidence hardly portrays a breakdown in British social ethics.[17]

Johnston's analysis suggests that frequency at religious worship [he did not separate churchgoers from those attending services in other faiths] is a relevant factor in all of the nine ethical situations reviewed. It is mostly matched by differences of age (the younger respondents being both less honest and less inclined to attend religious worship than the older respondents), but as he noted three years earlier, 'religious observance had an independent relationship to people's views ... religion appeared to have more influence on evaluations of everyday personal transactions than it did on judgements of more distant relationships in business and government'.[18] Personal situations envisaged here are employees fiddling expenses to make an extra £50, a milkman overcharging customers by £200, an antique dealer concealing woodworm in furniture to make £50, and a householder over-claiming on insurance by £500. The greater the dishonesty on such issues, the more respondents tended to believe it to be wrong, whether they currently attended religious worship or not. In contrast, issues such as expensive entertainment for business managers or council officials, showed little or no influence by religious observance.

More interesting questions were asked in BSA 1991 and 2005, involving not just ethical judgements about situations but also the additional question, 'Might you do this if the situation came up?'. Asked in this form, rather sharper differences appeared between churchgoers and non-churchgoers, as well as between those who had been brought up regularly going to church and those who had not. Particularly striking were the responses to this situation:

A man gives a £5 note for goods he is buying in a big store. By mistake, he is given change for a £10 note. He notices but keeps the change. Please say

---

[17]   Michael Johnston, 'The Price of Honesty', in Roger Jowell, Sharon Witherspoon and Lindsay Brook (eds), *British Social Attitudes: The 5th Report*, Aldershot, Hants: Dartmouth, Social and Community Planning Research, 1988, pp. 12–13.

[18]   Michael Johnston and Douglas Wood, 'Right and Wrong in Public and Private Life', in Roger Jowell and Sharon Witherspoon (eds), *British Social Attitudes: The 2nd Report*, Aldershot, Hants: Dartmouth, Social and Community Planning Research, 1985, p. 131.

which comes closest to what you think ... Nothing wrong; Bit Wrong; Wrong;
Seriously Wrong; Very Seriously Wrong.

In the sample as a whole, three-quarters thought this to be wrong (that is, 'wrong'
through to 'very seriously wrong'), but only one quarter said they might do it
themselves. A high level of moral consensus was obviously present here as
well. Yet significantly different and directional levels between churchgoers and
non-churchgoers were still evident. In 1991 those believing this to be wrong
showed this pattern clearly (94 per cent; 83 per cent; 79 per cent; 76 per cent: and
no-religion 67 per cent) as did those questioned in 2005 (87 per cent; 86 per cent;
76 per cent; 73 per cent: and no religion 60 per cent). (The slight drop in overall
levels might reflect that, with inflation, the loss of £5 may not be regarded as quite
so serious by 2005.) Among those saying in 1991 that they might do it themselves
a similar pattern is evident (6 per cent; 15 per cent; 18 per cent; 25 per cent: and
no-religion 37 per cent).

Although both of these patterns are statistically significant using directional
analysis, age and gender appear to be more significant factors here than
churchgoing. So older respondents and women are considerably less likely to say
they might keep the extra £5 than the younger male respondents. Nevertheless,
the churchgoing patterns of those saying they might do this among the 18–34
age-group (6 per cent; 35 per cent; 39 per cent; 44 per cent: and no-religion
54 per cent) and among men (4 per cent; 25 per cent; 27 per cent; 33 per cent: and
no-religion 39 per cent), both show that regular churchgoers are distinctive. There
is also a sharp difference between two groups of non-churchgoers (including
no-religion respondents here): among those who had never been to church as
children 51 per cent said that they might do this, whereas only 21 per cent did of
those who had been regularly as children. Some caution is needed here, since this
second group is more elderly and female than the first. However this is a large
difference and it is, once again, consonant with the cultural paradigm defended in
Volume 1 (that is, people brought up involuntarily in a church culture still retain
some of its values in adulthood even if they no longer go to church).

Two other questions were asked in this double form in BSA 1991. Both show
differences, although not quite such sharp differences, in these various groups.
One of these suggested that, 'In making an insurance claim, a man whose home

has been burgled exaggerates the value of what was stolen by £150.' Differences are evident between churchgoers and non-churchgoers both in those believing this to be wrong (87 per cent; 83 per cent; 73 per cent; 71 per cent: and no-religion 66 per cent) and those saying they might do it themselves (10 per cent; 17 per cent; 19 per cent; 28 per cent: and no-religion 31 per cent). A very similar question in BSA 1987 found the same pattern. BSA 1991 also found sharp differences between the two groups of non-churchgoers saying they might do it (41 per cent and 23 per cent respectively). The final situation in BSA 1991 suggested, 'A householder is having a repair job done by a local plumber. He is told that if he pays cash he will not be charged VAT. So he pays cash'. Rather narrower differences were found among those believing this to be wrong (55 per cent; 44 per cent; 49 per cent; 44 per cent: and no-religion 38 per cent) and those saying they might do it themselves among both churchgoers and non-churchgoers (58 per cent; 64 per cent; 70 per cent; 73 per cent: and no-religion 78 per cent) and the two groups of non-churchgoers (87 per cent and 75 per cent).

Questions about capital punishment also show distinctive patterns among and between churchgoers. Clear, statistically significant differences between churchgoers and non-churchgoers have been consistently shown in BSA data on this issue. Despite having been abolished in Britain in the 1960s, BSA regularly tested public support for capital punishment until the 1990s, usually by giving people three different scenarios. In the first respondents are asked if they 'favour capital punishment' for terrorist murder. The results show clear directionality in 1983–85 (61 per cent; 76 per cent; 81 per cent; 80 per cent) and in 1993–94 (61 per cent; 69 per cent; 77 per cent; 78 per cent) albeit with a slight overall decline in support. A very similar pattern is evident when respondents are asked if they favour capital punishment for police murder in 1983–85 (58 per cent; 73 per cent; 77 per cent; 76 per cent) and 1993–94 (63 per cent; 65 per cent; 74 per cent; 76 per cent), and when asked if they favour it for 'other murders' in 1983–85 (49 per cent; 62 per cent; 68 per cent; 72 per cent) and 1993–94 (49 per cent; 56 per cent; 67 per cent; 67 per cent). This is impressively consistent data. Age was a very significant factor in shaping attitudes on capital punishment, with the young less supportive than the old. However, churchgoing remained influential on this issue among the young who did go to church. To give a single example, there is clear directional support in the 1980s data about capital punishment for police murder in the 18–34 age-group (37 per cent; 60 per cent; 62 per cent; 75 per cent).

If data from all these scenarios is added together, then support for capital punishment in the sample as a whole dropped slightly over the decade from 71 per cent to 68 per cent. The effect of this was to bring irregular churchgoers and non-churchgoers closer to the position of weekly churchgoers, as a comparison of the pattern for 1983–85 (56 per cent; 70 per cent; 75 per cent; 76 per cent: and no-religion 70 per cent) with that for 1993–94 (57 per cent; 63 per cent; 73 per cent; 74 per cent: and no-religion 66 per cent) shows.

It appears, then, that many weekly churchgoers were hesitant about supporting capital punishment. Similarly, as analysed in Volume 2, they were more hesitant than the public at large about supporting abortion on economic grounds or euthanasia. This does seem to be consistent with a theological conviction that life is God-given. However, BSA data (combined with NISA data) suggest that there is a difference between regular churchgoers who are biblical literalists and those who are non-literalists. This is especially important for testing Robert Putnam's claim, noted in the previous chapter, that theological differences are epiphenomenal. On both of the BSA/NISA 1991 questions on capital punishment, the views of the literalists were closer to those of the whole sample, who generally supported capital punishment, than they were to the views of the non-literalists, who more typically opposed it.[19]

In their analysis of BSA 1995 data, David Donnison and Caroline Bryson found that in the sample as a whole those supporting euthanasia also tended to support abortion, suicide and (rather curiously) capital punishment. In contrast, 'those attending religious services regularly are more likely to think of life as God-given, and so something that individuals have no right to end. Given the growing secularization of Britain, these findings suggest that support for the legalisation of euthanasia will increase over time.'[20] It can now be seen that this analysis is not quite accurate: churchgoers are somewhat less predictable than this suggests. As was seen in Volume 2, there is evidence of many (but certainly not all) churchgoers

---

[19]   See *Churchgoing and Christian Ethics*, Table 13.

[20]   David Donnison and Caroline Bryson, 'Matters of Life and Death: Attitudes to Euthanasia', in Roger Jowell, John Curtice, Alison Park, Lindsay Brook and Katarina Thomson (eds), *British Social Attitudes: The 13th Report*, Aldershot, Hants: Dartmouth, Social and Community Planning Research, 1996, p. 172.

shifting over time to a position more in line with that of secularists on abortion and euthanasia. Yet on capital punishment it appears to be the other way around, with secularists and occasional churchgoers moving over time to a position nearer to that of regular churchgoers. In addition, both of the weekly churchgoing groups do indeed accept that life is God-given, but the literalists appear more inclined than the non-literalists to believe that in the context of murder the demands of order may over-rule the requirement not to take human life.

BSA data in 2008 again suggest that theological factors remain important in shaping and re-shaping the moral responses of churchgoers. Respondents were asked to respond to the statement that: 'Some people think that scientists should be allowed to use cells from human embryos for certain types of medical research.' The responses of those deciding that this should definitely or probably be allowed show significant directionality (51 per cent; 52 per cent; 73 per cent; 77 per cent: and 75 per cent no-religion). However, when the responses of weekly churchgoers are analysed by denomination, a significant difference emerges: 72 per cent of Anglican weekly churchgoers agreed that such research should be allowed, in contrast to 43 per cent of Catholic weekly churchgoers. Not unexpectedly, the next statement and question – 'People have different views about the beginning of human life. In your opinion, is an embryo a human being at the moment of contraception?' – gained greater support from Catholics than Anglicans (or other religious groups).

A further statement and question in BSA 2008 tested differences on euthanasia: 'Suppose a person has a painful incurable disease. Do you think that doctors should be allowed by law to end the patient's life?' As might again be expected from Volume 2, clear directionality was evident here in those responding that this form of euthanasia should definitely or probably be allowed (49 per cent; 77 per cent; 86 per cent; 87 per cent: and no-religion 87 per cent), albeit with a majority of Anglican weekly churchgoers agreeing (61 per cent). However, this time around, a majority of Catholic weekly churchgoers (57 per cent) also agreed. It was only among 'other Christians' (41 per cent) and 'non-Christians' (34 per cent) who attended weekly that there was less than a majority who agreed. Framed in *this* way, lay religious opposition to euthanasia seems to lessen. Arguably the Anglican and Catholic churchgoers were responding altruistically, on the basis of compassion, to those with 'a painful incurable disease'.

Very similarly, in response to a BSA 2005 question about whether abortion should be allowed 'if there is a strong chance of a defect in the baby', four-fifths of all respondents agreed that it should, but only 59 per cent of weekly churchgoers. However support rose to 72 per cent among Anglican weekly churchgoers (albeit dropping to 41 per cent among Catholics). In contrast, support for abortion as a 'mother's right' dropped to just 37 per cent among Anglican weekly churchgoers (compared with 72 per cent of those with no religion), with sharp differences between even infrequent churchgoers and others for abortion on demand. Weekly churchgoers (Anglican and sometimes Catholic) suggest that compassion – for abortion for foetal disabilities, euthanasia for those with a painful incurable disease and the use of embryos for medical research – may indeed trump strongly held principles.[21]

If all of this suggests the presence of a variety of altruistic attitudes among churchgoers, there is one piece of evidence which is usually thought to count against. It has often been claimed that churchgoers tend to be more racist than other people.[22] Responses to a number of BSA questions asked over the years tend to suggest that the opposite is the case. One question that has been asked many times is, 'How would you describe yourself … as very prejudiced against people of other races … a little prejudiced … or, not prejudiced at all?'. A significant directionality is once again evident. In the 1983–87 surveys combined, this can be seen in the pattern of those responding 'not prejudiced at all' (76 per cent; 65 per cent; 63 per cent; 58 per cent: and no-religion 60 per cent). Overall rates rose somewhat by 2010 but the significant directionality remains (82 per cent; 72 per cent; 68 per cent; 64 per cent: and no-religion 70 per cent). It is also evident, in 1994, among those responding 'very' or 'a little' prejudiced (28 per cent; 32 per cent; 36 per cent; 42 per cent: and no-religion 37 per cent) and again in 2010 (17 per cent; 27 per cent; 32 per cent; 35 per cent: and no-religion 27 per cent). Age is an important factor here, yet the same pattern is present in the 18–34 age-group in 1994 (13 per cent; 29 per cent; 35 per cent; 40 per cent: and no-religion 37 per cent).

Similarly, the pattern of those agreeing in 1994 that 'attempts to give equal opportunities to black people and Asians in Britain have gone too far' (19 per cent;

---

[21]   See further my *Health Care and Christian Ethics*, Cambridge: Cambridge University Press, 2006, chapter 4.

[22]   For a discussion of this, see section five of my *A Textbook of Christian Ethics*.

27 per cent; 30 per cent; 24 per cent: and no-religion 26 per cent) suggests that churchgoers are, if anything, less prejudiced than other people. When asked whether they would mind if a black person or Asian were appointed as their boss or married a close relative, churchgoers do not appear to be any more prejudiced than other people. Frankly it is difficult to find any support in the BSA data for this long-standing belief about churchgoers.

Even on the issue of specifically religious prejudice, evidence of greater prejudice among churchgoers was difficult to find a generation ago. The combined 1989–91 data of those saying that they were 'not prejudiced at all ... against other religions' (91 per cent; 91 per cent; 88 per cent; 88 per cent: and no-religion 89 per cent) suggest very little prejudice among both churchgoers and non-churchgoers. However the shocking events of 9/11 and 7/7 and increased levels of hostility, especially towards radical Muslims, reflected in many newspapers surveyed in Volume 1, seem to have changed this situation. In 2008 BSA asked people to respond to the statement that: 'Nearly all Muslims living in Britain want to fit in.' Significant directionality was found this time among those who 'strongly agreed' or 'agreed' (51 per cent; 41 per cent; 35 per cent; 35 per cent: and no-religion 37 per cent). The first result was undoubtedly skewed by the 85 per cent approval of weekly attending 'non-Christians' (many of whom may well be Muslims). However, the 51 per cent approval of 'Other Christians' (who may include Black Pentecostals) and the 47 per cent approval of Catholics weekly churchgoers suggest a comparative lack of religious hostility. Of weekly churchgoers it is Anglicans (35 per cent) who appear to reflect the level of suspicion present in the wider population and in many national newspapers.

Churchgoing and Charity

There is another area which consistently shows that regular churchgoers are different from other people, namely in their views and actions on charity. As seen in the previous chapter, Robert Putnam focuses on actions rather than views. BSA data provide no evidence about levels of charitable giving, but they do offer some evidence about regularity. So, in 2004 respondents were asked how often they gave money to charity. There were significant and mostly directional churchgoing differences for both those who replied that they never gave (6 per cent; 7 per cent; 4 per cent; 9 per cent: and no-religion 16 per cent) and for those who said that they gave once a week or more (26 per cent; 13 per cent; 7 per cent; 8 per cent: and no religion 4 per cent). However the most striking feature of BSA evidence is that churchgoers have distinctive views about where charity should be directed. And even when they disagree among themselves about the relative importance of particular charities, that does not prevent them from giving more readily than other people.

In BSA 1993 respondents were given two choices to name the 'most important cause to raise money for in Britain' out of six options: medical supplies to Africa; homeless people in the UK; starving people in poor countries; protecting rare animals throughout the world; kidney machines in the UK; and preventing cruelty to animals in the UK. If the two overseas options involving people are combined – namely, medical supplies to Africa and starving people in poor countries – then a very distinctive churchgoing pattern emerges (67 per cent; 50 per cent; 38 per cent; 32 per cent: and no-religion 36 per cent). If the two options involving animals are taken, then the pattern is reversed (6 per cent; 8 per cent; 9 per cent; 15 per cent: and no-religion 15 per cent), albeit at a much lower level of general support. The mean score for those opting for either homeless people or kidney machines in the UK shows a similar pattern (46 per cent; 69 per cent; 76 per cent; 77 per cent: and no-religion 72 per cent) but at a higher level. Weekly churchgoers evidently take the needs of the poor overseas more seriously than do other people.

Exactly the same point emerges from an analysis of BSA 1994 choices of what would be 'an excellent' or 'very good' way for national lottery money to be spent. In this instance respondents were not asked to choose between different options, but instead were allowed to consider each of the 11 options separately. This helps to adjust some of the distortion that may have resulted from the previous question. In that there was no way of telling whether or not someone, say, who opted for overseas aid was actually against animal or British-bound causes. In other words, it tested preferential options but not discrete sympathies. The lottery question provides a fuller picture of the latter.

The three lottery options which show a highly significant directionality among churchgoers and non-churchgoers are: 'helping starving people in poor countries'; 'helping ex-prisoners to find homes and jobs'; and 'helping to prevent cruelty to animals in Britain'. Frequency of churchgoing has a positive influence on agreeing with the first two options, but a negative influence on agreeing with the third. Hence, regular churchgoers are far more likely than other people to support money going to help the starving and ex-prisoners (as the parable of the sheep and the goats requires), and far less likely to support it going to help animals. This is shown clearly in the patterns of those believing that it is *not* a good way to spend the money on the starving (22 per cent; 42 per cent; 48 per cent; 54 per cent), ex-prisoners (29 per cent; 37 per cent; 48 per cent; 51 per cent) and, quite oppositely, animals (35 per cent; 23 per cent; 26 per cent; 14 per cent).

It is worth exploring this relationship in a little more depth. Attitudes towards spending lottery money on the starving overseas are strongly influenced by both age and by churchgoing. Yet, among both young and old, weekly churchgoers differ from irregular and non-churchgoers – those believing that this is not a good way among respondents aged 18–34 (15 per cent; 33 per cent; 29 per cent; 44 per cent: and no-religion 40 per cent) and those aged 60+ (23 per cent; 54 per cent; 57 per cent; 58 per cent: and no-religion 63 per cent). The overall pattern of those agreeing that this 'an excellent' or 'very good' way to spend the money also shows significant directionality (48 per cent; 35 per cent; 23 per cent; 19 per cent: and no-religion 22 per cent). This finding also matches negative responses to the BSA statement, 'We should support more charities which benefit people in Britain, rather than people overseas', as the significant patterns for 1991 (37 per cent; 44 per cent; 61 per cent; 74 per cent: and no-religion 54 per cent) and 1993 (42 per cent; 56 per cent; 66 per cent 77 per cent: and no-religion 66 per cent) both show.

The evidence here is clear; regular churchgoers in Britain seem to be significantly more concerned than other people about charitable money going to the poor overseas. Why is this? A straightforward theological answer would point to such biblical passages as Matthew 25 (as I have just done). Churchgoers have this concern because a bias towards the poor and needy is present in so many parts of Jewish and Christian Scripture.[23] A cultural answer might differ somewhat. Churchgoers are part of a culture which presents the needs of the poor and suffering in many different ways ... not just in biblical readings and sermons, but also in intercessions, in appeals to give to *Christian Aid* or to *Tear Fund*, in pictures and

---

[23] See Garth L. Hallett, *Priorities and Christian Ethics*, New York and Cambridge: Cambridge University Press, 1998.

posters decorating churches, and even in the words of many modern hymns. In cultural terms, people gathering regularly for Christian worship, especially in mainline denominations, are sensitized from many different directions about the poor overseas.

This may be a cultural answer, but it is not necessarily a 'theology free' answer. Involved in this culture is not simply a network of charitably minded friends (as Putnam concludes), but also a context that is already theologically sensitized. On theological grounds, biblical non-literalists may be inclined to view the poor overseas as more in need of economic help than evangelism. In contrast, biblical literalists may regard evangelism as their priority. This may explain why in the combined BSA/NISA 1991 data 51 per cent of weekly churchgoing biblical literalists agreed that, 'We should support more charities which benefit people in Britain, rather than people overseas,' whereas only 31 per cent of non-literalists did so. Yet on home-based charity there was little disagreement between them. In their response to the statement, 'I can't refuse when someone comes to the door with a collecting tin' there was very little difference between these two groups of regular churchgoers. Most of those going to church every week agreed with each other and differed significantly from those who went to church less regularly, as combined BSA data for 1991 and 1993 suggests (60 per cent; 48 per cent; 52 per cent; 51 per cent: and no-religion 41 per cent).

Theological factors also seem to have influenced churches in the 2005 English Church Census.[24] With responses from almost 19,000 English churches across denominations, a quarter were identified by their leaders as 'evangelical' and another quarter as 'broad'. When these two groups are compared with 'liberals' (about a tenth of respondents) clear differences emerge between them on social and community issues. So, 37 per cent of evangelicals agreed that churches should 'fight for justice', compared with 48 per cent of broads and 54 per cent of liberals. Similarly 14 per cent of liberals responded that their church actually 'engaged in social action' but only 10 per cent of broads and evangelicals (compared with just 5 per cent of churches that identified with none of these labels). In contrast, evangelicals were more likely (46 per cent) to see Christian mission movements as 'transforming' than liberals (42 per cent) or especially broads (29 per cent).

---

[24]   Data analysed here were again made available through Data Archive.

Nevertheless, it could be argued that responses to the BSA lottery questions show that regular churchgoers are less concerned than other people about the non-human environment. In turn, this might confirm the much discussed Lynn White thesis, to the effect that Judaism and Christianity have been responsible for fostering a negative and destructive view of the natural environment. In words that have been repeated many times over within the ecological movement, White (himself a churchgoer) concluded:

> Especially in its Western form, Christianity is the most anthropocentric religion the world has seen. As early as the second century both Tertullian and Saint Irenaeus of Lyons were insisting that when God shaped Adam he was foreshadowing the image of the incarnate Christ, the Second Adam. Man shares, in great measure, God's transcendence of nature. Christianity, in absolute contrast to ancient paganism and Asia's religions (except, perhaps, Zoroastrianism), not only established a dualism of man and nature, but also insisted that it is God's will that man exploit nature for his proper ends.[25]

Even in the 1990s there was now a growing literature of international sociological research assessing whether or not White's thesis could be corroborated empirically.[26] Overwhelmingly, it found no significant correlation between religious belief/ belonging and environmentally damaging beliefs, attitudes or behaviour. Two pieces of evidence from BSA appear to confirm this. The first is that most weekly

---

[25] Lynn White, 'The Historical Roots of our Ecologic Crisis', in *Science*, vol. 155, no. 3767, 10 March 1967, pp. 1203–1207.

[26] See Andrew Greeley, 'Religion and Attitudes Toward the Environment', *Journal for the Scientific Study of Religion*, 32:1, 1993, pp. 19–28; Michael P. Hornsby-Smith and Michael Procter, 'Catholic Identity, Religious Context and Environmental Values in Western Europe: Evidence from the European Values Surveys', *Social Compass*, 42:1, 1995, pp. 27–34; Douglas Lee Eckberg and T. Jean Blocker, 'Christianity, Environmentalism, and the Theoretical Problem of Fundamentalism', *Journal for the Scientific Study of Religion*, 35:4, 1996, pp. 343–355; Alan W. Black, 'Religion and Environmentally Protective Behaviour in Australia', *Social Compass*, 44:3, 1997, pp. 401–412; and Paul Dekker, Peter Ester and Masja Nas, 'Religion, Culture and Environmental Concern: An Empirical Cross-National Analysis', *Social Compass*, 44:3, 1997, pp. 443–458. For a significant theological response see Michael S. Northcott, *The Environment and Christian Ethics*, Cambridge: Cambridge University Press, 1996 and *Climate Change and Christian Ethics*, Cambridge: Cambridge University Press, 2013.

churchgoers (86 per cent) in BSA 1993 agree that, 'Human beings should respect nature because it was created by God'. Sometimes it is forgotten in this debate that belief in a creator God might actually enhance rather than diminish respect for the environment. The second, as already noted, is that churchgoers in both BSA and BHPS (but not in ESS) are actually more likely than non-churchgoers to be members of an environmental group. The lottery questions, too, suggest that churchgoers are just as concerned about the environment as other people. The only exception to this is the question about allocating money 'helping to prevent cruelty to animals in Britain'. In contrast, the option 'helping to protect the environment' suggests no significant difference between churchgoers and non-churchgoers.

Other questions in BSA 1994 suggest that churchgoers are more likely than other people to act on environmental issues. In one scenario it was suggested that 'A housing development was being planned in a part of the countryside you knew and liked' and respondents were asked what if anything they might do about this. Churchgoers differed from non-churchgoers in that they said that they would contact their MP or councillor (47 per cent; 41 per cent; 37 per cent; 29 per cent: and no-religion 29 per cent) and contact a government or planning department (21 per cent; 11 per cent; 20 per cent; 12 per cent: and no-religion 12 per cent). In a second scenario it was suggested that 'A site where wildflowers grew was going to be ploughed for farmland'. On this, too, churchgoers appeared different in that they 'would take action' (15 per cent; 5 per cent; 8 per cent; 9 per cent: and no-religion 4 per cent). Asked more bluntly what they had actually done 'to help to protect the countryside', more churchgoers than non-churchgoers said that they had contacted their MP or councillor (16 per cent; 7 per cent; 10 per cent; 6 per cent: and no-religion 6 per cent). These patterns do not suggest that churchgoers are particularly apathetic about, let alone hostile to, environmental issues.

Social Capital Mediated Through Churchgoing

After the wealth of new evidence provided in this chapter it is time to summarize.

1. There is abundant evidence from Britain, Europe and Australia confirming Putnam's finding in the United States of a strong connection between

church membership and/or regular churchgoing with volunteering. Regular churchgoers express more positive attitudes toward volunteering, and are considerably more prepared to volunteer themselves, than non-churchgoers or those without any religion. This is a very secure finding indeed in terms of social capital.

2. In contrast to Putnam, there does seem to be evidence that styles and regularity of volunteering across Europe are influenced by theological factors.

3. There is also strong evidence that the regularity and objects of charitable giving in Britain are closely connected with regular churchgoing in ways that are similar to the findings of Putnam in the United States.

4. In contrast to Putnam, differing theological perspectives on the Bible in the United Kingdom do seem to affect beliefs about whether charitable giving should be primarily directed at home-based or overseas charities. There are also differences between evangelical and liberal English churches on their engagement in social action and on the importance they give to fighting for justice.

5. There is abundant British evidence that altruistic attitudes and responses – in addition to those directly connected with volunteering or charitable giving – are to be found especially among regular churchgoers. Helping others informally, unselfishness, personal honesty and compassion all have strong connections with regular churchgoers. There is even evidence that these characteristics may persist in adult non-churchgoers who went to church regularly as children.

6. In some areas of altruistic attitudes, such as responses to the use of embryonic cells for medical research, there is also evidence that theological factors affect the differing responses of British regular churchgoers.

7. Although British churchgoers, including occasional churchgoers, are generally more cautious than non-churchgoers and those with no religion about laws allowing abortion and euthanasia as human rights, regular churchgoers have led rather than followed non-churchgoers and those with no religion in opposing capital punishment and racial prejudice in Britain.

Taken as whole these summary points suggest that churchgoers, shaped by theological factors and not simply by networks of friends, do make a significant contribution to Western social capital. Across Europe, as noted already, some 29 per cent of the population claim to go to church at least once a month. In the United States it is nearer to half. Even if such claims are exaggerated,[27] those who see themselves as regular churchgoers appear, from many different indicators, to be significantly more altruistic than those who do not.

In *Health Care and Christian Ethics* (2006) I examined extensive evidence that churchgoing is also correlated with significant benefits in health and longevity.[28] Critics have pointed out the obvious dangers of doctors making faith-based interventions on the basis of this evidence.[29] I was also critical, on theological grounds, of the instrumentality all too often involved in such interventions. Worship for Christians is primarily a response to God not a method for obtaining better health or for enhancing life-expectancy. However, although this evidence is sometimes cited by proponents of social capital (including Putnam), it is difficult to see how it contributes to *social* capital in the sense of helping other people and acting as good citizens. Health benefits relate more obviously to personal well-being than to social capital. They only become a help to other people in the sense that a healthy individual is likely to be less of a burden upon others. Ironically, however, a person with enhanced life-expectancy *is* more likely to become a burden.

---

[27]   C. Kirk Hadaway, Penny Long Marler and M. Chavers, 'What the Polls Don't Show: A Closer Look at US Church Attendance', *American Sociological Review*, 58, 1993, pp. 741–752.

[28]   For useful summaries see: Harold G. Koenig, Michael E. McCullough and David B. Larson, *Handbook of Religion and Health*, New York: Oxford University Press, 2001; and Byron R. Johnson, Ralph Brett Tompkins and Derek Webb, *Objective Hope: Assessing the Effectiveness of Faith-Based Organizations: A Review of the Literature*, Philadelphia: Center for Research on Religion and Urban Civil Society, University of Pennsylvania, 2001 [www.crrucs.org].

[29]   See R.P. Sloan, E. Bagiella and T. Powell, 'Viewpoint: Religion, Spirituality and Medicine', *The Lancet*, 353, 1999, pp. 664–667.

A long-term reduction in churchgoing in the Western world might well have a radical effect upon overall levels of altruism, charitable giving and volunteering (and perhaps personal well-being). In theological terms (which Putnam studiously avoids), altruism, volunteering and charitable giving might be seen as outward and partial signs of the three Pauline theological virtues of faith, hope and love (*pistis*, *elpis* and *agape*). Altruistic attitudes form an important part of *pistis* even in modern society. A concern for others is fundamental to Jewish, Christian and Islamic ethics and, beyond them, to many forms of Buddhism and Hinduism. Volunteering is often based upon *elpis*. It as an aspect of longing for a better and more caring society embedded (as Lisa Sowle Cahill argues)[30] in praxis and solidarity. Charitable giving, within many religious traditions, is a practical form of expressing *agape*. While altruism, volunteering and charitable giving do not constitute the whole of a faithful life, they are still important features of that life. If churchgoing in many Western countries is slowly eroding, then there is an understandable fear that, over time, *pistis*, *elpis* and *agape* will also be eroded in the West. Putnam's instincts do seem to be justified, even if some of his conclusions appear too blunt.

---

[30] Lisa Sowle Cahill, *Global Justice, Christology and Christian Ethics*, New York and Cambridge: Cambridge University Press, 2013, chapter 8.

PART III
Theological Virtues Transposed

Chapter 8

Virtues in the Synoptic Healing Stories

In *Health Care and Christian Ethics* (2006) I wrestled with a problem – what exactly should *a theologian* bring to national medical ethics committees? As explained in Volume 2, for the last two decades I have become increasingly involved in medical ethics committees, now in the British Medical Association, the Medical Research Council, the Nuffield Council on Bioethics and the Royal College of Obstetricians and Gynaecologists. At times this has led me into territories at odds with more conservative theological colleagues, especially concerning the beginning of life and sometimes also the end of life. However, having discovered that most of my moral positions in these areas are also shared by a majority of lay Anglican weekly churchgoers (as reported in the previous chapter), my unease has been considerably reduced. I have concluded that one function of a public theologian on such committees is to offer something other than a religious veto. Religious and secular people alike can and do conclude that it is compassionate not to prolong intolerable life, not to ban abortions and thereby risk a return to the horrors of septic illegal abortions, nor to stop the use of embryonic stem cells in medical research on serious (and currently untreatable) genetic, neural and optic conditions.

However, this function of public theology offers few positive conclusions about what a theologian might actually bring to such committees. Having read what theological colleagues had to say,[1] and by now being deeply influenced by Alasdair MacIntyre's *After Virtue* and Charles Taylor's *Sources of the Self*, I needed to start afresh – with an intuition that the healing stories in the Synoptic Gospels might offer an obvious and abundant resource for a critical identification of some of the specific virtues in tension that a public theologian needs to bring to the discourse of medical ethics committees.

---

[1] See further, chapters one and two of my *Health Care and Christian Ethics*, Cambridge: Cambridge University Press, 2006.

But this raises an obvious problem. Most commentators discuss these Synoptic stories as *miracle* stories rather than *healing* stories. Doubtless this is appropriate in other theological contexts, but in this context it could hardly be less helpful. The liberal pastoral theologian Hugh Melinsky, writing in 1968 in *Healing Miracles*, illustrates this clearly. He took an approach based upon synthesis rather than conflict between healing miracles and modern medicine. For him a 'miracle' occurs under the following conditions:

> First an event is claimed to have happened which does not conform with the normal run of human experience. This is a source of wonder (which is the basic meaning of the word 'miracle'). But, second, in and through this event a claim is made for a particular disclosure of God, his power, his activity, indeed his concern and love. In this respect a miracle is also a sign.[2]

The words 'does not conform with the normal run of human experience' are especially problematic in this context. With hindsight, the example that he gave (an early instance of chemotherapy) demonstrates just how changeable human experience is in modern medicine. He detected a miraculous, even if temporary, healing in a patient who received this treatment, whereas today we would regard some remission after chemotherapy as 'normal'. By looking for the miraculous in events currently not consistent with the 'normal run of human experience', the theologian risks being pushed into an ever tighter corner with every medical discovery.

What about a more conservative theological approach to miracles in the context of modern medicine? Writing from an explicitly evangelical perspective, Colin Brown has been particularly critical of fellow evangelicals who argue for what they term 'covenanted healing':

> Many bereaved people are prone to depression and guilt because of the nagging feeling that they did not love enough or care enough for the one whom they have now lost. If the bereaved are taught that God has covenanted to heal those who

[2]   M.A.H. Melinsky, *Healing Miracles: An Examination from History and Experience of the Place of Miracle in Christian Thought and Medical Practice*, Oxford: Mowbrays, 1968, p. 2.

are prayed for in faith, this depression and guilt can be intensified. It can make them feel that they are personally responsible for the death of their loved one because they did not pray enough or believe enough. Instead of finding comfort and hope in the assurances of God's gift of eternal life to those who turn to him, such people can be subjected to the Satanic temptation to self-recrimination and despair.[3]

So what is the alternative? I soon discovered that John Pilch's work offers a rather different approach. In a series of articles[4] and in his fascinating book *Healing in the New Testament: Insights from Medical and Mediterranean Anthropology*[5] he sets the healing stories into a fresh context. Appropriating insights from medical anthropology, he seeks to show how health and sickness, and then suitable therapies, are variously understood in different cultures. In the process he is able to demonstrate important points of comparison as well as contrast between modern medicine and healing in New Testament times.

Pilch makes a fundamental distinction between 'healing' and 'cure':

In Western, scientifically-oriented cultures, therapies are aetiological, that is, they focus on the causes of diseases: germs or viruses ... Clearly such a situation requires the existence of a microscope and a host of other relatively recent inventions, technologies, and the like. The name given to this specific kind of therapy is *cure*, that is, the taking of effective control of a disordered biological and/or psychological process, usually identified as a *disease* ... In cultures that are not scientifically oriented, therapies are symptomatic, that is, aimed at alleviating or managing the symptoms. This process invariably entails creating new meaning for the sufferer ... The name given to this kind of therapy is *healing*, namely 'a process by which (a) disease and certain other worrisome circumstances are made into illness (a cultural construction and therefore

3   Colin Brown, *That You May Believe: Miracles and Faith Then and Now*, Grand Rapids, MI: William B. Eerdmans, 1985, p. 204.

4   E.g. John Pilch, 'Understanding Healing in the Social World of Early Christianity', *Biblical Theology Bulletin*, 22:1. 1992, pp. 26–33 (see his bibliography for other articles by him going back to 1981).

5   John Pilch, *Healing in the New Testament: Insights from Medical and Mediterranean Anthropology*, Minneapolis, MN: Fortress Press, 2000.

meaningful), and (b) the sufferer gains a degree of satisfaction through the reduction, or even the elimination of the psychological, sensory, and experiential oppressiveness engendered by his medical circumstances'.[6]

Expressed like this the contrast between 'cure' and 'healing' – the first representing the modern world and the second the New Testament world – functions almost as an ideal type in Pilch's writings. He is well aware, for example, that not everything that happens in Western medicine today is aetiological and that medical practice is not always about 'cure' rather than 'healing'. Rather it is that aetiology and cure are the ultimate aims of Western medicine and practice. In contrast, the fundamental aims and assumptions of healing in the New Testament (and in the ancient world generally) are radically different. Viewed in summary terms Western medicine is primarily concerned with: doing or achieving; individualism; future-orientation; mastery over nature; and views human nature as good or neutral and thus correctable. In similar summary terms New Testament healing is primarily concerned with: being and/or becoming; collateral or linear relationships; present and past time orientation; and views nature as uncontrollable and human nature as both good and bad.

On the basis of this distinction he is amazed at fellow Christians today who go to their doctors requiring aetiological medicine, based upon properly scientific investigations, and yet who go to church and treat healing stories in the Gospels at face value as 'cures' but without being able to make any similar investigations. In contrast, he insists that:

> The sickness problems presented to Jesus in the New Testament are concerned
> with a state of being (blind; deaf; mute; leprosy [an 'unclean' skin condition
> rather than Hansen's disease]; death; uncontrolled haemorrhaging, rather than
> an inability to function). What a Westerner reader might interpret as a loss of
> function, namely lameness, an ancient reader would see as a disvalued state of
> being. This is expressed in the Levitical code where, among those descendants
> of Aaron who may not offer the bread, it lists: 'a man blind or lame, or one who

---

[6]   Pilch, *Healing in the NT*, pp. 13–14 [Pilch is quoting from Arthur Kleinman, *Patients and Healers in the Context of Culture*, Berkeley: University of California Press, 1980, p. 265].

has a mutilated face or a limb too long, or a man who has an injured foot or an injured hand' (Lev. 21:18–19). Thus the real problem for the paralytics in the Synoptics (Mk. 2:1–11 and parallels) and in John 5 is not their obvious inability to do something, but their disvalued state.[7]

Here, of course, there is a point of contact between the ancient and modern worlds. Manifestly not all surgery today is aimed at restoring function. Cosmetic surgery, for example, is much more to do with 'being' than 'doing' and is frequently about 'disvalued states'.

Pilch's aim is not to make the healing stories in the Gospels redundant in the modern world, but rather to understand them better and to help 'an interpreter to be a respectful reader of biblical material'.[8] In a poignant conclusion to his book he tells of how his wife died from ovarian cancer. After initial surgery she was told by her surgeon that she was definitely in remission. She asked him: 'Do you mean that I am cured?' But he responded quite properly: 'We can't use that word until you are in remission for five years'. In the event she only lived for three. Pilch comments:

> As modern Western medicine admits, cure is a relatively rare occurrence in human experience. For most of the twentieth century, human sickness has peaked and subsided before modern medicine discovered a cure. Often the human body accommodates and learns how to defeat the sickness. In some cases this takes longer than in others. Healing, on the other hand, occurs always, infallibly, 100 per cent of the time. Healing is the restoration of meaning to life. All people, no matter how serious their condition, eventually come to some resolution. My wife was healed even before she went into remission and continued in her healed state until she died. She and I discovered new meaning in life, meaning specific to this shared experience of battling the disease, and ultimately – in our case – recognizing that the disease had won.[9]

---

[7] Ibid., p. 13.
[8] Ibid., p. 116.
[9] Ibid., p. 141.

This account is very close to the one offered by Melinsky, yet there is a crucial difference. Melinsky continued to talk about the 'miraculous' in his account and appeared to move from an initial belief that some miraculous physical cure had been effected to a more spiritual interpretation instead. Pilch makes no mention of the miraculous here and distinguishes between 'cure' and 'healing'. For Pilch, 'healing' seems finally to take precedent over physical cure – despite the fact that the sights of Western medicine are so firmly set at such cure.

Pilch's judicious use of social science as a means of understanding the context of these stories, albeit without eliminating their theological significance, is also helpful. The discussions within medical anthropology about cultural differences and similarities do help to avoid the conflations between healing within the New Testament and modern medicine against which both Gerd Theissen and Howard Clark Kee have warned.[10] The specific distinction between 'healing' and 'cure' is also helpful. He is certainly not suggesting that modern medicine should abandon its quest for 'cure', based upon aetiological diagnosis and functional therapy, and return instead to New Testament 'healing'. But he is saying that the latter can add an important dimension even to our understanding of health in the modern world.

Healing Virtues

This is an important start, but it does not identify specifically Christian virtues. How might such resources be identified from the healing stories in the Synoptic Gospels? To achieve this the skills of the social scientist might once more be helpful. Identifying implicit assumptions, beliefs and practices – sometimes at odds with those that are explicitly stated – is germane to social science and, I believe, to sociological theology. Both quantitative and qualitative methods can be used to achieve this in the modern world, as the last chapter has suggested. In the ancient world it is likely to be qualitative methods that are more appropriate.

---

[10]   Gerd Theissen, *The Miracle Stories of the Early Christian Tradition*, Edinburgh and Philadelphia, PA: T&T Clark and Fortress Press, 1983 [German original 1974], pp. 277–278; Howard Clark Kee, *Medicine, Miracle and Magic in New Testament Times*, Cambridge: Cambridge University Press, 1986, pp. 128–129. See also his *Miracle in the Early Christian World*, New Haven: Yale University Press, 1983, chapter 5.

However, by using such methods effectively it might be possible to analyse the healing stories in the Synoptic Gospels to uncover the virtues implicit within them.

Qualitative methods in social science typically look for regularities and correlations. So qualitative research using extended interviews with subjects is often based upon a loosely structured framework (allowing, as far as possible, subjects to express their thoughts on a particular topic using their own words). The interviews are recorded and then transcribed. In turn, the transcriptions can be analysed (often using an appropriate software programme) in order to see which explicit words or phrases – or implicit notions – recur or are combined most regularly within the transcriptions. Qualitative research of this sort lacks the 'objectivity' of randomized, stratified quantitative sampling. Yet it gains a depth and specificity that would otherwise not be possible. Individual subjects can be given a real opportunity to express themselves in their own terms and not simply in those of the interviewers.

Empirical research using such qualitative methods often focuses upon details within a recorded interview or written story that might otherwise appear trivial. Social anthropologists and qualitative sociologists are trained to look beyond public explanations, in the belief both that human beings have complex forms of behaviour of which they are only partially aware and that interpersonal communication usually consists of more than verbal expressions. For example, those social scientists who are trained to observe non-verbal body language learn to identify patterns of social communication among human subjects who are themselves largely unconscious of these patterns. Seemingly trivial gestures, body movements, eye contact and non-verbal noises are used as evidence by these social scientists of complex forms of social communication. Indeed, among those people with Asperger's Syndrome it is often these seemingly trivial gestures, movements and noises that are either absent in their social interactions or are present but in forms that are unfamiliar to most other people. So although some of those with this Syndrome may be highly skilled in verbal logic, other people may be confused by the asymmetry between their verbal and non-verbal skills of communication. They literally 'send out mixed messages'.

If the healing stories within the texts of the earliest Gospel traditions are inspected in this way, what patterns of reported behaviour – or, more specifically, what values or virtues – recur? Caution is needed at this point. Vernon Robbins reminds the incautious that 'there is not simply a text; texts were produced by authors and they are meaningless without readers. There are not simply readers; readers are meaningless without texts to read and authors who write texts. All three presuppose historical, social, cultural and ideological relations among people and the texts they write and read.'[11] In the light of the considerable advances of biblical interpretation over the last two decades it would be naïve to claim that any focus upon particular biblical texts – let alone my own – is free from an element of 'reader response'. My own focus here is quite explicit – namely a concern for healing within the context of Western medicine. Any focus of this sort inevitably involves some 'historical, social, cultural and ideological relation' between a personal response and the Synoptic texts.

Nonetheless, some approximate way of counting might help to identify the most prevalent patterns that might be present within these texts whether or not it is me that is involved in the study of them. It would be a mistake to attempt to turn this into a formal, quantitative exercise. The very nature of the Synoptic Gospels precludes this, since they contain so much duplicate material as well as variant textual readings. In any case it is sometimes a matter of personal judgement whether or not a particular virtue is thought to be implicit within a particular story. At most any system of counting is a means of identifying rough prevalence. With this in mind, the system used here will be to give a full weighting to a primary occurrence in one of the Synoptic sources and just half a weighting for a parallel occurrence (judging the latter to be not without significance yet not as significant as the former).

Passionate emotion is a very strong feature of the Synoptic healing stories. This takes several forms: sometimes it is Jesus who is portrayed as angry; sometimes it is the healing that is set in a situation of sharp confrontation; and sometimes it is the crowd which is portrayed as being afraid or amazed. In all of these forms taken together (and they do often occur together) passionate emotion has a very high rating of some 18. Crowd amazement/fear occurs usually at the end of a number of stories in Mark: the man in synagogue (1:27), the paralytic (2:12), the Gadarene demoniac (5:15), Jairus' daughter (5:42) and the deaf mute (7:37). Matthew and/ or Luke have parallels with all of these stories and in addition share a further story

---

[11]   Vernon Robbins, *The Tapestry of Early Christian Discourse: Rhetoric, Society and Ideology*, London: Routledge, 1996, p. 39.

of the blind/dumb demoniac (Mt. 12:23/Lk. 11:14). Matthew also has a crowd 'wondering' (15:31) and Luke has a crowd afraid (after the raising of the widow of Nairn's son in 7:16). Sharp controversy also features in several healing stories: sometimes because the healing is on a sabbath – the man with the withered hand (Mk 3:1–6/Mt. 12:9–14/Lk. 6:6–11) and in Luke's stories of the woman with an 18-year infirmity (13:10–21) and the man with dropsy (14:1–6); on another occasion the sharp controversy involves supposed healing by Beelzebub (Mt. 12:22–32/Lk. 11:14–20); and on another it is about the power to forgive sins (Mk 2:3–12/Mt. 9:2–8/Lk. 5:18–26). Jesus himself variously shows anger or compassion, according to differing texts, towards the leper in Mark (1:43), anger towards the Pharisees in the story of the man with the withered hand (3:5), and in Matthew the two blind men are told 'sternly' by Jesus to tell no one (9:30).

Faith (with a weighting of some 15) is another very strong feature in the Synoptic healing stories. The phrase 'your faith has made you well', said by Jesus directly to the one who has just been healed, is addressed in all three Gospels to the woman with a haemorrhage (Mk 5:34/Mt. 9:22/Lk. 8:48), in Mark and Luke to blind Bartimaeus (Mk 10:52/Lk. 18:42) and in Luke alone to one of the ten lepers (17:19). In a Matthew story (9:28) Jesus asks the two blind men 'Do you believe that I am able to do this?' before healing them, whereas in Mark's story of the epileptic boy (9:24) it is the father who declares 'I believe, help my unbelief' before his son is healed. In a number of other healing stories Jesus recognizes the faith of those close to the one who was to be healed: the paralytic man in all three Gospels (Mk 2:5/Mt. 9:2/Lk. 5:20), the centurion's servant in Matthew and Luke (Mt. 8:10/Lk. 7:9), and in Matthew's version of the Markan story of the Canaanite woman (15:28). A lack of faith on the part of the would-be healer is given as the reason in all three Gospels for the inability of the disciples to heal the epileptic boy (Mk 9:19/Mt. 17:17/Lk. 9:41) and a lack of faith by others is associated in Mark and Matthew with Jesus' inability to heal many in his home country (Mk 6:5–6/ Mt. 13:58).

Mercy or compassion features in several forms within the Synoptic healing stories (with a weighting of at least 14). The most common of these is for a story to begin with a plea to Jesus for mercy from the ill or their relatives. This form can be found explicitly in Mark's story of blind Bartimaeus (Mk 10:47/Lk. 18:37) and in both of Matthew's parallel stories of two blind men (9:27 and 20:30);

in Luke's story of the 10 lepers (17:13); in Matthew's versions of the Canaanite/
Syro-Phoenician woman (15:22) and the epileptic boy (17:15). An initial plea
for mercy may also be present implicitly in those stories which involve people
begging Jesus and/or prostrating themselves before him asking for a healing: in
all three Gospels the leper (Mk 1:40/ Mt. 8:2/Lk. 5:11) and Jairus (Mk 5:22–23/
Mt. 9:18/Lk. 8:41), and in Mark the Syro-Phoenician woman (7:26) and the blind
man at Bethsaida (8:22). In Mark's original story of the epileptic, the boy's father
asks Jesus not for 'mercy' but for 'pity' or 'compassion' (9:22) – using the verb
splankgnizesthai rather than *eleos* (mercy). In a number of stories it is compassion
that is explicitly attributed to Jesus himself: in Luke's story of the widow at Nain
(7:13); in two of Matthew's accounts of crowds associated with healing (9:36 and
14:14); and in some texts of Mark's story of the leper (1:41). In Matthew's story
of the two blind men at Jericho (20:29–34) 'mercy' and 'compassion' uniquely are
both used: the blind men cry to Jesus 'Have mercy on us' and again 'Lord, have
mercy on us' and Jesus responds in 'compassion' touching their eyes. In a context
of care, rather than healing as such, 'compassion' is attributed to Jesus as a reason
for the feeding of the four thousand in both Mark and Matthew (Mk 8:2/Mt. 15:32)
and the feeding of the five thousand in Mark (6:34). Compassion also features at
pivotal points in Luke's parables of the Good Samaritan (10:33) and Prodigal Son
(15:20) and in Matthew's parable of the Unmerciful Servant (18:27).

Another prevalent feature of the healing stories (with an overall weighting
of at least 12) involves touching. Jesus touching the person to be healed is a
very strong feature indeed. In Mark Jesus touches Peter's mother-in-law (1:31),
the leper (1:41), Jairus' daughter (5:41), some sick people (6:5), the deaf-mute
(7:33), the blind man (8:23) and the epileptic boy (9:27). Two of these stories
have parallels in Matthew and Luke and a further one in Matthew but not Luke.
In addition, Luke has two separate stories involving Jesus touching – the bier of
the widow's son (7:14) and the woman with an 18-year infirmity (13:13) – and
Matthew tells of Jesus touching two blind men (9:29). In addition to all of these
reports of touching there are two other stories – the woman with the issue of
blood (Mk 5:27/Mt. 9:20/Lk. 8:44) and the crowd at Gennesaret (Mk 6:56/Mt.
14:36) – in which the people to be healed touch Jesus' garments.

A related feature, namely uncleanness, is explicitly linked to two of these
stories – the leper, found in all three Gospels, and the epileptic boy, in Mark

alone – and may be implicitly present in several more of the stories. The overall prevalence weighting for uncleanness/cleansing is almost as high as for touching. So in Mark it also features in the man in synagogue (1:23 and 27), the crowd (3:11), the Gadarene demoniac (5:2 and 13) and the Syro-Phoenician woman's daughter (7:25). Luke has parallels with the first three of these and an additional story featuring cleansing – the 10 lepers (17:14). Matthew also has Jesus' command to the 12 disciples to 'cleanse lepers' (10:8).

A feature of healing stories that has attracted much scholarly attention during the last century is reticence or restraint (with a weighting of around 10). Jesus gives a command at the end of several stories that no one should be told: in Mark and Luke he commands cast-out demons not to speak (Mk 1:34/Lk. 4:41); in all three Gospels (Mk 1:44/Mt. 8:4/Lk. 5:14) he tells the leper to tell no one (with Mark including the adverb 'sternly'); in Mark he orders unclean spirits not to make him known and in the parallel Matthew story he gives the same order to those that have been healed (Mk 3:12/Mt. 12:16); in Mark and Luke he tells Jairus and his family to tell no one after his daughter has been healed (Mk 5:43/Lk. 8:56); in Mark Jesus charges people more than once to tell no one after the healing of the deaf mute (7:36) and tells the blind man 'Do not even enter the village' after his healing (8:26); and in Matthew Jesus 'sternly' charges the two blind men 'See that no one knows it' (9:30). This feature of reticence or restraint is not wholly consistent. For instance, Jesus tells unclean spirits in Mark and Luke to be silent (Mk 1:25/Lk. 4:35), but in the same Gospels the Gadarene demoniac once healed is told to go home and tell what 'the Lord' (in Mark) or 'God' (in Luke) 'has done for you' (Mk 5:19/Lk. 8:39). In addition, in both Matthew and Luke Jesus uses his healings as evidence for John the Baptist (Mt. 11:4–5/Lk. 7:22) and in Luke for Herod (13:32).

Although these are all frequent within the Synoptic healing stories, there are other features that occur but less often. Ironically such minority features have sometimes been given particular attention within biblical commentaries. For example, only in Matthew and Luke is a direct link made between healing and the Kingdom of God (Mt. 12:28/Lk. 11:20) and even within these two Gospels this link is most unusual. Again, an explicit identification of healing as a 'sign' is a feature of John (4:54) rather than the Synoptic Gospels. Yet considerable attention has been given to both of these features in discussions of healing stories within the Synoptic Gospels. Another feature that has received considerable attention is the use of Aramaic commands at the very moment of healing. For example, it encouraged early form critics to identify this as a magical technique similar to other ancient miracle stories. It is indeed a feature of two of Mark's stories (5:41 and 7:34), but it does not occur in parallels or elsewhere in the Synoptic healing stories and may be explained simply as being appropriate to their original context (as in 3:17, 7:11, 14:36 and 15:22 and 34).[12] In Mark there are a number of other links that are occasionally made: synagogues feature in five of the healing stories (1:23, 1:39, 3:1, 5:36 and 6:2), 'authority' is explicit in three stories (1:27, 2:10 and 3:15), sin and forgiveness in one (2:5–10), power in another (5:30) and 'prayer' in yet another (9:29). It certainly must not be assumed that these less frequent features are unimportant. However, a qualitative approach to evidence does carry an a priori assumption that if features regularly and spontaneously recur within interviews or written stories, then they may well be an indication of values or commitments that might otherwise be overlooked. On this basis particular attention needs to be given to those six features – passionate emotion, faith, mercy/compassion, touching, uncleanness and reticence/restraint – that occur most often in the Synoptic healing stories.

So far these six features have been discussed in the order of their rough prevalence. Given the crude way that their different weightings have been measured, this is hardly satisfactory. All that has been established up to this point is that it is these features – rather than a link with the Kingdom of God, signs, Aramaic commands, synagogues, authority, sin/forgiveness, power or prayer – which are the most characteristic features of the Synoptic healing stories. It might, though, be more logical to order these most characteristic features in terms of their sequence actually within healing stories. On this basis, mercy/compassion typically occurs at the beginning of stories, faith soon after the healing and reticence/restraint at the end. The remaining features – passionate emotion, touching and uncleanness – tend to cluster in association in the middle of healing stories. An overall four-fold pattern begins to emerge: an initial plea for mercy/compassion, followed by passionate emotion/unclean touching –

---

[12]   See further Vincent Taylor, *The Gospel According to St Mark*, London: Macmillan, 1959, p. 296, and Morna D. Hooker, *The Gospel According to St Mark*, London: A & C Black, 1991, p. 150.

then the healing itself – followed by a recognition of faith, and concluding with a command for restraint.

In sociological terms this is an 'ideal' typology (or, in Wittgenstein's philosophical terms, 'family resemblance'): it depicts the characteristic pattern of a Synoptic healing but not the actual pattern of any particular story. Only in the combined stories of the healing of Jairus' daughter and the woman with a haemorrhage can all four elements be found: the prostrate opening plea of Jairus/ the weeping and wailing in Jairus' house, the touching of the daughter by Jesus and the unclean touching of Jesus by the woman/the faith of the woman/and the command to Jairus and his family to tell no one. All of the Synoptic stories contain at least one (and usually more) of the four, but none contains them all.

Compassion

A plea for mercy/compassion typically initiates a healing story. Melinsky states bluntly and inaccurately:

> To attempt to understand the healing miracles in terms of nineteenth-century philanthropy is to try measuring a patient's temperature with a slide-rule. In fact, compassion for a sick person is never in the gospels a primary motive for Jesus' healing.[13]

He forgets, of course, Matthew's accounts of Jesus' response to crowds seeking healing (9:36 and 14:14), his story of the two blind men (20:34) and Luke's story of the widow at Nain (7:13) (Melinsky, in line with Vincent Taylor, discounts the variant reading in Mk 1:41). However, even biblical commentators have been apt to play down the role of compassion in the Synoptic healing stories. So, all that A.H. M'Neile comments on Matthew 20:34 is: 'An expression of emotion in Mt., absent from Mk, is unusual',[14] and all that C.F. Evans comments on Luke 7:13 is: 'Only here and Matt. 20:34 as the motive for performing a miracle.'[15]

---

[13]   Melinsky, *Healing Miracles*, p. 18.

[14]   A.H. M'Neile, *The Gospel According to St. Matthew*, London and New York: Macmillan and St. Martin's Press, 1965, p. 292.

[15]   C.F. Evans, *Saint Luke*, London and Philadelphia, PA: SCM Press and Trinity Press, 1990, p. 348.

Given the combined evidence within the earliest Gospel traditions just rehearsed – including explicit and implicit pleas for mercy alongside direct depictions of Jesus' compassion – this does seem to be too narrow an interpretation. It is interesting that in the second edition of his influential book *Conflict, Holiness and Politics in the Teaching of Jesus*, one of the major changes that Marcus Borg makes is to change 'mercy' and 'merciful' to 'compassion' and 'compassionate':

> The justification for the change is very simple. Namely the most common connotations of 'mercy' and 'merciful' in modern English do not express the meanings of the relevant gospel and biblical texts. In English 'mercy' and 'merciful' commonly have two closely related dimensions of meaning. First, showing mercy typically presumes a situation of wrongdoing. One is merciful to somebody who has done wrong ... Second, the language of mercy commonly presumes a power relationship of superior to inferior ... But in most synoptic contexts, these meanings are not only not called for, but are often inappropriate. The word 'compassion avoids these connotations. As its Latin roots suggest, compassion means 'to feel with'. To be compassionate means to feel the feelings on another, and then to act accordingly.[16]

Even in the later traditions of healing stories to be found in John and Acts compassion does not seem to be absent: in John, Jesus responds to the official who begs him to come down and heal his son (4:47) and is reported at the outset of the Lazarus story to 'love' Martha, Mary and Lazarus (11:5), and, in Acts, the first healing story is depicted by Peter as 'a good deed' (4:9). Compassion does seem to be more significant in the early Christian narratives than some allow.

Care

After compassion in the Synoptic healing stories comes a cluster of actions and attitudes which collectively, and in the context of health today, might most appropriately be termed 'care'. This term embraces actions as well as attitudes in

---

[16] Marcus J. Borg, *Conflict, Holiness and Politics in the Teaching of Jesus*, 2nd edition, Harrisburg, PA: Trinity Press International, 1998, p. 16.

that, properly understood, it involves both 'caring for' and 'caring about' those in need.

This combination of caring for and caring about is apparent in a number of the healing stories, but it is particularly a feature of Mark's versions of the healing the leper (1:40–45) and the epileptic boy (9:14–29). Placed so early in Mark's Gospel, the story of the leper contains a powerful combination of Jesus deliberately touching someone who is deemed to be ritually unclean with deep emotions attributed to Jesus in the course of this healing. Unlike the parallel stories in Matthew and Luke, the story in Mark contains three separate words ('anger' or 'compassion' in verse 41 and 'stern' and 'sent away' in verse 45), which, as Morna Hooker suggests, indicate 'agitation or strong emotion in Jesus' part'.[17] Only John's powerful account of Jesus' emotions at the centre of the Lazarus story (11:33–38) can rival this. She argues that 'it is probable that Mark himself understood Jesus' anger and emotion as caused by the forces of evil and disease with which he is here in conflict'.[18] The next chapter will return to this important story.

A combination of anger and touching someone who is unclean is also a strong feature of the story of the epileptic boy. In Mark Jesus 'rebuked the unclean spirit' (9:25) and then took the boy 'by the hand and lifted him up' (9:27). However, the story also starts with controversy involving the scribes, as well as the crowd, for once, 'amazed' at the outset (9:15). And Jesus, in turn, is angry in this unusually long story for Mark, apparently with the disciples, denouncing them in all three Gospels as 'O faithless generation' (9:19).

Caring about those in need properly involves attention to their social and physical context as well as to their immediate cause of concern. The passionate emotions depicted in the Synoptic healing stories are sometimes directed at the disease itself or at the 'unclean spirits'. Yet at other times they involve the faithlessness of the disciples or the religious authorities of the time. Even the crowd emotions, which more typically come at the end of a healing story (as in Lk. 9:43), can be a source of concern to Jesus. The early narrative in Mark is punctuated with crowd-induced difficulties for Jesus: 'Jesus could no longer openly enter a town' (1:45); 'Jesus withdrew with his disciples to the sea, and a great multitude from

---

[17] Hooker, *The Gospel According to St Mark*, p. 79.
[18] Ibid., p. 81.

Galilee followed' (3:7); and he withdrew in a boat 'lest they should crush him; for he had healed many, so that all who had diseases pressed upon him to touch him' (3:9–10).

Faith

The third feature in the healing stories – faith – is multilayered as well, both within the Synoptic Gospels and (implicitly) within modern health care. At the most basic level the 'faith' required of those to be healed (or their families/friends) in the Synoptic stories appears to be a faithful trust in Jesus as healer. In the later traditions of healing stories in John and Acts *pistis* is clearly more than this: in a context of healing, people become 'believers' (for example John 4:53 and Acts 5:14) and *pistis* is explicitly in Jesus or in his name (for example John 11:25 and Acts 3:16). Yet in the Synoptic stories faith appears more ambiguous and commentators tend to have different ways of interpreting it (doubtless reflecting their own particular theological positions or 'reader responses'). For example, among those commentators concerned primarily with *pistis* in the healing stories in Mark: for Vincent Taylor it primarily 'denotes a confident trust in Jesus and in his power to help';[19] for J.M. Robinson 'Mark has no single person or act as the object of faith, and no specific credal statement as the content of faith. Rather it is faith in the action recorded in Marcan history';[20] Christopher D. Marshall, in contrast, considers that Robinson 'is much too vague, for the object of faith is, in a sense, quite specific: the presence of God's eschatological power in the person of Jesus'[21] (but note here Marshall's phrase 'in a sense', especially since he has earlier admitted to 'some ambiguity concerning the intended object of faith').[22] Among commentators more widely there are also differences: for A.H. M'Neile *pistis* is 'not belief in Him as divine, but confidence that He could perform a miracle';[23]

---

[19]   Taylor, *The Gospel According to St Mark*, p. 194.

[20]   J.M. Robinson, *The Problem of History in Mark*, London: SCM Press, 1957, p. 13.

[21]   Christopher D. Marshall, *Faith as a Theme in Mark's Narrative*, Cambridge: Cambridge University Press, 1989, p. 232.

[22]   Marshall, *Faith*, p. 230.

[23]   M'Neile, *The Gospel According to St. Matthew*, p. 105.

for Davies and Allison it is 'belief in Jesus and his power as miracle worker';[24] and for C.F. Evans it is simply 'confidence in Jesus as the source of power'.[25] Despite these differences there does seem to be widespread agreement that *pistis* here has less to do with confessional belief, let alone intellectual assent (as in Mk 13:21), than with trust/confidence.

It is a feature of several of the Synoptic healing stories that faith is demonstrated by action rather than declared verbally, and it is not always even the one to be healed who actually does this demonstrating. So in the story of the paralytic man in Mark and Luke it seems to have been the determined action of friends which was responsible for Jesus seeing their faith (Mk 2:5/Lk. 5:20). Commentators have again differed among themselves about whether or not the paralytic man was included in the faith that Jesus saw. There is obviously no way of telling what the Gospel writers themselves intended here (let alone what happened in reality). In any case in those stories involving someone presumed to be dead her/his faith was clearly not involved. Another instance of determined but silent action, in all three Gospels here, followed by Jesus' commendation of faith, is the woman with a haemorrhage (or, perhaps more accurately, with ritually unclean vaginal bleeding). In Mark and Matthew, significantly, the silent touching of Jesus' clothes is preceded by her trust that if this can be done 'I shall be made well' (Mk 5:28/ Mt. 9:21).

In a number of stories faithful trust in Jesus as healer takes the form of verbal persistence rather than determined silent action. It is this which Jesus appeared to commend in Mark's story of blind Bartimaeus and in Luke's parallel story (Mk 10:52/Lk. 18:42); in Matthew and Luke's story of the centurion and his servant (Mt. 8:10/Lk. 7:9), albeit in Luke's version this is heightened by the centurion using his friends to relay his messages to Jesus; and in Matthew's version of the Canaanite woman (15:28). In the last two stories the non-Jewish origins of those begging for healing enhances both their persistence and the subsequent commendation of their faith.

---

[24]   W.D. Davies and Dale C. Allison Jr, *A Critical Commentary on The Gospel According to Saint Matthew*, Edinburgh: T&T Clark, 1991, volume 2, p. 25.

[25]   Evans, *Saint Luke*, p. 391.

There is one particular story where *pistis* understood as 'faithful trust in Jesus as healer' becomes explicit, namely Matthew's story of the two blind men. After their initial persistence:

> Jesus said to them, 'Do you believe [*pisteuete*] that I am able to do this?' They said to him, 'Yes, Lord.' Then he touched their eyes, saying, 'According to your faith [*pistin*] be it done to you.' And their eyes were opened. (Mt. 9:28b–30a)

So the 'faith' of the two blind men here seems to have been simply 'that I am able to do this'. Once they had demonstrated this faith – perhaps both by their initial persistence and by their actual assent to Jesus' direct question – then healing followed. Is that all that 'faith' denotes in the Synoptic healing stories?

Mark's account of the healing of the epileptic boy might suggest as much until, that is, the mention of prayer in the final verse. There was an initial failure of the disciples to heal the boy; Jesus' response about a faithless generation; the account of the illness by the boy's father with a request to have pity 'if you can do anything'; Jesus' response about all things being possible 'to him who believes'; the father's cry of faith; and then the healing. All of this fits a similar pattern of the 'faith' required being simply 'that I am able to do this'. But then (in Mark alone) the disciples asked Jesus why they had been unable to cast out the boy's unclean spirit and Jesus responded that, 'This kind cannot be driven out by anything but prayer' (9:29). Faith is now set at a quite different level – that is, as response to God.[26] Similarly the story of the paralytic man, in all three Gospels here, concludes with the crowd giving glory to God for the healing. Luke also has the man himself giving glory to God separately (5:25) and Matthew adds significantly that, 'they glorified God, who had given such authority to men' (9:7). When it is also recalled how often healing stories in Mark are associated with Jesus teaching in a synagogue, it is clear that *pistis* within the assumptions of the Synoptic healing stories cannot be limited simply to the mundane trust that someone is able to effect a healing. It *is* that, but it is also clearly more than that: beyond the mundane, faith, properly understood, is response to God.

'Faith' is present in both of these senses – faith as trust in the healer and faith as response to God. However, there is also a third sense, based upon mutuality, which

---

[26] C.f. Marshall, *Faith*, pp. 221–223.

is present in some of the stories. It seems to be present in Luke's puzzling story of the 10 lepers. C.F. Evans points out the problem with this particular story ending with the formula 'your faith has made you well':

> Elsewhere this either effects the healing or accompanies it (cf. 8:48; 18:42 and the parallels in Mark), but here it comes belatedly as a comment on it, and as a somewhat conventional rounding off of the story as a miracle story. For Luke cannot have meant that only the Samaritan was healed by faith, the rest being healed without faith. The sharp point for which the story is told, and which cannot be made without it, is Jesus' commendation, not of faith as such, nor of thanksgiving in general, but of the genuine piety of a non-Israelite manifesting itself in gratitude.[27]

In Luke's story the other nine lepers apparently did show faith, both in appealing to Jesus for mercy in the first place and then in obeying his command to go and show themselves to the priests. Although they were healed, they did not reciprocate with either praise to God or prostrate gratitude to Jesus [and therefore, so more conservative scholars than Evans tend to argue, they were not actually 'saved'.[28] Malina, in contrast, argues that to 'thank Jesus would mean that the relationship is over'[29]]. There was healing but little mutuality. And in one incident in Mark and Matthew, despite being set in a synagogue, there was apparently such an absence of faith/mutuality that there was little healing at all (Mk 6:5/Mt. 13:58). A full account of faith in the Synoptic healing stories needs to add mutuality to the two other levels of trust in the healer and response to God.

Humility

The fourth and concluding feature of the healing stories is a command for restraint. How is this to be understood in a context of healing? It is surprising how little attention is given to this question in biblical commentaries. The basic

---

[27]   Evans, *Saint Luke*, p. 623.

[28]   E.g. I. Howard Marshall, *The Gospel of Luke*, Exeter: Paternoster, 1978, pp. 648–649.

[29]   Bruce J. Malina, *The New Testament World*, 3rd edition, Louisville, KY: Westminster John Knox, 2001, p. 93.

problem seems to be that, despite a widespread agreement that it does not actually work, many commentators still feel obliged to focus upon Wrede's theory of the so-called Messianic Secret when considering commands to silence within the Synoptic healing stories.

Writing 50 years ago, even then Vincent Taylor admitted that 'in the form in which Wrede presented it, the theory has been widely rejected, but it continues to exert a great influence … the citadel has caved in; but the flag still flies'.[30] For Wrede the commands to silence were an unhistorical device of the early church to explain why Jesus was not recognized as the Messiah during his life-time. In Taylor's revised form the theory becomes an expression of Jesus' own conception of Messiahship: knowing himself to be already the Messiah, not least through his healings, he nonetheless commanded silence until his destiny was fulfilled after the Resurrection. Yet even in this modified form this theory hardly fits the exceptions to silence already noted (Mk 5:19/Lk. 8:39, Mt. 11:4–5/Lk. 7:22 and 13:32).

Another four decades later, Morna Hooker's discussion of the commands to silence is still dominated by Wrede. She rejects Taylor's revised theory and agrees with Wrede that the commands are (largely) an unhistorical device. However, she differs from Wrede in her interpretation of the function of this device:

> It seems clear the commands to secrecy are largely (though not necessarily entirely) artificial, and that they are a narrative device which has been used by Mark to draw his reader's attention to the real significance of his story. Secrecy and disclosure are part of a theme which pervades the whole of Mark's gospel. Throughout the narrative, Jesus acts with supreme authority yet makes no open claims for himself … Yet for those with eyes and ears to see and hear, the meaning is plain … The truth about Jesus is at once hidden from view and yet spelt out on every page of the gospel.[31]

It is only at this point in her discussion that Hooker suggests that there may be another plausible explanation of the commands. She regards it as an open question whether Mark created these commands entirely himself or whether some might

30 Taylor, *The Gospel According to St Mark*, pp. 122–123.
31 Hooker, *The Gospel According to St Mark*, pp. 68–69.

actually have come from an earlier tradition reflecting Jesus' own ministry (interestingly, and in sharp contrast, the form critic Gerd Theissen concluded that 'probably all the commands to silence in miracle stories are from the tradition'[32]). However, on the supposition that some of commands may not be Mark's own creations, she suggests:

> If we believe that Jesus' actions were characterized by an authority which may fairly be termed 'messianic', then it is possible that the so-called messianic secret reflects not simply the tension between Jesus as he was perceived in his lifetime and as he was confessed after the resurrection, but the reluctance of Jesus to make claims about himself: for his message was centred on God and on his Kingdom, not on himself, and if he believed himself to be in any sense the Messiah, the last thing he would do was to claim the title for himself.[33]

In other words, reticence may have been an expression of humility.

Once Wrede's theory is no longer allowed to dominate interpretations of the commands to silence, it is possible that this final suggestion may actually be more fruitful in the specific context of healing. Within this context there are some very obvious and pressing reasons for taking humility seriously. Public and personalized claims to have special powers of healing – although often made by crusading faith healers – are notoriously treacherous. Unless they are to resort to chicanery, mundane faith healers soon find them impossible to fulfil. Even Jesus within the Synoptic Gospels, as just noted, was unable to heal many in a context that lacked faith/mutuality. Worse still, such claims soon attract unwelcome crowd expectations, both within the ancient world and, rather oddly, within modern pluralistic societies. Crowd elation, hysteria, recriminations, exaggerated claims and polemical counter-claims are soon made.

A pattern of reticence in a context of exaggerated crowd expectations can soon be detected in the Synoptic Gospels. The threatening role of the crowd in the early chapters of Mark has already been noted. Yet it is also a feature of Matthew. In their commentary on Matthew, Davies and Allison appear to agree with Wrede's conclusion that 'the idea of the messianic secret no longer has the importance

---

[32] Gerd Theissen, *Miracle Stories*, p. 150.
[33] Hooker, *The Gospel According to St Mark*, p. 69.

for Matthew that it has for Mark'.[34] They note, for example, that Matthew drops six of Mark's commands to silence. However, this conclusion fails to observe the overall pattern of, say, chapters 8 and 9 in Matthew. Although two of Mark's commands are dropped here, another is introduced from Matthew's own source and then placed in a strategic point in the narrative. An overall pattern of reticence, movement and troubled crowds emerges: Jesus comes down from the mountain and great crowds follow him (8:1); Jesus commands the leper to silence (8:4); Jesus enters Capernaum (8:5); Jesus sees great crowds surrounding him and gives orders to get away (8:18); Jesus crosses over by boat to the country of the Gadarenes (8:28); all the city come out to meet Jesus and beg him to leave (8:34); Jesus crosses back by boat (9:1); the crowds see the healing of the paralytic and are afraid (9:8); Jesus puts the crowd outside before raising the ruler's daughter (9:25); Jesus sternly commands the two blind men to silence (9:30); crowds are moved at the healing of the dumb demoniac (9:33); but the Pharisees make hostile counter-claims (9:34); Jesus goes about cities and villages preaching and healing (9:35); Jesus has compassion for the crowds (9:36).

Reticence following exaggerated crowd expectations might also be detected in the later traditions of healing stories to be found in John and Acts. Earlier commentators tended to make much of the contrast between Mark and these later sources, since the latter lack explicit commands to silence either by Jesus (in John) or by the apostles (in Acts). Both of these later sources also make much about healings as 'signs' (for example John 4:54 and Acts 4:16: in this Acts context Peter even preaches two sermons on the strength of a single healing). Yet, viewed from the specific perspective of healing: Jesus apparently withdrew because of the crowd after healing a sick man at the pool (John 5:13); he could no longer go 'about among the Jews' after raising Lazarus (John 11:54); 'jealousy' against the apostles was prompted by crowds being healed by them (Acts 5:12–18); and Peter put all the weeping women outside before healing a woman at Joppa (Acts 9:40).

Of course such reticence in a context of exaggerated crowd expectations can never be absolute. Despite being sternly commanded to silence by Jesus, Matthew recounts that the two blind men 'went away and spread his fame through all that district' (9:31). And, away from pressing crowds, the exceptions to commands

---

[34]   Davies and Allison, *A Critical Commentary on The Gospel According to Saint Matthew*, volume 2, p. 14.

to silence even in the earliest Gospel traditions no longer appear so odd. It is precisely within a context of exaggerated crowd expectations that the boastful claims of ancient or modern faith healers become so damaging. In contrast, the healer who is really concerned to heal will be much more humble and cautious about public claims.

Humility, compassion, care and faith are all virtues expressed in many religious traditions. In the next chapter I will argue that they also have a distinctive and important contribution to make to theological responses to AIDS.

Chapter 9

Theological Virtues in the Public Forum

One of the recent and interesting features of public discourse about bioethics in Britain and elsewhere is that a number of key religious virtues are gradually being used. This is a conscious borrowing from religious traditions made because it adds something significant to otherwise secular ethical discourse. The concepts of 'covenant' and 'stewardship' are increasingly borrowed from Judaism, the concepts of 'solidarity' and 'the common good' from Catholic social ethics and occasionally in the West, but more frequently in South Africa, the concept of *ubuntu* from African traditional ethics.

From serving on the Nuffield Council on Bioethics I have been able to see some of this borrowing at first hand. The independent Nuffield Council on Bioethics – funded by the Nuffield Foundation, the Welcome Foundation and the Medical Research Council – is the nearest body that Britain has to a National Bioethics Committee. A number of its reports have been highly influential in shaping public policy. Recently the Nuffield Council on Bioethics has made significant use of the concepts of 'stewardship', 'solidarity' and 'the common good'. Stewardship was first used as a key ethical concept in its 2007 report *Public Health: Ethical Issues*,[1] solidarity in its 2009 report *Dementia: Ethical Issues* and common good in its 2011 report *Biofuels: Ethical Issues*. Following these reports *Human Bodies: Donation for Medicine and Research* (October 2011) makes significant use of all three concepts in its defence of altruism in organ donation. Commissioned by the Nuffield Council on Bioethics, Barbara Prainsack and Alena Buyx took this work a step further, as the title of their independent report indicates, *Solidarity: Reflections on an Emerging Concept in Bioethics*. They explicitly acknowledge that 'Christian writing contributed significantly to the development of the concept'

---

[1]   Nuffield Council on Bioethics reports can be accessed at http://www. nuffieldbioethics.org or obtained from Nuffield Council on Bioethics, 28 Bedford Square, London, WC1B 3JS.

of solidarity.[2] They also offer their own definition of solidarity as 'shared practices reflecting a collective commitment to carry "costs" (financial, social, emotional, or otherwise) to assist others'[3] – a definition that aligns well with a specifically theological understanding.

Or to give another striking example of the virtues of solidarity and the common good, linked to altruism, being used in the public forum today, the Harvard political philosopher Michael Sandel ended his 2009 Reith Lectures as follows:

> Rather than focus on access to private consumption, a politics of the common good would make the case for rebuilding the infrastructure of civic life; public schools to which rich and poor alike would want to send their children; public transportation systems reliable enough to attract commuters from all walks of life; public health clinics, playgrounds, parks, recreation centres, libraries and museums that would, ideally at least, draw people out of their gated communities and into the common spaces of a shared democratic citizenship.

> In the course of these lectures, I've argued for a greater role for a moral argument in public life, and for the need to keep markets in their place … . The notion that ethics, altruism and fellow-feeling are scarce resources, whose supply is fixed once and for all and depleted with use, this idea seems to me outlandish – outlandish but deeply influential. My aim in these lectures has been to call this idea into question. I've tried to suggest that the virtues of democratic life – community, solidarity, trust, civic friendship – these virtues are not like commodities that are depleted with use. They are rather like muscles that develop and grow stronger with exercise. A politics of moral and civic renewal depends, it seems to me, on a more strenuous exercise of these civic virtues.[4]

Covenant and stewardship are interrelated within the *Torah*. God establishes a covenant first with Noah, then with Abraham and finally with Moses. This covenant promises God's blessing upon the people of Israel, protection from their

---

2   Barbara Prainsack and Alena Buyx, *Solidarity: Reflections on an Emerging Concept in Bioethics*, London: Nuffield Council on Bioethics, November 2011, p. ix.

3   Prainsack and Buyx, *Solidarity*, p. 46.

4   Reith Lecture 4, Radio 4, 30 June 2009: http://www.bbc.co.uk/programmes/b00kt7sh [accessed: 26 April 2012].

enemies and an assurance of land and food security. In turn, the people must use the land responsibly (that is, act as good stewards), care for the poor and worship God alone. The two concepts thus link both human justice and protection of the environment with faithful and obedient worship of God:

> If you follow my statutes and keep my commandments and observe them faithfully, I will give you your rains in their season, and the land shall yield its produce, and the trees of the field shall yield their fruit. Your threshing shall overtake the vintage, and the vintage shall overtake the sowing; you shall eat your bread to the full, and live securely in your land. And I will grant peace in the land ... I will look with favour upon you and make you fruitful and multiply you; and I will maintain my covenant with you. (NRSV Lev. 26:3–6a and 9)

This link between land and justice has been able to make an important contribution to the debate about the environment. Within many parts of the developing world it is the poor who suffer most from environmental destruction and climate change. The notion of covenant has contributed in areas such as doctor-patient relationships:[5] instead of viewing these relationships as impersonal contracts, some have argued that properly understood they should be seen more as covenants with mutual duties and responsibilities.

The concepts of 'solidarity' and 'the common good' have been particularly developed within Catholic social ethics, although other religious traditions use them as well. Solidarity is the idea that we are all 'fellow-travellers' and that we have duties to support and help each other and in particular those who cannot readily support themselves. It directs ethical attention to the most vulnerable within societies. Justice, which is at the root of solidarity, is often seen as a fair distribution of benefits and burdens, particularly in connection with misfortunes for which we cannot be held personally responsible. At a social level the concept of solidarity requires countries to ensure that benefits are shared fairly and that burdens are not laid upon the most vulnerable in society. Solidarity reminds us that we have a 'shared humanity', a 'shared life'. Solidarity was, very appropriately, the name given to the workers' movement in Poland that challenged the former

---

[5]   See William F. May, *The Physician's Covenant: Images of the Healer in Medical Ethics*, Philadelphia, PA: Westminster Press, 1983.

totalitarian regime there. A number of its leaders were indeed committed Catholics with a strong sense of social justice.

The ethical concept of the common good goes back at least to Aristotle who argued that a good life is oriented to goods shared with others – the common good of the larger society of which one is a part. In *Nicomachean Ethics* he argued that individual goods and the common good are linked, but that the latter is finally more important: 'The attainment of the good for one person alone is, to be sure, a source of satisfaction; yet to secure it for a nation or for city-states is nobler' (109b). It was Thomas Aquinas who borrowed this concept from Aristotle and then developed it further in Catholic social thought.

There are several important features of this ethical concept:[6]

- Some global issues (such as world peace, climate change and AIDS) raise ethical issues that cannot adequately be addressed using more individualistic ethical concepts.
- Even stewardship and solidarity are often concerned with the inter-dependence within societies rather than inter-dependence across societies and across generations.
- Common good arguments require us to identify 'goods' that we believe all should share equitably (including those in developing countries) whatever society they live in or whether or not they have yet been born.
- Common good arguments often assume that there is a common ownership of, or right to use, essential resources.
- Common good arguments might require all those living now to reduce their demands for the sake of future generations (for developed countries, this could mean some restrictions on lifestyle; for developing countries, this could mean reducing their expectation of achieving the same lifestyle currently prevalent in developed countries).
- Common good arguments do not, therefore, depend upon simply balancing the self-interests of those living now.

---

[6]   See David Hollenbach, *The Common Good and Christian Ethics*, Cambridge: Cambridge University Press, 2002; T.J. Gorringe, *The Common Good and the Global Emergence: God and the Built Environment*, Cambridge: Cambridge University Press, 2011; and Alasdair MacIntyre, *Dependent Rational Animals*, London: Duckworth, 1999.

- Rather common good arguments (like stewardship and solidarity arguments) explicitly seek to evoke altruism especially among those who are at present most privileged.

Of course common good arguments can be abused by totalitarian regimes (religious or secular). Yet even within Western democracies today global issues such as world peace, climate change and (as will be seen in a moment) AIDS, suggest that an account of the common good as understood in these bullet points is still important. A common good perspective encourages scientists, politicians and religious leaders to strive for effective measures that protect common social goods across societies and generations.

The fifth concept is *ubuntu*. This is a Bantu word from South Africa but many people argue that it has resonances in other parts of Black Africa as well. It emphasizes the interconnectedness of people and is often contrasted with Western individualism. *Ubuntu* assumes that the identity of individuals is located in their relationships with other people: human beings cannot function adequately in isolation – we need each other and should be responsible for each other. *Ubuntu* expects people to be generous to each other and to be good neighbours. It is part of the cross generational African concept: the living, the unborn and ancestors, all in an ongoing mutual relationship.[7] *Ubuntu* encourages people to see themselves as always part of a greater whole, which includes their family, their neighbours, their kinspeople and others in their language group. People should offer hospitality when it is required by others and can expect to receive hospitality themselves when they require it.

Compassion, care, faith and humility can be, and also are being, increasingly added to bioethical discourse in the public forum. This can be seen, for example, when looking at the present debate about legalizing euthanasia or assisted dying in Britain. The Director of Public Prosecutions used 'compassion' as a key criterion in the 2010 guidelines on assisted dying.[8] Indeed, it is now quite common for all sides in the euthanasia debate to appeal for compassion. Yet a search of some of

---

[7]   See Bénézet Bujo, 'Differentiations in African Ethics' in William Schweiker (ed.), *The Blackwell Companion to Religious Ethics*, New York and Oxford: Blackwell, 2005, p. 432.

[8]   http://www.cps.gov.uk/publications/prosecution/assisted_suicide_policy.html [accessed: 26 April 2012].

the leading textbooks in secular bioethics soon suggests that compassion has in the recent past been relatively ignored. By some it was even dismissed (as it was at times in the classical world) for being too emotional and passionate. Yet some concept of compassion (albeit not always an identical concept) is present in many different sacred texts. In the *Qur'an* every chapter (*sura*) but one starts with an appeal to God who is merciful/compassionate. It is even present in the *Gita* and the *Nikayas* despite their strong suspicion of passion. The Dalai Lama speaks for many across Jewish, Christian, Islamic, Buddhist and Hindu religious traditions: 'Love and compassion are most important, most precious, and most sacred … They are the basic elements supporting our life and happiness'.[9] From roots within different religious traditions, compassion does seem to be increasingly important within bioethics today.

There are obvious overlaps between these different concepts. Both solidarity and *ubuntu* emphasize the importance of people working together and helping each other. Both stewardship and the common good encourage people to look carefully at the wider world or environment. Yet it can be seen that each also has a distinctive focus. What is interesting, here, is that each has made a significant contribution to wider ethical debate even within pluralistic settings. Each brings a particular wisdom that can be recognized even by those who do not share the beliefs and practices of the religious tradition from which it comes.

AIDS: A Case Study

In 2003 UNAIDS, the Joint United Nations Programme on HIV and AIDS, took an unexpected step. It convened a group of Catholic and non-Catholic theologians, meeting at Windhoek in Namibia, to address the issue of how religious communities might be able to help reduce the spread of the HIV virus. Sub-Saharan Africa has been particularly affected by AIDS and Namibia itself has one of the highest rates of infection. It is now generally recognized that the virus is predominantly spread there through unprotected heterosexual intercourse. Of course it is not only spread in this way. It can be spread from mothers to their babies and people can

---

[9]   Dalai Lama, *How to Expand Love: Widening the Circle of Loving Relationships*, New York: Atria Books, 2005, p. 209.

be infected from dirty needles and blood donations. Nevertheless unprotected heterosexual (or homosexual) intercourse is the way that it is mostly spread. An activity which is intensely desirable and enjoyable is directly linked to the spread of the deadly HIV virus. UNAIDS concluded that, if this spread is to be halted, human behaviour needs to be changed, and that, especially in the deeply religious cultures of Sub-Saharan Africa, local churches acting in solidarity for the common good might be able to facilitate such a change. Yet UNAIDS was also aware that some local religious leaders had made highly misleading and inflammatory claims about AIDS – for instance, stating that it was a punishment from God for homosexuality. Catholic authorities were also insisting at the time that condoms should never be used even to prevent HIV infection. Even today in Britain some fundamentalist faith healers actually encourage their HIV-positive followers to stop taking anti-retroviral medication.

The report that came out of this UNAIDS meeting stated its aims as follows:

> In the context of HIV and AIDS, the most powerful obstacle to effective prevention, treatment and care is proving to be the stigmatization of people living with HIV and AIDS. Christian theology has, sometimes unintentionally, operated in such a way as to reinforce stigma, and to increase the likelihood of discrimination. However, at other times, Christian theology has also, often, been successful in challenging society's injustices and bringing about change … The purpose of the present document is to identify those aspects of Christian theology that endorse or foster stigmatizing attitudes and behaviour towards people living with HIV and AIDS and those around them, and to suggest what resources exist within Christian theology that might enable churches to develop more positive and loving approaches.[10]

UNAIDS also realized that if this issue is to be addressed adequately, with hearts and minds changed, then as many religious traditions as possible (they soon included Islamic, Hindu and Buddhist leaders as well) need to be involved. Central to the

[10] Robin Gill (ed.), *Reflecting Theologically on AIDS: A Global Challenge*, London: SCM Press, 2007, pp. 19–20. The full report can be found at: http://data.unaids.org/publications/irc-pub06/jc1119_theological_en.pdf [accessed: 26 April 2012].

UNAIDS position (with some emerging empirical evidence of success)[11] is that faith communities acting for the common good could make a positive contribution in this important area. On 11 April 2012, Michel Sidibé, Executive Director of UNAIDS, met Pope Benedict XVI, encouraging his personal engagement in ending mother-to-child transmission of HIV. Interviewed on Vatican Radio he said at the time:

> My visit is a very simple one. I am convinced that we will never change the face of our people who are suffering from HIV if we are not fostering the link between science, religions and social change. For me the Church is playing a critical role to help us to reach those people at the grassroots levels, through their mechanisms every Sunday ... they have families coming so we need to use this strength to help us to fight stigma, discrimination; and also to inform people that being sexually responsible is important when you really want to prevent new infections.[12]

Religious traditions do not have a monopoly on moral passion but they do have particular reason for having strong, even passionate, moral convictions. Within those religious traditions that believe in a creator God a crucial and emphatic connection is usually made between this belief and human moral behaviour. God who created us is righteous, so we in turn should be righteous. God who created us is compassionate towards us, so we in turn should be compassionate towards each other. This is not simply a form of divine command ethic, it is also a response ethic to divine goodness.[13] The philosopher John Cottingham expresses this clearly (albeit in language that is not inclusive):

> If God himself is in his essential nature merciful, compassionate, just and loving, then when we humans act in [good] ways we are drawn closer to God, the source

---

[11]   Rachel Mash and Robert J. Mash, 'A quasi-experimental evaluation of an HIV prevention programme by peer education in the Anglican Church of the Western Cape, South Africa. BMJ Open 2012;2: e000638.doi:10:1136/bmjopen-2011–000638 [accessed: 24 April 2012].

[12]   AJA News 108, Mau 2012: ajanews@jesuits.net [accessed: 3 June 2012].

[13]   Mark C. Murphy terms this 'moral concurrentism' in his *God and Moral Law: On the Theistic Explanation of Morality*, Oxford: Oxford University Press, 2011.

of our being, and the source of all that is good. Such acts command our allegiance in the strongest way, since they bring us nearer to the 'home' where our true peace and fulfilment lie; and, conversely, in setting our face against them, we are cutting ourselves off from our true destiny, from the ultimate basis of joy and meaningfulness in our lives. If, on the other hand, there is no God, if God is 'dead', then there might (as Nietzsche frighteningly suggested) be conclusive reasons to steel ourselves *against* impulses of love and mercy, to harden our hearts against compassion and forgiveness, since such sentiments might get in the way of our will to power, or our passion for self-realization, or some other grand project we happen to have.[14]

John Cottingham writes this (as he admits) from a perspective shaped by Jewish and Christian traditions. It does not do justice to a Buddhist perspective, or even to some Hindu perspectives. However, it does capture the contrast between Western theists like himself and Western atheists who follow in the tradition of Nietzsche. It is a contrast that can be found readily within Muslim, Jewish and Christian sacred texts as the following passages illustrate:

From the *Qur'an*:

> We command you, to be mindful of God. Even if you do ignore him, everything in the heavens and the earth belongs to him, and he is self-sufficient, worthy of all praise ... You who believe, uphold justice and bear witness to God, even if it is against yourselves, your parents, or your close relatives. Whether the person is rich or poor, God can best take care of both. Refrain from following your own desire, so that you can act justly – if you distort or neglect justice, God is fully aware of what you do. You who believe, believe in God and his Messenger and in the Scripture he sent down to his Messenger, as well as what he sent down before. Anyone who does not believe in God, his angels, his Scriptures, his messengers, and the Last Day has gone far, far astray. (4:135)[15]

---

[14] John Cottingham, *Why Believe?* London: Continuum, 2009, p. 41.

[15] M.A.S. Haleem (trans.), *The Qur'an*, Oxford: Oxford University Press, 2005.

From the *New Testament*:

> Beloved, let us love one another, because love is from God; everyone who loves
> is born of God and knows God. Whoever does not love does not know God, for
> God is love. God's love was revealed among us in this way: God sent his only
> Son into the world so that we might live through him. In this is love, not that we
> loved God but that he loved us and sent his Son to be the atoning sacrifice for our
> sins. Beloved, since God loved us so much, we also ought to love one another.
> (NRSV, 1 John 4:7–11)

From the Hebrew *Bible*:

> Happy are those whose help is the God of Jacob,
> whose hope is in the LORD their God,
> who made heaven and earth,
> the sea, and all that is in them;
> who keeps faith for ever;
> who executes justice for the oppressed;
> who gives food to the hungry. (NRSV, Psalm 146)

There are obvious differences between these passages (for example the threat of
the Last Day in the first and the atoning sacrifice in the second), yet each makes
a strong link between belief in the goodness of God and human moral behaviour.
Ethics and faith are emphatically connected.

What about forms of Buddhism that have no belief in God at all – especially
the Theravada Buddhism of South and South East Asia? Do non-theistic
Buddhists (or polytheistic/ pantheistic Hindus) suffer from the moral weaknesses
of atheism suggested by John Cottingham? Would such Buddhists be tempted to
find conclusive reasons to steel themselves *against* impulses of love, mercy and
compassion? In reality there is considerable evidence of the rigorous life expected
of the Buddhist monk, such as the following:

From the Buddhist *Nikayas*:

> A monk refrains from killing living creatures. He discards sticks and swords, and is gentle and full of compassion, remaining sympathetic and well disposed towards all creatures and beings. This is one aspect of his moral behaviour.
>
> Letting go of what has not been given to him, he refrains from taking what is not given. Accepting and wanting only what is given, he lives honestly, without stealing. This is a further aspect of his moral behaviour.
>
> Giving up the non-celibate life, he follows a life of celibacy. He lives detached, refraining from the vulgar practice of copulation. This is a further aspect of his moral behaviour. (19–20)[16]

Far from pursuing some will to power or passion for self-realization, the monk is 'letting go' and 'giving up' with the positive aim of attaining enlightenment. Here is the crucial difference between the non-theistic monk of Theravada Buddhism and Nietzsche's atheistic superman. The former is attempting to go beyond self and the cycle of rebirth in order to attain enlightenment whereas the latter is exalting in self. In one famous passage an ascetic who 'as a consequence of his energy, application, practice, and attentiveness ... reaches that state of concentration where, with his mind concentrated, he sees with godlike vision, purified and surpassing that of men,' the consequences of bad action:

> Bad actions certainly do exist. Bad conduct has its result. Indeed, I have seen that person who here in this life harmed living creatures, took what is not given, behaved improperly sexually, spoke what is untrue, talked maliciously ... and had mistaken views; and I have seen that at the breaking up of the body, after death, that person was reborn in a state of misfortune, an unhappy destiny, a state of affliction, hell. (198)[17]

---

[16]   Rupert Gethin (trans.), *Nikayas: Sayings of the Buddha*, Oxford: Oxford University Press, 2008.

[17]   Gethin, *Nikayas*.

Clearly this is not individualistic atheism in John Cottingham's (Western) sense at all. Non-theistic forms of Buddhism do have a powerful sense of meaning structuring reality independent of self. From a Western perspective it manifestly constitutes some form of sacred belief and myth quite unlike the beliefs of the person depicted by Nietzsche.

A Buddhist sense of meaning structuring reality independent of self is also expressed, albeit in more modern terms, by the Dalai Lama:

> When we come to see that everything we perceive and experience arises as a result of an indefinite series of interrelated causes and conditions, our whole perspective changes. We begin to see that the universe we inhabit can be understood in terms of a living organism where each cell works in balanced cooperation with every other cell to sustain the whole. If then, just one of these cells is harmed, as when disease strikes, that balance is harmed and there is danger to the whole. This, in turn, suggests, that our individual well-being is intimately connected both with that of all others and with the environment within which we live.[18]

What all of this suggests is that these different religious traditions do tend to have a rich variety of remarkably strong positive and negative drivers. A committed belief in a loving and compassionate God is closely related to a passionate belief that people should, in turn, be loving and compassionate to each other acting for the common good. So does an ascetic life that seeks enlightenment for self as well as for others (the Dalai Lama frequently appeals for compassion and 'balanced cooperation'). Negatively, a fear of judgement on the Last Day (to be found in parts of the *Qur'an* and the *New Testament* but seldom in the *Hebrew Bible*) or a desire to escape the cycle of rebirth (within Theravada Buddhism) and/or a harmful lack of balance can also be a strong driver within religious traditions.[19]

---

[18]   Dalai Lama, *Ethics for the New Millennium*, New York: Riverhead Books, 1999, p. 4.

[19]   See further my 'AIDS and Religious Virtues', *Ecumenical Review*, 63, 19 December 2011, pp. 419–431.

Leprosy and AIDS within Sociological Theology

In seeking to make an appropriate response to the challenge of AIDS today a connection is frequently made by Christian theologians with the response of the Synoptic Jesus to the challenge of leprosy. This connection is made explicitly, but in passing, in the Windhoek Report. It is also made in many thousands of other statements, articles and sermons (as a Google search soon reveals).[20] But this connection is complicated by a widespread agreement among biblical scholars that 'leprosy' in the Bible (*sara'at* in the Jewish Bible or *lepra* in the New Testament) is not simply to be identified with Hansen's disease (*Elephantiasis Graecorum*).[21]

Using his medical knowledge, S.G. Browne argued that none of the biblical references to 'leprosy' includes 'any of the indubitable signs and symptoms of leprosy, and those that are mentioned tell against rather than for leprosy'. In addition, 'none of the pathognomonic features of leprosy are so much as hinted at: these are, anaesthetic areas of the skin, painless and progressive ulceration of the extremities, and facial nodules'.[22] So despite the tempting clinical association that is sometimes reported between leprosy (Hansen's disease) and AIDS in the modern world,[23] the theological connection has more to do with social perceptions than with epidemiology.

From the perspective of sociological theology this conclusion makes the connection more rather than less interesting. Once seen in terms of social perceptions both biblical leprosy and modern-day AIDS have quite a number of startling and theologically significant similarities. Just as leprosy in the Bible was surrounded by social fears, interdictions and stigmatization that had little or

---

[20]   I am most grateful to Jeff Astley for the observation that entering 'leprosy' and 'AIDS' together in an Advanced Google Search clearly demonstrates this connection.

[21]   See, for example, Vincent Taylor, *The Gospel According to St Mark*, London: Macmillan, 1959, p. 186; W.D. Davies and Dale C. Allison Jr, *A Critical Commentary on The Gospel According to Saint Matthew*, volume 2, Edinburgh: T&T Clark, 1991, pp. 10–11; Martin Noth, *Leviticus*, London: SCM Press, 1965, p. 106; and Gordon J. Wenham, *The Book of Leviticus*, London: Hodder and Stoughton, 1979, p. 195.

[22]   S.G. Browne, *Leprosy in the Bible*, London: Christian Medical Fellowship, 1970, p. 8.

[23]   The Indian Association of Leprologists reported an association between leprosy and AIDS at a clinical level (http://www.rediff.com/news/2004/nov/05med.htm) [accessed: 23 June 2012]. If, as some argue, biblical 'leprosy' was a form of contagious TB, this association is even stronger.

no relation to aetiological medicine, so AIDS in the modern world has spawned similar social fears, interdictions and stigmatization – once again with little or no relation to aetiological medicine. And some of the cruder theological responses to disease and natural disaster illustrated by Job's critics in the Bible have sadly been replicated by some church leaders in the modern world.

Using the frame of social perception it is possible to construct a typology of leprosy, first in the Jewish Bible and then in the Synoptic Gospels. It is from a critical comparison of these two typologies that a more appropriate Christian theological response to AIDS might then be sought. This is not of course to maintain that social perceptions of biblical leprosy and modern-day AIDS are identical. Inescapably AIDS is strongly associated with sexual activity (even though, epidemiologically, HIV has often been contracted through needles and blood transfusions and transmitted from HIV-positive mothers to their babies) whereas biblical leprosy was not (albeit, as Mary Douglas pointed out, in Africa today 'leprosy is widely associated with incest').[24] It is sufficient to claim that there are some instructive social similarities, especially pertinent for sociological theology, between biblical leprosy and modern-day AIDS.

A ten-fold typology of social perceptions of leprosy (*sara'at*) in the Jewish Bible (located particularly in the priestly code) might be constructed as follows:

First, **Leprosy is visibly shocking**: Moses (Ex. 4:6), Miriam (Num. 12:10) and Gehazi (2 Kgs 5:27) are all depicted as being 'leprous, as white as snow'. Wenham objects to the addition of 'white' in this translation and argues instead that 'the point of comparison may well be the flakiness of snow'.[25] Whether white or flaky, leprosy is regarded as visible and shocking (and different, of course, from the visibly shocking ulceration of the extremities and facial nodules characteristic of Hansen's disease).

Second, **Leprosy requires vigorous testing by the priest**: Leviticus 13 is the primary source for this testing. 'The priest shall examine the disease on the skin of his body, and if the hair in the diseased area has turned white and the disease appears to be deeper than the skin of his body, it is a leprous disease' (Lev. 13:3). The priest must re-examine those suspected of leprosy seven days later to see if

---

24   Mary Douglas, *Leviticus as Literature*, Oxford: Oxford University Press, 1999, p. 185.
25   Wenham, *The Book of Leviticus*, p. 195.

'the disease is checked and ... has not spread in the skin' (13:9) and again seven days later. As Martin Noth observes: 'It was the priest's business to pronounce on the state of cleanness and uncleanness; hence it is a case here of fixing the priestly professional knowledge in writing.'[26] Later Rabbinic texts discussed (a) whether the 'colours of leprosy signs were sixteen, thirty-six or seventy-two' and (b) whether priests should 'inspect leprosy-signs for the first time the day after the Sabbath, since [the end of] that week will fall on the Sabbath'.[27]

Third, **Leprosy involves (dangerous) impurity**: Mary Douglas emphasizes that not all forms of impurity depicted in the priestly code involve danger or deep disgust. But leprosy does: 'Leviticus certainly plays upon disgust at bodily exudations in its long disquisition on uncleanness of bleeding and leprosy ... if impure was not originally a term of vilification it certainly has become one'.[28] 'The Lord spoke to Moses, saying: Command the Israelites to put out of the camp everyone who is leprous, or has a discharge, and everyone who is unclean through contact with a corpse ... they must not defile their camp, where I dwell among them' (Num. 5:1–3). Leprosy supposedly endangers the common good.

Fourth, **Lepers fearfully render other people/objects impure**: Leprosy can even affect a house (appearing as 'greenish or reddish spots' deeper than the surface of the walls) and 'the priest shall command that they empty the house before the priest goes to examine the disease, or all that is in the house will become unclean' (Lev. 14:36). Mary Douglas again showed how leprosy is believed to spread, to defile and to become ever more dangerous. It starts with the postulating body, it then spreads to the garments, then to the house, and finally and disastrously to the tabernacle: 'If there is no cure, the incurably defiled house must be destroyed (Lev. 14:39–42), as also the incurable leprous garment (Lev. 13:52), and eventually the incurable leper can expect to be destroyed by the disease. In the last case, defilement of the tabernacle, chapter 16 enjoins the rite of atonement for the tabernacle. If defilement of the tabernacle were not remedied, the people could expect the curses of chapter 26 to be unleashed upon them as a punishment for failing to keep the covenant.'[29]

---

[26] Noth, *Leviticus*, p. 103.

[27] Jacob Neusner, *The Rabbinic Traditions about the Pharisees before 70: Part I The Masters*, Leiden: E.J. Brill, 1971, p. 406.

[28] Douglas, *Leviticus as Literature*, p. 145.

[29] Ibid., pp. 191–192.

Fifth, ***Leprosy can result from sin***: In three of the leprosy stories in the Jewish Bible the disease does seem to be associated with sinful behaviour resulting in God's anger or the anger of God's representatives. Miriam angered God for speaking against Moses (Num. 12:8), Gehazi angered Elisha because of his greed (2 Kgs 5:25) and King Uzziah angered the priests because he rather than they made an offering (2 Chr. 26:17).

Sixth, ***Leprosy is inflicted by God***: Even when such sinful behaviour does not seem to be associated with leprosy, the disease is still inflicted by God. So in the Moses leprosy story, the Lord said to Moses '"Put your hand inside your cloak." He put his hand into the cloak; and when he took it out, his hand was leprous, as white as snow' (Ex. 4:6). Again in Leviticus, 'The Lord spoke to Moses and Aaron saying: When you come into the land of Canaan, which I give you for a possession, and I put a leprous disease in a house ...' (Lev. 14:33–34). And in the Uzziah story, although it did involve sin, the king 'was leprous in his forehead ... because the Lord had struck him' (2 Chr. 26:20).

Seventh, ***Leprosy requires extensive reparation***: Whether leprosy involves sinful behaviour or not, it does require priestly reparation, set out in great detail in Leviticus 14: 'The priest shall offer the sin offering, to make atonement for the one to be cleansed from his uncleanness. Afterwards he shall slaughter the burnt offering' (Lev. 14:19).

Eighth, ***Leprosy necessitates social exclusion, interdictions and stigmatization***: Leviticus 13 is again the primary source, supplying a recipe for the social exclusion and stigmatization of lepers for many centuries to come: 'The person who has the leprous disease shall wear torn clothes and let the hair of his head be dishevelled; and he shall cover his upper lip and cry out, "Unclean, unclean." He shall remain unclean as long as he has the disease; he is unclean. He shall live alone; his dwelling shall be outside the camp' (Lev. 13:45–46). The leper is of course a source of dangerous impurity to other people, to buildings and, especially, to the tabernacle (and, in medieval Europe, to church buildings). Emphatically lepers 'must not defile their camp, where I dwell among them' (Num. 5:3). Royal status was no exception; even King Uzziah 'being leprous lived in as separate house, for he was excluded from the house of the Lord' (2 Chr. 26:21).

Ninth, *Leprosy consumes flesh uncontrollably*: Aaron pleads with Moses on behalf of Miriam: 'Do not let her be like one still-born, whose flesh is half consumed when it comes out of its mother's womb' (Num. 12:12).

Tenth, *Leprosy can remain until (and even beyond) death*: Gehazi is told by Elisha: 'Therefore the leprosy of Naaman shall cling to you, and to your descendants forever' (2 Kgs 5:27) and 'King Uzziah was leprous to the day of his death' (2 Chr. 26:21).

Not all of this ten-fold typology relates to social perceptions of AIDS today but much of it does, especially in parts of sub-Sahara where HIV infection is so tragically rife. In parts of Africa today AIDS is depicted as 'slims' disease because of the shocking physical degeneration of many suffers; it is widely regarded as a dangerous impurity – albeit an impurity that might be removed by sleeping with virgins or by remedies supplied by traditional (priestly) healers; it is closely associated with sin and viewed (even by some church leaders) as a punishment from God; it is believed to necessitate social exclusion, interdictions and stigmatization in the supposed interests of the common good; as 'slims' disease it consumes flesh uncontrollably; and of course it can remain at least until death.

Within Western countries, too, especially in the 1980s when AIDS was still widely seen as 'the gay disease', some of these social perceptions were present. Against medical explanations at the time HIV was widely regarded as contagious to touch (Princess Diana's hugging of a small child with AIDS is often depicted as an iconic breaking of this social perception) and some deemed AIDS to be God's punishment of homosexuality. Members of the gay community sought anonymous testing precisely because they feared exclusion and stigmatization by society at large. And only the effectiveness of cocktails of anti-retroviral drugs in recent years has reduced apocalyptic fears of early/untimely death.

Allied to this there have frequently been public (even government) denials based upon social perceptions rather than upon rigorous empirical research: denials of a link between HIV infection and AIDS disease; denials that a particular country or church had any prevalence of HIV infection (or even any gay people); denials that unprotected heterosexual (rather than homosexual) intercourse also spreads HIV infection; and denials by individuals that they have been party to this spread of HIV infection. Social exclusion, stigmatization and a lack of truth-telling have all too often been responses to the challenge of AIDS.

How does this social perception of *sara'at* in the Jewish Bible compare with that of *lepra* in the Synoptic Gospels? There are six discrete mentions of the disease in the Synoptic Gospels and none elsewhere in the New Testament. The most elusive of these is the mention of Jesus being 'in the house of Simon the leper' when a woman anoints him with costly ointment (Mk 14:3 and Mt. 26:6). John Nolland argues that 'it is most natural to think in terms of Simon as someone whose identity is expected to be known in the Christian folk memory of the Gospel readership, and who is remembered as one cured of leprosy by Jesus'.[30] Vincent Taylor suggests more vaguely that this house 'must have been known to the circle from which the story comes'.[31] In Matthew the 12 disciples are charged to 'cure the sick, raise the dead, cleanse the lepers, cast out demons' (10:8). In both Matthew and Luke (significantly adding the reference to lepers to the original quotation from Isaiah) John the Baptist's disciples are told to report back that 'the blind receive their sight, the lame walk, the lepers are cleansed, the deaf hear, the dead are raised, (and) the poor have good news brought to them' (Mt. 11:5 and Lk 7:22). Then there are two extended leper stories. There is the story of the cleansing of the leper contained in all three Synoptic Gospels (Mk 1:40–45; Mt. 8:1–4; Lk. 5:12–16). And there is the story of the 10 lepers recounted only by Luke (17:11–19).

The fascinating sixth allusion to leprosy, given only in Luke – Jesus (in a story foundational for Liberation theology) declared in the synagogue: 'There were also many lepers in Israel in the time of the prophet Elisha, and none of them was cleansed except Naaman the Syrian' (Lk. 4:27) – suggests an illuminating typology for these leprosy stories and depictions. Setting out the Elisha/Naaman story in eight phases – Prelude, Prophet's Initial Response, Encounter, Required Ritual, Cleansed Leper's Return, Prophet's Response, Dismissal and Follow-up – clear Synoptic parallels can be seen with all but the last. And even the last may have a parallel in the broader Lucan corpus.

---

[30]   John Nolland, *The Gospel of Matthew*, Grand Rapids, MI: William B. Eerdmans, 2005, p. 1051.

[31]   Taylor, *The Gospel According to St Mark*, p. 530.

Prelude

In the Elisha/Naaman story the latter, in contrast to the prophet himself, is depicted as being a 'commander of the army of the king of Aram … a great man and in high favour with his master' (2 Kgs 5:1). Yet, of course, 'the man, though a mighty warrior, suffered from leprosy'. None of the lepers that feature in the Synoptic stories are depicted in this way (unless Nolland's supposition about 'Simon the leper' is extended). However, in Matthew the centurion in the story immediately following his main leper story is similarly depicted as 'a man under authority, with soldiers under me; and I say to one, "Go," and he goes, and to another, "Come," and he comes, and to my slave, "Do this," and the slave does it' (Mt. 8:9).

Prophet's Initial Response

Elisha's initial response to hearing about Naaman's plight was, 'Let him come to me, that he may learn that there is a prophet in Israel' (2 Kgs 5:8). Similarly the Synoptic Jesus responded 'Go and tell John [the Baptist] what you hear and see: the blind receive their sight; the lame walk; the lepers are cleansed … What did you come out to see? A prophet?' (Mt. 11:5f/Lk. 7:22f).

Encounter

Naaman came to Elisha with chariots and gifts whereas Elisha issued a command from within his house without meeting him. Similarly, the 10 lepers are depicted as 'keeping their distance' from Jesus (Lk. 17:12) and the centurion's servant is healed at a distance (Mt. 8:5f).

Required Ritual

Elisha required Naaman to 'Go, wash in the Jordan seven times, and your flesh shall be restored and you shall be clean' (2 Kgs 5:10). In the two Synoptic extended stories both the single leper and the ten lepers are commanded to go to the priest(s) in accord with the rituals required in Leviticus 13 and 14:

'See that you say nothing to anyone; but go, show yourself to the priest, and offer for your cleansing what Moses commanded, as a testimony to them' (Mk 1:44) and 'Go and show yourselves to the priests' (Lk. 17:14).

Cleansed Leper's Return

Naaman, an Aramean, freshly cleansed 'returned to the man of God, he and all his company; he came and stood before him and said, "Now I know that there is no God in all the earth except in Israel; please accept a present from your servant"' (2 Kgs 5:15). In the extended Luke story, one of the ten lepers, a Samaritan, 'when he saw that he was healed, turned back, praising God with a loud voice. He prostrated himself at Jesus' feet and thanked him' (Lk. 17. 15–16).

Prophet's Response

Elisha would accept no payment from Naaman: 'As the Lord lives, whom I serve, I will accept nothing!' (2 Kgs 5:16). And in the Synoptic Gospels the disciples were told by Jesus to 'give without payment' (Mt. 10:8) and a leper was told to say 'nothing to anyone' (Mk 1:44/Mt. 8:4/Lk. 5:14).

Dismissal

Elisha said to the cured Naaman 'Go in peace' (2 Kgs 5:19). In Luke Jesus said to one of the ten cured lepers: 'Get up and go on your way; your faith has made you well' (Lk. 17:18).

Follow-up

In the (perhaps added) sequel to the Elisha/Naaman story Gehazi was chastised by Elisha because of his financial deception: 'the leprosy of Naaman shall cling to you, and to your descendents, forever' (2 Kgs 5:27). A very tentative parallel might be made with Ananias and Sapphira being chastised by Peter because of their financial deception: 'How is it that you have agreed together to put the Spirit of the Lord to the test? Look, the feet of those who have buried your husband are at the door, and they will carry you out' (Acts 5:9).

Yet, despite the many parallels suggested by this typology, there are also some crucial and highly instructive differences between the Elisha/Naaman story and the leprosy stories and depictions in the Synoptic Gospels. Jesus' very declaration in the synagogue that 'There were also many lepers in Israel in the time of the prophet Elisha, and none of them was cleansed except Naaman the Syrian' (Lk. 4:27) is followed (not very logically suggests Christopher Evans)[32] by a threat of violence from those in the synagogue: 'They got up, drove him out of the town, and led him to the brow of the hill on which their town was built, so that they might hurl him off the cliff' (Lk. 4:29). In the Elisha/Naaman story no violence is directed against the prophet, despite Naaman's anger at the prophet's required ritual. Violence is rather directed in the sequel by the prophet himself at his greedy servant, just as earlier he had directed extreme violence on 42 boys who had 'jeered at him, saying, "Go away, baldhead! Go away, baldhead!" (2 Kgs 2:23).

Another important difference is that the required ritual action (at a distance from Elisha) effects the cleansing of Naaman from leprosy: 'So [Naaman] went down and immersed himself seven times in the Jordan, according to the word of the man of God; his flesh was restored like the flesh of a young boy, and he was clean' (2 Kgs 5:14). In contrast, in the two extended leper stories in the Synoptic Gospels the cleansing takes place in the presence of Jesus and the required ritual to go to 'the priest' is not in order to be cleansed of the leprosy but in order to be pronounced clean (as required by Lev. 13).

Most important of all, in a context of seeking a theologically appropriate response to the challenge of AIDS today, the cleansing in the Synoptic stories involves direct touching by Jesus. Elisha, while keeping his distance, issued a command from inside his house through a messenger to Naaman the leper outside. Only once the latter had been cleansed at a distance was it that 'he returned to the man of God, he and all his company; he came and stood before him' (2 Kgs 5:15). In contrast the 10 lepers approach Jesus directly, albeit 'keeping their distance', calling out 'Jesus, Master have mercy on us!' (Lk. 17:12). Jesus sees them and

---

[32] C.F. Evans, *Saint Luke*, London and Philadelphia, PA: SCM Press and Trinity Press, 1990, p. 275.

responds to them directly. Even more striking, in the other extended story in all three Synoptic Gospels Jesus responded to the leper's plea for compassion and 'stretched out his hand and touched' the leper (Mk 1:41/Mt. 8:3/Lk. 5:13). Luke's version of the story is particularly vivid (the words in italics are unique to Luke):

> Once, when he was in one of the cities, there was a man *covered with leprosy.*
> When he saw Jesus, he *bowed with his face to the ground* and begged him,
> 'Lord, if you choose, you can make me clean.' Then Jesus stretched out his hand,
> touched him, and said, 'I do choose. Be made clean.' Immediately the leprosy
> left him. (NRV Lk. 5:12–13)

The previous chapter noted just how important is this combination of responding to a plea for compassion and touching the one perceived to be so unclean. Especially in a context of AIDS today, if there is a single element in the Synoptic healing stories that has attracted Christian commentators, it is precisely this. In sermons on the web it is noted again and again. One, for example, from a minister of the Faithful Central Bible Church in California argues passionately (albeit confusing Matthew and Luke) that:

> I suggest that if we understand Jesus' attitude about leprosy, the AIDS of His
> day, we will know how we ought to respond to it. Let the position and posture
> of Jesus be your position and posture as you deal with the issue of AIDS. The
> account of the incident in the book of Matthew says the man was 'full of leprosy,'
> which means he was in the final stages of the disease. He was dying, and praise
> the Lord, Jesus did not waste time satisfying his curiosity or passing judgment.
> The man needed help … He saw to the man's need.'[33]

The Jesuit Kenneth Overberg makes a similar, albeit more sophisticated, theological point on the web in seeking to develop 'a biblical vision of AIDS':

> Jesus … crosses the boundaries of purity laws to touch the alienated … with a
> simple touch, Jesus breaks down the barriers, challenges customs and laws that

---

[33] http://healingbeginshere.org/sremon/kculmer_sermon.htm [accessed: 26 April 2012 in 'Sermon Notes for Clergy'].

alienate, and embodies his convictions about the inclusive meaning of the reign of God (Mk 1:40–42) ... This event not only reveals Jesus' care for an individual in need but also his concern about structures of society. Jesus steps across the boundaries separating the unclean and actually touches the leper. In doing so, Jesus enters into the leper's isolation and becomes unclean.[34]

Biblical scholars might sound a note of caution about such connections. James Dunn, for example warns that 'we cannot say that Jesus touched the leper (Mk 1:41) in defiance of the purity code. And the probable testimony of 1:44 is that Jesus instructed the leper to follow the required procedure for a person with a contagious skin disease to be readmitted to society. In which case Jesus acted in accord with the purity laws.'[35] For Dunn, 'the point is rather that Jesus seems to disregard the impurity consequences in such cases, so that it may be fairly concluded that Jesus was indifferent to such purity issues'.[36] For the present theological connection this is probably sufficient. The Synoptic Jesus does indeed seem to disregard the impurity consequences of *lepra*. In this respect he differs sharply from crucial aspects of the ten-fold typology based upon social perceptions of *sara'at* in the Jewish Bible. The Synoptic Jesus also differs, despite many other similarities, specifically from the Elisha/Naaman story. Jesus touches the unclean leper, but Elisha does not (neither did the priests in Leviticus nor the rabbis subsequently). More than that the Synoptic Jesus' touching is a direct and personal response to a plea for compassion.

Amid all the continuities between these biblical stories, these discontinuities are theologically crucial in a context of AIDS today. Learning to deconstruct (socially perceived) impurity consequences is essential for developing an appropriate theological response to AIDS, just as it was to Jesus to challenge the dire impurity consequences of *lepra*. The ten-fold typology demonstrates just how dire the latter were for those nurtured within the priestly code of the Jewish Bible. *Lepra* then and AIDS in much of Africa today are both visibly shocking, involve dangerous and defiling impurity, are deemed to be inflicted by God characteristically as

---

[34] http://www.americancatholic.org/Newsletters/SFS/an1098.asp [accessed: 26 April 2012 in 'Scripture from Scratch'].

[35] James D.G. Dunn, 'Jesus and Purity: An Ongoing Debate', *New Testament Studies*, 48, 2002, p. 461.

[36] Ibid., p. 461.

punishment for sin, necessitate social exclusion, interdictions and stigmatization in the supposed interests of the common good, consume flesh uncontrollably and signal early death, leaving children as orphans and the elderly without carers. Yet the Synoptic Jesus, moved by compassion or responding to pleas for compassion, habitually disregarded such consequences when approached by those deemed to be impure by the priestly code. Even if the Synoptic Jesus is considered to be an otherwise observant Jew, instructing cleansed lepers to follow the rituals required in Leviticus 13 and 14, he still allowed compassion to trump deeply embedded scruples about dangerous and defiling impurity.

Herein I believe lies one of the sharpest theological challenges both to much secular ethics and to a number of versions of Christian ethics. As seen already, within the Synoptic healing stories compassion is not simply about feeling sorry for the vulnerable, nor is it even just about empathy, a preparedness to identify with the vulnerable. Rather, compassion is both a response to the vulnerable and a determination to help and to act in solidarity with them, sometimes at the expense of principled scruples.

HIV Prevention

But there is more to be discovered in the 'leprosy' story from Mark about *solidaristic* compassion. This is after all a story that exemplifies a central tension. The norms of the local community are simultaneously both challenged and affirmed. The complex requirements of Jewish purity laws are both broken and sustained in a single story. For those biblical scholars who see Jesus as one who overturns Jewish laws the touching of the impure 'leper' confirms a pattern displayed in Jesus' table fellowship with sinners, breaking the sabbath and being touched by the woman made impure from menstrual blood. However, for those who see Jesus as an observant Jew there is his command to "show yourself to the priest, and offer for your cleansing what Moses commanded" as is required in Leviticus 13 and 14. Confusingly the story can be read either way.[37]

My own suggestion is to see this as a story, which upholds community norms when they do not conflict with the demands of compassion, but which challenges

---

[37]   Ibid., pp. 449–467.

them when they do. Such solidaristic compassion finally trumps even strongly held and principled scruples. So Jesus upholds the formal requirements of Leviticus 13 and 14, yet as a healer "moved with pity, Jesus stretched out his hand and touched" the 'leper'. The formal requirements of the community were sustained but the personal practice was quite different.

This pattern is shown even more clearly in Luke's story of the crippled woman healed on the sabbath (Lk. 13:10–17). Viewed from the synagogue community's perspective their leader was obviously correct: 'There are six days on which work ought to be done; come on those days and be cured, and not on the sabbath day.' The woman had been crippled for 18 years. One more day after all those years would have mattered little in the interests of keeping communal norms about the sabbath. Jesus' response was astonishingly sharp: 'You hypocrites!'

In the Synoptic Gospels the charge of hypocrisy is always made by Jesus (13 times in Matthew) and is characteristically levelled at the religiously observant and their leaders. In this story the religious leader and his congregation are denounced as hypocrites, as 'actors' who say one thing but do another.[38] Or, to express this in terms of Chapter 5, they break the relationship between faith and praxis. They claim the high ground of religious faith but in the process ignore the accompanying requirements of compassionate praxis.

In the context of HIV, hypocrisy by communal leaders has been only too evident. Perhaps it is the hypocrisy of leaders hiding information about prevalence, denying the link between HIV and AIDS, or claiming that HIV only affects the gay community. Or perhaps, and most shocking among religious leaders, it is the denial, mentioned earlier, that their own community and pastors are themselves living with HIV. Communal fidelity and truth-telling are key components in HIV prevention, yet the record of churches has all too often been riddled with hypocrisy. If Jesus responded to the vulnerable with compassion, care, faith and humility, he responded to those religious people who ignored their plight with a sharp denunciation of hypocrisy. And 'when he said this, all his opponents were put to shame'.

The issue of 'shame' is especially sensitive in the context of HIV and not surprisingly 'stigmatization' and 'shame' are often elided. All too often communities, even church communities, have seen fit to 'stigmatize' and 'shame'

---

[38]   See Evans, *Saint Luke*, p. 338.

those living with HIV. Stigmatizing and shaming people who cannot undo their condition is particularly cruel and deeply harmful. Those with disabilities have all too often been stigmatized in this way. The history of 'leprosy' demonstrates this all too clearly. Emphatically Jesus did not do that to the woman in this story. Yet he did 'put to shame' the community that had failed to show her solidaristic compassion.

Perhaps 'stigmatization' and 'shame' are not always the same even in the context of HIV. Perhaps communities that stigmatize those living with HIV, or that condone predatory male sexual behaviour that helps to spread HIV, can appropriately be shamed. This does appear to be possible in the so-called story of the 'woman who had been caught in adultery (John 8:2–11). It is generally recognized that this is indeed an ancient story about Jesus but that it did not originally form a part of the Fourth Gospel.[39] In the context of understanding compassion it is particularly important although it requires sensitive interpretation.

Once again it is the religiously observant who take the moral high ground but are finally put to shame by Jesus. This time they are not defending the sabbath. They have found a woman who has apparently flouted sexual norms: 'Teacher, this woman was caught in the very act of committing adultery.' Like many religious communities today it is sexual activity that is identified as being especially sinful. In the story Jesus does not deny the role of sin. The woman herself is finally told 'from now on do not sin again' and whatever she has done is not condoned. Yet she is explicitly not condemned by Jesus and everyone else is reminded that they are not 'without sin'. She is not stigmatized as an 'adulterer' but the religious community is apparently shamed, going away 'one by one, beginning with the elders'. They had been challenged by Jesus in public and, as a direct result, put to shame.

Taken together a socio-critical reading of these stories suggests that the Synoptic Jesus was prepared both to affirm and to challenge religious communities. In them he affirmed communal practices when they did not conflict with the demands of solidaristic compassion but challenged them sharply when they did. The virtues identified at an individual level in the healing stories – compassion, care, faith and humility – are supplemented at a communal level

---

[39] C.K. Barrett, *The Gospel According to St John: An Introduction with Commentary and Notes on the Greek Text*, London: SPCK, 1967, pp. 490–493.

with sharp challenges even denunciations. These virtues in tension might help to shape perceptions of AIDS.

Perhaps socially contextualized theology, filtered through a sociological gaze, really can still make an important contribution to such a global challenge.

Afterword

It will be evident from the previous chapter that my project is far from complete. How indeed could it ever be? Attention to religious virtues in the public forum of Western, pluralist countries raises important, but as yet largely unresolved, questions about how different faith traditions can responsibly interact for the common good. Some Christian theologians will strongly object to *any* such interaction, arguing that Christians should strive to create a society that is wholly Christian rather than seek to interact publicly with other faith or secular traditions. For them Christian faith alone offers 'truth'.

By now it will be obvious that I profoundly disagree. I regard 'Christian faith' itself as pluralistic and see continuities between various forms of Christian faith and various forms of Jewish and Muslim faith, as well as resonances (and dissonances) with various forms of Indian faith. I am also conscious of the malevolent connections between faith and power that soon emerge once particular faith or secular ideologies gain exclusive political control. The track record of medieval Christendom or Islamists today is hardly more encouraging than that of Soviet Union Stalinists in the mid twentieth century. Unchecked totalitarian ideologies whether religious or not – as Mannheim was well aware – all too readily persecute those whom they consider to be 'deviants'.

However this is to be achieved, I believe that there is an important task for theologians across different faith traditions to undertake. I am at one with Lisa Sowle Cahill in believing that: 'Global realities of human inequality, poverty, violence, and ecological destruction call for a twenty-first-century Christian response that can link the power of the gospel to cross-cultural and interreligious cooperation for change.'[1] This task might be called *Faith and Good Global Citizenship*. In a social context shaped in part by both aggressive secularity and fundamentalist resurgence (mutually feeding each other), theologians working

---

[1]   Lisa Sowle Cahill, *Global Justice, Christology and Christian Ethics*, New York and Cambridge: Cambridge University Press, 2013, p. 1.

together for the common good might offer a radically different and decidedly more eirenic perspective. Together we could focus upon constructive ways that different forms of faith might still contribute to good global citizenship – while remaining vigilant about the weaknesses and temptations to power of faith traditions.

If my three volumes of *Sociological Theology* encourage others to engage in this crucial task, I will be more than satisfied.

Works Cited

Aleshire, Daniel and Richard L. Gorsuch, 'Christian Faith and Prejudice: Review of Research', *Journal for the Scientific Study of Religion*, 13:3, 281–307, 1974.

Bäckström, Anders and Grace Davie, 'The WREP Project: Genesis, Structure and Scope', in Anders Bäckström, Grace Davie, Ninna Edgarth and Per Pettersson (eds), *Welfare and Religion in 21st Century Europe*, Volume 1, Farnham, Surrey: Ashgate, 2010.

Baillie, D.M., *God Was in Christ*, London: Faber and Faber, 1956.

Baillie, John, *God's Will for Church and Nation: Reprinted from the Reports of the Commission for the Interpretation of God's Will in the Present Crisis as Presented to the General Assembly of the Church of Scotland during the War Years*, London: SCM Press, 1946.

Bainton, Roland H., *Christian Attitudes toward War and Peace*, Nashville, TN: Abingdon, 1960.

Baker, Chris, with Jonathan Miles-Watson, 'Faith and Traditional Capitals: Defining the Public Scope of Spiritual and Religious Capital: A Literature Review', *Implicit Religion*, 13:1, 17–69, 2010.

Barber, Bernard, 'Toward a New View of the Sociology of Knowledge', in Lewis A. Coser (ed.), *The Idea of Social Structure*, San Diego, CA: Harcourt Brace Jovanovich, 1975.

Baron, Stephen (ed.), with John Field and Tom Schuller, *Social Capital: Critical Perspectives*, Oxford: Oxford University Press, 2000.

Barrett, C.K., *The Gospel According to St John: An Introduction with Commentary and Notes on the Greek Text*, London: SPCK, 1967.

Barton, John (ed.), *The Cambridge Companion to Biblical Interpretation*, Cambridge: Cambridge University Press, 1998.

Baum, Gregory, *Religion and Alienation: A Theological Reading of Sociology*, New York: Paulist Press, 1975 [reprinted Ottawa: Novalis, 2006].

——*The Social Imperative: Essays on the Critical Issues that Confront the Christian Churches*, New York: Paulist Press, 1979.

——*Theology and Society*, New York: Paulist Press, 1986.

——*Essays in Critical Theology*, Kansas City, MO: Sheed and Ward, 1994.

Becker, Penny Edgell, *Congregations in Conflict*, Cambridge and New York: Cambridge University Press, 1999.

Beckford, James A., 'The Embryonic Stage of a Religious Sect's Development: The Jehovah's Witnesses', in Michael Hill (ed.), *A Sociological Yearbook of Religion in Britain*, SCM Press, 11–32, 1972.

——*The Trumpet of Prophecy*, Oxford: Blackwell, 1975.

Bentley, Peter and Philip J. Hughes, *Australian Life and the Christian Faith: Facts and Figures*, Kew, Victoria, Australia: Christian Research Association, 1998.

Berger, Peter L., *The Precarious Vision*, New York: Doubleday, 1961.

——*The Social Reality of Religion*, London: Faber and Faber, 1969 [US title: *The Sacred Canopy of Religion*, Garden City, NY: Doubleday, 1967]].

——*A Rumour of Angels*, Garden City, NY: Doubleday, 1969 and Harmondsworth, Middlesex: Penguin, 1970.

——, with Thomas Luckmann, *The Social Construction of Reality*, New York: Anchor, 1966 and London: Penguin, 1971.

——, with Brigitte Berger and Hansfried Kellner, *The Homeless Mind: Modernization and Consciousness*, New York: Random House and London: Penguin 1973.

——'Second Thoughts on Defining Religion', *Journal for the Scientific Study of Religion*, 13:2, 125–134, 1974.

——*Facing up to Modernity: Excursions in Society, Politics and Religion*, New York: Basic Books and London: Penguin, 1977.

——*The Heretical Imperative: Contemporary Possibilities of Religious Affirmation*, New York: Anchor, 1979 and London: Collins, 1980.

——*A Far Glory: The Quest for Faith in an Age of Credulity*, New York: Anchor Books, 1992.

——(ed.), *The Desecularization of the World*, Grand Rapids, MI: Eerdmans, 1999.

Black, Alan W., 'Religion and Environmentally Protective Behaviour in Australia', *Social Compass*, 44:3, 401–412, 1997.

Bonino, José Miguez, *Revolutionary Theology Comes of Age*, London: SPCK, 1975 [US title: *Doing Theology in a Revolutionary Situation*, Minneapolis, MN: Fortress, 1975].

Borg, Marcus J., *Conflict, Holiness and Politics in the Teaching of Jesus*, 2nd edition, Harrisburg, PA: Trinity Press International, 1998.

Bouma, Gary D., 'Recent "Protestant Ethic" Research', *Journal for the Scientific Study of Religion*, 21:2, 141–155, 1973.

——, with Beverly R. Dixon, *The Religious Factor in Australian Life*, MARC, Australia: World Vision and the Zadok Centre, 1986.

Bridge, A.C., *Images of God*, London: Hodder & Stoughton, 1960.

Brock, Peter, *Twentieth-Century Pacifism*, New York: Van Nostrand Reinhold, 1970.

——*Pacifism in Europe to 1914*, Princeton, NJ: Princeton University Press, 1972.

Brown, Callum, 'Did Urbanisation Secularise Britain?', *Urban History Yearbook*, 1–14, 1988.

——*The Death of Christian Britain*, London: Routledge, 2001.

Brown, Colin, *That You May Believe: Miracles and Faith Then and Now*, Grand Rapids, MI: William B. Eerdmans, 1985.

Browne, S.G., *Leprosy in the Bible*, London: Christian Medical Fellowship, 1970.

Bruce, Steve, *The Rise and Fall of the New Christian Right: Protestant Politics in America 1978–88*, Oxford: Clarendon, 1988.

——*A House Divided: Protestantism, Schism and Secularization*, London: Routledge, 1989.

——*Religion in the Modern World: From Cathedrals to Cults*, Oxford: Oxford University Press, 1996.

——*Choice and Religion: A Critique of Rational Choice Theory*, Oxford: Oxford University Press, 1999.

——*God Is Dead: Secularization in the West*, Oxford and Malden, MS: Blackwell, 2002.

——*Politics and Religion*, Oxford: Polity Press, 2003.

——*Secularization: In Defence of an Unfashionable Theory*, Oxford: Oxford University Press, 2011.

Brunner, Emil, *Justice and the Social Order*, Leicester: Lutterworth, 1945.

Bultmann, Rudolf, 'New Testament and Mythology', in H.W. Bartsch (ed.), *Kerygma and Myth*, London: SPCK, 1953.

Buyx, Alena, with Barbara Prainsack, *Solidarity: Reflections on an Emerging Concept in Bioethics*, London: Nuffield Council on Bioethics, 2011.

Cadoux, C.J., *The Early Christian Attitude to War*, London: Headley Brothers, 1919.

Cahill, Lisa Sowle, *Global Justice, Christology and Christian Ethics*, New York and Cambridge: Cambridge University Press, 2013.

Campbell, Colin, 'The Cult, the Cultic Milieu and Secularization', in Michael Hill (ed.), *A Sociological Yearbook of Religion in Britain*, London: SCM Press, 119–136, 1972.

Campbell, David E., *American Grace: How Religion Divides and Unites Us*, with Robert D. Putnam, New York: Simon & Schuster, 2010.

Carrette, Jeremy, 'The Paradox of Globalisation: Quakers, Religious NGOs and the United Nations', in B. Hefner, J. Hutchinson, S. Mels and C. Timmerman (eds), *The Local and the Global in Renegotiating Religious Praxis*, London: Routledge, 2013.

Carroll, Robert P., *When Prophecy Failed*, London: SCM Press, 1979.

Casanova, José, *Public Religions in the Modern World*, Chicago: University of Chicago Press, 1994.

Catto, Rebecca (ed.), with Linda Woodhead, *Religion and Change in Modern Britain*, London: Routledge, 2012.

Clark, O. Fielding, *For Christ's Sake*, London: Religious Education Press, 1963.

Clements, Kevin, *The Churches and Social Policy: A Study in the Relationship of Ideology to Action*, Wellington, New Zealand: Victoria University of Wellington, 1970.

——'The Religious Variable: Dependent, Independent or Interdependent?', in Michael Hill (ed.), *A Sociological Yearbook of Religion in Britain*, London: SCM Press, 4, 1971.

Coser, Lewis A. (ed.), *The Idea of Social Structure*, San Diego, CA: Harcourt Brace Jovanovich, 1975.

Cottingham, John, *Why Believe?* London: Continuum, 2009.

Cullmann, Oscar, *The Christology of the New Testament*, London: SCM Press, 1959.

Curtis, J.E. (ed.), with J.W. Petras, *The Sociology of Knowledge: A Reader*, London: Duckworth, 1970.

Dalai Lama, *Ethics for the New Millennium*, New York: Riverhead Books, 1999.

Davie, Grace, *Religion in Britain since 1945: Believing without Belonging*, Oxford: Blackwell, 1994.

——*Religion in Modern Europe: A Memory Mutates*, Oxford: Oxford University Press, 2000.

——*Europe: The Exceptional Case*, London: Darton, Longman & Todd, 2002.

——*The Sociology of Religion*, London: Sage, 2007.

——, with Anders Bäckström, 'The WREP Project: Genesis, Structure and Scope', in Anders Bäckström, Grace Davie, Ninna Edgarth and Per Pettersson (eds), *Welfare and Religion in 21st Century Europe*, Volume 1, Farnham, Surrey: Ashgate, 2010.

Davies, Douglas J., *Meaning and Salvation in Religious Studies*, Leiden: E.J. Brill, 1984.

Davies, W.D. and Dale C. Allison Jr, *A Critical Commentary on The Gospel According to Saint Matthew*, 3 volumes, Edinburgh: T&T Clark, 1991.

Dawkins, Richard, *The God Delusion*, London: Bantam Press, 2006, and Boston: Houghton Mifflin, 2008.

Day, Abby, *Believing in Belonging*, Oxford: Oxford University Press, 2011.

Dekker, Paul, Peter Ester and Masja Nas, 'Religion, Culture and Environmental Concern: An Empirical Cross-national Analysis', *Social Compass*, 44:3, 443–458, 1997.

Dennett, Daniel, *Breaking the Spell: Religion as a Natural Phenomenon*, New York: Viking, and London: Allen Lane, 2006.

Derrida, Jacques, *Psyché: Inventions de l'autre*, Paris: Editions Galilée, 1987.

Dinham, Adam, with Robert Furbey, Richard Farnell, Doreen Finneron and Guy Wilkinson, *Faith as Social Capital: Connecting or Dividing?*, Bristol: Policy Press, 2006.

——*Faith in Social Capital after the Debt Crisis*, London: Palgrave Macmillan, 2012.

——, with Robert Jackson, 'Religion, Welfare and Education', in Linda Woodhead and Rebecca Catto (eds), *Religion and Change in Modern Britain*, London: Routledge, 272–294, 2012.

Donnison, David and Caroline Bryson, 'Matters of Life and Death: Attitudes to Euthanasia', in Roger Jowell, John Curtice, Alison Park, Lindsay Brook and Katarina Thomson (eds), *British Social Attitudes the 13th Report*, Dartmouth, Hants: Social and Community Planning Research, 161–183, 1996.

Douglas, Mary, *Leviticus as Literature*, Oxford: Oxford University Press, 1999.

Dunn, James D.G., *Unity and Diversity in the New Testament*, London: SCM Press, 1977.

——, with James P. Mackey, *New Testament Theology in Dialogue*, London: SPCK 1987.

——'Jesus and Purity: An Ongoing Debate', *New Testament Studies*, 48:4, 449–467, 2002.

Durkheim, Emile, *Suicide*, London: Routledge & Kegan Paul, 1970 [1897].

——*The Elementary Forms of the Religious Life*, London: George Allen & Unwin, 1976 [1915].

Eckberg, Douglas Lee and T. Jean Blocker, 'Christianity, Environmentalism, and the Theoretical Problem of Fundamentalism', *Journal for the Scientific Study of Religion*, 35:4, 343–355, 1996.

Edwards, David L. and John A.T. Robinson (eds), *The Honest to God Debate*, London: SCM Press, 1963.

Engels, Frederick, with Karl Marx, *The German Ideology*, ed. C.J. Arthur, London: Lawrence & Wishart, 1970 (1846).

Evans, Christopher F., *Saint Luke*, London and Philadelphia, PA: SCM Press and Trinity Press, 1990.

Field, John (ed.), with Stephen Baron and Tom Schuller, *Social Capital: Critical Perspectives*, Oxford: Oxford University Press 2000.

——*Social Capital*, London and New York: Routledge, 2003.

Fierro, Alfredo, *The Militant Gospel*, Maryknoll, NY: Orbis, and London: SCM Press, 1977.

Fletcher, Joseph, *Situation Ethics*, Philadelphia, PA: Westminster, and London: SCM Press, 1966.

Francis, Leslie J., with William K. Kay, *Teenage Religion and Values*, Leominster, Herefordshire: Gracewing Fowler Wright Books, 1995.

Frank, Dan, *The Word and the World: Religion after the Sociology of Knowledge*, London: Continuum, 2007.

Furbey, Robert, with Adam Dinham, Richard Farnell, Doreen Finneron and Guy Wilkinson, *Faith as Social Capital: Connecting or Dividing?*, Bristol: Policy Press, 2006.

Gill, Robin, 'British Theology as a Sociological Variable', in Michael Hill (ed.), *A Sociological Yearbook of Religion in Britain*, London: SCM Press, 1–12, 1974.

——*The Social Context of Theology*, Oxford: Mowbrays, 1975.

——*Theology and Social Structure*, Oxford: Mowbrays, 1977.

——(ed.), *Theology and Sociology: A Reader*, London: Geoffrey Chapman, 1987, New York: Paulist Press, 1988 [revised edition London: Cassell, 1996].

——*Competing Convictions*, London: SCM Press, 1989.

——*The Myth of the Empty Church*, London: SPCK, 1993 [revised as *The 'Empty' Church Revisited*, Aldershot, Hants: Ashgate, 2003].

——*Churchgoing and Christian Ethics*, Cambridge: Cambridge University Press, 1999.

——*A Textbook of Christian Ethics*, 3rd edition, London: T&T Clark, 2006.

——*Health Care and Christian Ethics*, Cambridge: Cambridge University Press, 2006.

Glasner, Peter E., *The Sociology of Secularisation*, London: Routledge & Kegan Paul, 1977.

Glock, Charles Y. and Rodney Stark, *Christian Beliefs and Anti-Semitism*, New York: Harper, 1966.

——(ed.), with Phillip E. Hammond, *Beyond the Classics: Essays in the Scientific Study of Religion*, New York: Harper & Row, 1973.

Gorer, Geoffrey, *Exploring English Character*, London: Cresset Press, 1955.

Gorringe, T.J., *The Common Good and the Global Emergence: God and the Built Environment*, Cambridge: Cambridge University Press, 2011.

Gorsuch, Richard L. and Daniel Aleshire, 'Christian Faith and Prejudice: Review of Research', *Journal for the Scientific Study of Religion*, 13:3, 281–307, 1974.

Greeley, Andrew M., *Unsecular Man: The Persistence of Religion*, New York: Schocken Books, 1972 [English title: *The Persistence of Religion*, London: SCM Press, 1973].

——'Religion and Attitudes toward the Environment', *Journal for the Scientific Study of Religion*, 32:1, 19–28, 1993.

Gutierrez, Gustavo, *A Theology of Liberation*, London: SCM Press, 1974.

Hadaway, C. Kirk, Penny Long Marler and M. Chavers, 'What the Polls Don't Show: A Closer Look at US Church Attendance', *American Sociological Review*, 58, 741–752, 1993.

——, with Robin Gill, 'Is Religious Belief Declining in Britain?', *Journal for the Scientific Study of Religion*, 37:3, 507–516, 1998.

Hallett, Garth L., *Priorities and Christian Ethics*, New York and Cambridge: Cambridge University Press, 1998.

Halmos, Paul, *The Faith of the Counsellors*, London: Constable, 1965.

Halpern, David, *Social Capital*, Cambridge: Polity, 2005.

Hammond, Phillip E. (ed.), with Charles Y. Glock, *Beyond the Classics: Essays in the Scientific Study of Religion*, New York: Harper & Row, 1973.

Harris, Margaret, *Organizing God's Work: Challenges for Churches and Synagogues*, Basingstoke, Hants: Macmillan and New York: St. Martin's Press, 1998.

Hick, John, 'Theology and Verification', in John Hick (ed.), *The Existence of God*, London: Macmillan, 1964.

Hill, Michael (ed.), *A Sociological Yearbook of Religion in Britain*, London: SCM Press, 4, 1971.

——(ed.), *A Sociological Yearbook of Religion in Britain*, SCM Press, 5, 1972.

——(ed.), *A Sociological Yearbook of Religion in Britain*, SCM Press, 7, 1974.

Hinchliff, Peter, 'Religion and Politics: The Harsh Reality', in Haddon Willmer (ed.), *Christian Faith and Political Hopes: A Reply to E.R. Norman*, London: Epworth, 1979.

Hollenbach, David, *The Common Good and Christian Ethics*, Cambridge: Cambridge University Press, 2002.

Hooker, Morna D., *The Gospel According to St Mark*, London: A & C Black, 1991.

Hornsby-Smith, Michael P. and Michael Procter, 'Catholic Identity, Religious Context and Environmental Values in Western Europe: Evidence from the European Values Surveys', *Social Compass*, 42:1, 27–34, 1995.

Howes, Graham, 'A Response to Dan Frank', in Dan Frank, *The Word and the World: Religion after the Sociology of Knowledge*, London: Continuum, 57–97, 2007.

Hughes, Philip J. and Peter Bentley, *Australian Life and the Christian Faith: Facts and Figures*, Kew, Victoria, Australia: Christian Research Association, 1998.

Jackson, M.J., *The Sociology of Religion*, London: Batsford, 1974.

Jenkins, David, *Guide to the Debate about God*, London: SCM Press, 1966.

Jones, G. Vaughan, *Christology and Myth in the New Testament*, London: Allen & Unwin, 1956.

Johnson, Byron R., Ralph Brett Tompkins and Derek Webb, *Objective Hope: Assessing the Effectiveness of Faith-Based Organizations: A Review of the Literature*, Philadelphia: Center for Research on Religion and Urban Civil Society, University of Pennsylvania, 2001 [www.crrucs.org].

Johnston, Michael, with Douglas Wood, 'Right and Wrong in Public and Private Life', in Roger Jowell and Sharon Witherspoon (eds), *British Social Attitudes: The 2nd Report*, Aldershot, Hants: Dartmouth, Social and Community Planning Research, 1985.

——'The Price of Honesty', in Roger Jowell, Sharon Witherspoon and Lindsay Brook (eds), *British Social Attitudes: The 5th Report*, Aldershot, Hants: Dartmouth, Social and Community Planning Research, 1988.

Kay, William K., with Leslie J. Francis, *Teenage Religion and Values*, Leominster, Herefordshire: Gracewing Fowler Wright Books, 1995.

Kee, Alistair (ed.), *A Reader in Political Theology*, London: SCM Press, 1974.

——*Marx and the Failure of Liberation Theology*, Philadelphia, PA and London: Trinity Press International and SCM Press, 1990.

Kee, Howard Clark, *Miracle in the Early Christian World*, New Haven: Yale University Press, 1983.

——*Medicine, Miracle and Magic in New Testament Times*, Cambridge and New York: Cambridge University Press, 1986.

Kerkhofs, Jan, 'Between "Christendom" and "Christianity"', *Journal of Empirical Theology*, 1:2, 88–101, 1988.

King, Christine E., *The Nazi State and the New Religions: Five Case Studies in Non-Conformity*, New York: Edwin Mellen, 1982.

——'Jehovah's Witnesses under Nazism', in Michael Berenbaum (ed.), *A Mosaic of Victims: Non-Jews Persecuted and Murdered by the Nazis*, New York: New York University Press, 1990.

—— 'Responses outside the Mainstream Catholic and Protestant Traditions', in C. Rittner, S.D. Smith and I. Steinfeldt (eds), *The Holocaust and the Christian World*, London: Kuperard, 2000.

Koenig, Harold G., Michael E. McCullough and David B. Larson, *Handbook of Religion and Health*, New York: Oxford University Press, 2001.

Knott, Kim, with Jolyon Mitchell, 'The Changing Faces of Media and Religion', in Linda Woodhead and Rebecca Catto (eds), *Religion and Change in Modern Britain*, London: Routledge, 243–264, 2012.

Knox, John, *The Church and the Reality of Christ*, New York: Harper & Row, 1962, and London: Collins, 1963.

Lam, P-Y, 'Religion and Civil Culture: A Cross-National Study of Voluntary Association Membership', *Journal for the Scientific Study of Religion*, 45:2, 177–193, 2006.

Lee, Lucy, 'Religion', in *British Social Attitudes 28th Report*, London: Sage, 173–184, 2011.

Lenski, Gerhard E., *The Religious Factor*, New York: Doubleday, 1961.

Lindblom, Johannes, *Prophecy in Ancient Israel*, Oxford: Blackwell, 1962.

Luckmann, Thomas, with Peter L. Berger, *The Social Construction of Reality*, New York: Anchor, 1966, and London: Penguin, 1971.

Lynch, Gordon, *The Sacred in the Modern World: A Cultural Sociological Approach*, Oxford: Oxford University Press, 2012.

MacCulloch, Diarmaid, *A History of Christianity: The First Three Thousand Years*, London: Allen Lane, 2009.

MacGregor, G.H.C., *The New Testament Basis of Pacifism*, London: James Clarke, 1936.

MacIntyre, Alasdair, *A Short History of Ethics*, London: Routledge & Kegan Paul, 1967.

——*Against the Self-Images of the Age*, London: Duckworth, 1971.

——*After Virtue: A Study in Moral Theory*, 2nd edition, London: Duckworth, 1985. [1981].

——*Dependent Rational Animals*, London: Duckworth, 1999.

M'Neile, A.H., *The Gospel According to St. Matthew*, London and New York: Macmillan and St Martin's Press, 1965.

Macquarrie, John, *The Scope of Demythologizing*, London: SCM Press, 1960.

——*God-Talk*, London: SCM Press, 1967.

Malina, Bruce J., *The New Testament World*, 3rd edition, Louisville, KY: Westminster John Knox, 2001.

Mannheim, Karl, *Ideology and Utopia*, London: Routledge & Kegan, 1936.

Marshall, Christopher D., *Faith as a Theme in Mark's Narrative*, Cambridge: Cambridge University Press, 1989.

Marshall, I. Howard, *The Gospel of Luke*, Exeter: Paternoster, 1978.

Martin, David, *Pacifism: An Historical and Sociological Study*, London: Routledge & Kegan Paul, 1965.

——*The Religious and the Secular*, London: Routledge & Kegan Paul, 1969.

——*Tracts against the Times*, Cambridge: Lutterworth, 1973.

——'The Secularisation Question', *Theology*, 76:630, 86, 1973.

——'Ethical Commentary and Political Decision', *Theology*, 76:638, 527–536, 1973.

——*A General Theology of Secularization*, Oxford: Blackwell, 1978.

——*Reflections on Sociology and Theology*, Oxford: Clarendon Press, 1996.

——*Christian Language and its Mutations: Essays in Sociological Understanding*, Aldershot, Hants: Ashgate, 2002.

——*On Secularization: Towards a Revised General Theory*, Aldershot, Hants: Ashgate, 2005.

——*The Future of Christianity: Reflections on Violence, Democracy, Religion and Secularization*, Farnham, Surrey: Ashgate, 2011.

Martin, Roderick, 'Sociology and Theology', in D.E.H. Whitley and R. Martin (eds), *Sociology, Theology and Conflict*, Oxford: Blackwell, 1969.

Marx, Karl, with Frederick Engels, *The German Ideology*, ed. C.J. Arthur, London: Lawrence & Wishart, 1970 (1846).

Mascall, Eric L., *Existence and Analogy*, London: Darton, Longman & Todd, 1949.

——*Up and Down in Adria*, London: Faith Press, 1962.

——*Theology and Images*, Oxford: Mowbrays, 1963.

——*The Secularisation of Christianity*, London: Libra, 1967.

Mash, Rachel and Robert J. Mash, 'A quasi-experimental evaluation of an HIV prevention programme by peer education in the Anglican Church of the Western Cape, South Africa. BMJ Open 2012;2:e000638.doi:10.1136/bmjopen-2011–000638.

Mass Observation, *Puzzled People: A Study of Popular Attitudes to Religion, Ethics, Progress and Politics in a London Borough*, London: Gollancz, 1947.

Maurice, F.D., *The Kingdom of Christ, or, Hints on the Principles, Ordinances and Constitution of the Catholic Church: In Letters to a Member of the Society of Friends*, Everyman edition, London: J.M. Dent, 1906 (1837).

——*The Church and Family*, London: Macmillan, 1850.

——*The Life of Frederick Denison Maurice Chiefly Told in His Own Letters*, London: Macmillan, 1884.

Mealand, David, *Poverty and Expectation in the Gospels*, London: SPCK, 1980.

Mehl, Roger, *The Sociology of Protestantism*, London: SCM Press, 1970.

Melinsky, M.A.H., *Healing Miracles: An Examination from History and Experience of the Place of Miracle in Christian Thought and Medical Practice*, Oxford: Mowbrays, 1968.

Milbank, John, *Theology and Social Theory: Beyond Secular Reason*, Oxford: Blackwell, 1990 [revised 2006].

Milford, T.R., *The Valley of Decision: The Christian Dilemma in the Nuclear Age*, London: British Council of Churches, 1961.

Miranda, José Porfirio, *Marx and the Bible*, Maryknoll, NY: Orbis, 1974.

Mitchell, Jolyon, with Kim Knott, 'The Changing Faces of Media and Religion', in Linda Woodhead and Rebecca Catto (eds), *Religion and Change in Modern Britain*, London: Routledge, 243–264, 2012.

Moule, C.F.D., *The Origin of Christology*, Cambridge: Cambridge University Press, 1977.

Murphy, Mark C., *God and Moral Law: On the Theistic Explanation of Morality*, Oxford: Oxford University Press, 2011.

Nelson, Geoffrey K., 'The Concept of the Cult', *The Sociological Review*, 16:3, 351–362, 1968.

Neusner, Jacon, *The Rabbinic Traditions about the Pharisees Before 70: Part I The Masters*, Leiden: E.J. Brill, 1971.

Niebuhr, H. Richard, *The Social Sources of Denominationalism*, New York: Henry Holt, 1929.

Niebuhr, Reinhold, *Moral Man and Immoral Society*, New York: Scribner, 1934.

Nolland, John, *The Gospel of Matthew*, Grand Rapids, MI: William B. Eerdmans, 2005.

Norman, Edward, *Christianity and the World Order: The BBC Reith Lectures, 1978*, Oxford: Oxford University Press, 1979.

Northcott, Michael S., *The Environment and Christian Ethics*, Cambridge: Cambridge University Press, 1996.

——*Climate Change and Christian Ethics*, Cambridge: Cambridge University Press, forthcoming 2013.

Noth, Martin, *Leviticus*, London: SCM Press, 1965.

Owen, Hugh Parry, *Keygma and Myth and Revelation and Existence*, Cardiff: University of Wales, 1957.

Packer, J.I., *Keep Yourselves from Idols*, London: Church Book Room Press, 1963.

Parsons, Talcott, *The Social System*, Glencoe, IL: The Free Press and London: Routledge & Kegan Paul, 1951.

——*Sociological Theory and Modern Society*, New York: Free Press, 1967.

Percy, Martyn, *Shaping the Church: The Promise of Implicit Theology*, Farnham, Surrey: Ashgate, 2010.

Pettersson, Per, 'Majority Churches as Agents of European Welfare', in Anders Bäckström, Grace Davie, Ninna Edgarth and Per Pettersson (eds), *Welfare and Religion in 21st Century Europe*, Volume 2, Farnham, Surrey: Ashgate, 2011.

Pilch, John 'Understanding Healing in the Social World of Early Christianity', *Biblical Theology Bulletin*, 22:1, 26–33, 1992.

——*Healing in the New Testament: Insights from Medical and Mediterranean Anthropology*, Minneapolis, MN: Fortress Press, 2000.

Prainsack, Barbara and Alena Buyx, *Solidarity: Reflections on an Emerging Concept in Bioethics*, London: Nuffield Council on Bioethics, 2011.

Preston, Ronald, 'Vision and Utopia', a letter in *Theology*, 81:684, 1978.

Prochaska, Frank, *Christianity and the Social Service in Modern Britain: The Disinherited Spirit*, Oxford: Oxford University Press, 2006.

Putnam, Robert D., *Bowling Alone: The Collapse and Revival of American Community*, New York: Simon & Schuster, 2000.

——, with David E. Campbell, *American Grace: How Religion Divides and Unites Us*, New York: Simon & Schuster, 2010.

Ramsey, A. Michael, *F. D. Maurice and the Conflicts of Modern Theology*, Cambridge: Cambridge University Press, 1951.

——*Images Old and New*, London: SPCK, 1963.

——*Sacred and Secular*, London: Longman, 1964.

——*God, Christ and the World*, London: SCM Press, 1969.

Ramsey, Ian T., *Religious Language*, London: SCM Press, 1957.

Ramsey, Paul, *Deeds and Rules in Christian Ethics*, Edinburgh: Scottish Journal of Theology Occasional Paper No. 11, 1965.

——*Deeds and Rules in Christian Ethics*, New York: Scribners, 1967 [expanded version].

Raven, Charles E., *Is War Obsolete?*, London: George Allen & Unwin, 1935.

——*War and the Christian*, London: Garland, 1938.

——*Lessons of the Prince of Peace*, London: Longmans Green, 1942.

——*The Theological Basis of Pacifism*, London: The Fellowship Publications, 1951.

Rex, John, *Key Problems of Sociological Theory*, London: Routledge & Kegan Paul, 1961.

Rhymes, Douglas, *No New Morality*, London: Constable, 1964.

Richardson, Alan, *Four Anchors from the Stern*, London: SCM Press, 1963.

——*Religion in Contemporary Debate*, London: SCM Press, 1966.

Robbins, Vernon, *The Tapestry of Early Christian Discourse: Rhetoric, Society and Ideology*, London: Routledge, 1996.

Robertson, Roland (ed.), *Sociology of Religion*, Harmondsworth, Middlesex: Penguin, 1969.

Robinson, John A.T., *On Being the Church in the World*, London: SCM Press, 1960.

——*Liturgy Coming to Life*, London: SCM Press, 1963.

——*Honest to God*, London: SCM Press, 1963.

——(ed.), with David L. Edwards, *The Honest to God Debate*, London: SCM Press, 1963.

——*Christian Morals Today*, London: SCM Booklet, 1964.

——*The New Reformation?*, London: SCM Press, 1965.

——*But That I Can't Believe*, London: SCM Press, 1967.

——*Exploration into God*, London: SCM Press, 1967.

Robinson, J.M., *The Problem of History in Mark*, London: SCM Press, 1957.

Sandel, Michael, Reith Lecture 4, Radio 4, 30 June 2009: http://www.bbc.co.uk/programmes/b00kt7sh [accessed: 26 April 2012].

Scharf, Betty, *The Sociological Study of Religion*, London: Hutchinson, 1970.

Scruton, Roger, *The Face of God*, London: Continuum, 2012.

Segundo, Juan Luis, *The Liberation of Theology*, Maryknoll, NY: Orbis, and London: Macmillan, 1977.

Sloan, R.P., E. Bagiella and T. Powell, 'Viewpoint: Religion, Spirituality and Medicine', *The Lancet*, 353, 664–667, 1999.

Smidt, Corwin (ed.), *Religion as Social Capital: Producing the Common Good*, Waco, TX: Baylor University Press, 2004.

Stark, Rodney, with Charles Y. Glock, *Christian Beliefs and Anti-Semitism*, New York: Harper, 1966.

Stark, Werner, *The Sociology of Knowledge*, London: Routledge & Kegan Paul, 1958.

Stassen, Glen (ed.) *Just Peacemaking*, Cleveland, OH: Pilgrim Press, 1999.

Taylor, Charles, *Sources of the Self: The Making of Modern Identity*, Cambridge, MS: Harvard University Press, 1989.

——*A Secular Age*, Cambridge, MA: Harvard University Press, 2007.

Taylor, Vincent, *The Gospel According to St Mark*, London: Macmillan, 1959.

Temple, William, *Christianity and the Social Order*, London: Pelican, 1956 [re-published, London: SPCK, 1976].

Theissen, Gerd, *The Miracle Stories of the Early Christian Tradition*, Edinburgh and Philadelphia, PA: T&T Clark and Fortress Press, 1983 [German original 1974].

Timms, Noel (ed.), with Mark Abrams and David Gerard, *Values and Social Change in Britain: Studies in the Contemporary Values of Modern Society*, London: Macmillan, 1985.

——*Family and Citizenship: Values in Contemporary Britain*, Aldershot, Hants: Dartmouth, 1992.

Towler, Robert, *Homo Religiosus: Sociological Problems in the Study of Religion*, London: Constable, 1974.

——*The Need for Certainty: A Sociological Study of Conventional Religion*, London: Routledge & Kegan Paul, 1984.

Troeltsch, Ernst, *The Social Teaching of the Christian Churches*, 2 volumes, New York: Harper, 1960 [1912].

Turner, Bryan S., 'The Sociological Explanation of Ecumenicalism', in C.L. Mitton (ed.), *The Social Sciences and the Churches*, Edinburgh: T&T Clark, 231–245, 1972.

United Reformed Church, *Non-Violent Action*, London: SCM Press, 1973.

van Buren, Paul, *The Secular Meaning of the Gospel*, New York: Macmillan and London: SCM Press, 1963.

Vidler, Alec R., *Witness to the Light: F.D. Maurice's Message for Today*, New York: Scribner, 1948.

——(ed.), *Soundings*, Cambridge: Cambridge University Press, 1962.

von Rad, G., *Old Testament Theology*, Volume 2, Edinburgh: Oliver & Boyd, 1965.

Wallis, Roy, *The Road to Total Freedom: A Sociological Analysis of Scientology*, London: Heinemann, 1976 and New York: Columbia University Press, 1977.

Ward, Graham, *Barth, Derrida and the Language of Theology*, Cambridge: Cambridge University Press, 1995.

——'Theology and Postmodernism', *Theology*, 100:794, November, 1997.

——*True Religion*, Oxford: Blackwell, 2003.

Weber, Max, *The Protestant Ethic and the 'Spirit' of Capitalism*, New York: Scribner, 1958 [1905].

——*The Sociology of Religion*, London: Methuen, 1965 [1920].

Welty, Eberhard, *A Handbook of Christian Social Ethics*, New York: Herder and Herder, 1963.

Wenham, Gordon J., *The Book of Leviticus*, London: Hodder and Stoughton, 1979.

White, Lynn, 'The Historical Roots of our Ecologic Crisis', in *Science*, 155:3767, 1203–1207, March 1967.

Wilson, Bryan, *Religion in Secular Society*, London: C.A. Watts, 1966, and Harmondsworth, Middlesex: Penguin, 1969.

——'A Typology of Sects', in Roland Robertson (ed.), *Sociology of Religion*, Harmondsworth, Middlesex: Penguin, 361–383, 1969.

——*Religious Sects*, London: Weidenfeld and Nicolson, 1970.

——'The Debate Over "Secularization"', *Encounter*, October 1975.

——*Contemporary Transformations of Religion*, Oxford: Oxford University Press, 1976.

——*Religion in Sociological Perspective*, Oxford: Oxford University Press, 1982.

——*The Social Dimension of Sectarianism*, Oxford: Clarendon Press, 1990.

Wilson, John and Thomas Janoski, 'The Contribution of Religion to Volunteer Work', *Sociology of Religion*, 56:2, 137–152, 1995.

Woodhead, Linda (ed.), with Rebecca Catto, *Religion and Change in Modern Britain*, London: Routledge, 2012.

Wuthnow, Robert, *Saving America? Faith-Based Services and the Future of Civil Society*, Princeton and Oxford: Princeton University Press, 2004.

Yinger, J. Milton, *The Scientific Study of Religion*, New York: Collier-Macmillan, 1970.

Index